EVALUATING TRAINING PROGRAMS

EVALUATING TRAINING PROGRAMS

THE FOUR LEVELS

THIRD EDITION

DONALD L. KIRKPATRICK

JAMES D. KIRKPATRICK

BERRETT-KOEHLER PUBLISHERS, INC.
San Francisco

Berrett-Koehler Publishers, Inc.
235 Montgomery Street, Suite 650
San Francisco, CA 94104-2916
Tel: (415) 288-0260 Fax: (415) 362-2512 www.bkconnection.com

ORDERING INFORMATION

Quantity sales. Special discounts are available on quantity purchases by corporations, associations, and others. For details, contact the "Special Sales Department" at the Berrett-Koehler address above.

Individual sales. Berrett-Koehler publications are available through most bookstores. They can also be ordered directly from Berrett-Koehler. Tel: (800) 929-2929; Fax: (802) 864-7626; www.bkconnection.com

Orders for college textbook/course adoption use. Please contact Berrett-Koehler. Tel: (800) 929-2929; Fax: (802) 864-7626.

Orders by U.S. trade bookstores and wholesalers. Please contact Ingram Publisher Services, Tel: (800) 509-4887; Fax: (800) 838-1149; E-mail: customer .service@ingrampublisherservices.com; or visit www.ingrampublisherservices .com/Ordering for details about electronic ordering.

Berrett-Koehler and the BK logo are registered trademarks of Berrett-Koehler Publishers, Inc.

Printed in the United States of America

Berrett-Koehler books are printed on long-lasting acid-free paper. When it is available, we choose paper that has been manufactured by environmentally responsible processes. These may include using trees grown in sustainable forests, incorporating recycled paper, minimizing chlorine in bleaching, or recycling the energy produced at the paper mill.

Library of Congress Cataloging-in-Publication Data

Kirkpatrick, Donald L.
  Evaluating training programs: the four levels/Donald L. Kirkpatrick and James D. Kirkpatrick—3rd ed.
    p. cm.
  Includes bibliographical references and index.
  ISBN–10: 1–57675–348–4; ISBN–13: 978–1–57675–348–4
  1. Employees—Training of—Evaluation. I. Kirkpatrick, James D., 1952-
II. Title.
HF5549.5.T7K569 2005
658.3'12404—dc22   2005048069

Third edition
12   10 9 8 7 6

Book production by Westchester Book Group

Contents

Foreword

Every year new challenges emerge in the field of training and development—for example, competency development, outsourcing, e-learning, and knowledge management, to name a few. In spite of the variety and complexity of these challenges, there is a common theme: business leaders want to see value for their investment. Do people's initial reactions to the learning experience indicate that the learning is relevant and immediately applicable to their needs? How effective is the learning and how sustainable will it be? What are people doing differently and better as a result? What results are these investments in learning and development having for the business?

These are the fundamental questions that have been asked every year about training and development since 1959, when Don Kirkpatrick put them on the agenda of business and learning leaders. Today, these questions are still being asked—and applied—to a wide variety of learning programs. E-learning may be less expensive than classroom learning; however, is it as effective as classroom learning? A knowledge management system may deliver the information to people; however, does it change their behavior? Kirkpatrick's four levels will help find the answer to these and many more questions.

Kirkpatrick's four levels—reaction, learning, behavior, results—have stood the test of time and are as relevant today as they were over four decades ago. They are perhaps even more relevant today, as the pressure on training professionals to deliver results, and not just positive "smile sheets," grows greater every year. So readers, take heart. This third edition of Kirkpatrick's classic book is chock-full of useful information for evaluating learning according to the four levels. Several case studies illuminate how the four levels can be applied to a wide variety of training and development programs.

I have personally found Kirkpatrick's four-level framework to be helpful in the evaluation work at Caterpillar, Inc., and with other organizations. This book contains a case study written by me and Chris Arvin, Dean of the College of Leadership at Caterpillar University, in which we used the four-level framework to illustrate the value created by a Caterpillar University leadership development program. In our story we wrote about what leaders learned, what new behaviors emerged, and how these new behaviors created sustainable business results. This is the essence of the four-level framework: it provides a structure to tell a compelling story of value creation.

This brings us to the original premise. Whatever the learning program, business leaders expect demonstrable value. They expect people to react in a positive way to their learning experience (level 1) and to learn critical information (level 2). Leaders want to see changes in behavior as a result of what people have learned (level 3) and may expect these new behaviors to deliver results for the business (level 4). With the third edition of this book, readers have an opportunity to update their understanding of this classic evaluation framework and to learn from the case studies about how to effectively apply the framework to a variety of learning programs. Readers are presented with the tools and the know-how to tell their own story of value creation.

Merrill C. Anderson, Ph.D.
Chief Executive Officer
MetrixGlobal, LLC
Johnston, Iowa

Foreword to the Third Edition

Reaction, Learning, Behavior, Results. Wake me up in the middle of the night and I will grind them out on demand.

I would like you to memorize these words too. Reaction, Learning, Behavior, Results. Learn them back and forth. Results, Behavior, Learning, Reaction. Everytime I sit down with a client, I find myself asking the same questions, over and over again. What are the results you want? What has to be done? What competencies or assets do we need in place? How can we organize our solution in such a way that people will react favorably to it?

The four levels are almost like a question. There's so much wisdom in the concept. It not only articulates an elusive term—evaluation of training—but it inspires us to look beyond our traditional classroom content delivery model. It opens windows to the many ways we can improve the performance of our organizations. Look at all the things we can do if we adopt the four levels and look at the world from four different perspectives. It gives us four platforms to improve performance in our organizations. Reaction, Learning, Behavior, Results. In other words, make sure your clients trust you and like what you're doing, offer them the best resources to enhance their perception, help them to improve their approach, and inspire them to get the results they need. What a way to empower people.

When I talk about measurement, testing, and evaluation, I always ask my audience where we can find the first written systematic evaluation procedure. Most of the time, they have no idea. Then I refer to the story of Gideon written down in the Christian Bible. Why is this relevant in this context? You're about to find out.

You have to know, Gideon was a judge. In his time Israel was delivered into the hands of Midianites. Gideon was chosen to save the people of Israel from the Midianites. Now, Gideon's level of self-esteem was a bit ramshackle. He came from a poor family and he was the least in his father's house. He did not think he was capable of doing the chore. Limiting beliefs, we might call them today. In order to build his self-esteem, Gideon asked for evidence that the Lord was with him. So he kind of tested the Lord. *"Shew me a sign that thou talkest with me."* Now, one sign was not enough for Gideon. He needed a few. Eventually Gideon was convinced he could beat the Midianite's. He gathered a bunch of people to fight the Midianites. Thirty-two thousand, to be precise. But now it was the Lord's time to do some testing. You test my power, I test your trust, the Lord must have been thinking. The Lord said: "You have too many men. Do some shifting. Ask anyone who is afraid to go home." Twenty-two thousand left the group. Gideon remained with ten thousand. But the Lord said: Yet too many. We need to try them again. And boy, the Lord is creative when it comes to evaluation. He let Gideon bring the remaining ten thousand down unto the water to let them drink. "And the Lord said unto Gideon, 'Every one that lappeth of the water with his tongue, as a dog lappeth, him shalt thou set by himself; likewise every one that boweth down upon his knees to drink.' The number that put their hand to their mouth were three hundred men." Gideon fought the Midianites with these three hundred and won.

By telling the story and showing the fear of Gideon, I introduce the concepts of risk and trust. A good evaluation procedure helps you generate indicators that explain or even predict success. But the story also touches the subject of recruiting the best people for a job. It's a rich story that was brought to me by loving parents. Later on I realized the story is a nice illustration of an evaluation procedure. So, I started to use it in the workshops I conduct. A few years later I met the man who introduced the four levels and started working with him. By coincidence I found out . . . guess what? Dr. Donald Kirkpatrick is an active member of The Gideons International, the organization we all know from the so-called Gideon Bible.

Don's four levels had, have, and will have major impact on the way we look at evaluating training programs. And if executed on all four levels, the frame will teach us a major and sometimes painful lesson. We cannot expect performance improvement if we just train. Training is just one solution in a row of many. In order to get sustainable results, we need to cooperate with our fellow staff members and managers. We need to come up with an integral plan where every stakeholder is involved. The four levels will help you to build a sequence of reinforcing interventions that will have significant impact. Use the four levels and align your training efforts with business strategy. I assure you, the stockholders will love the four levels.

Donald Kirkpatrick's framework is applicable not only to training but to numerous other disciplines. Marketing, for example. Imagine one of the daily commercials you saw today on the television. Did you like it? Did it change your posture? Will you go to shop? Will you eventually buy it? Or take politics. Are you a politician who just designed a new law to reduce speeding? To evaluate the execution, just answer the four questions. How will they receive the new law? Will they know what it's about? Will they change their driving behavior? And eventually, will the number of people speeding trim down?

The four levels are even applicable in the field of technology. Think of introducing a new software program. Do they like it? Do they know how it works? Can they work with it? Do they get the results they need?

When it comes to applying the four levels, Don gives us simple guidelines of how to proceed. PIE. PIE? Simple: we have to teach Practical, Interesting, and Enjoyable programs. Again, something everybody understands. Practical? If we train, we need to come up with something people can use in their lives and that works. It has to be applicable. Interesting? It has to stir our curiosity. It has to be obvious that the new way we demonstrate is better than the old way. It has to get us into a mode that is strong enough to get us out of our comfort zone. And last but not least: it has to be enjoyable. Not only fun but also safe and done with love and care. With the PIE approach Don rephrased a principle that originates from Peter Petersen, a German pedagogue in the beginning of the twentieth century. He proclaimed that our teaching had to appeal to our "Haupt, Hart und Handen"— the head, the heart, and the hands. To put it in Don's words: it has to be interesting, enjoyable, and practical. These are fundamental values. And I think this is why Don's work is recognized by so many people. Donald Kirkpatrick is connected to these values. He taps into these universal sources and that's why I think his work is so inspiring to many of us.

For me, working with Don is associated with these amazing insights and apparent coincidences. Don't ask me to explain. I will leave it to the scientist. The same goes for trying to find out whether the four levels are a model or a taxonomy. Or whether there is a causal relationship between the levels. The concepts themselves are inspiring enough. Reaction, Learning, Behavior, Results. All four equally important. 'Just' four levels.

I strongly recommend that you get acquainted with these concepts. Learn them by heart. They will help you to connect and make friends with the people within your organization who need to get connected with your job and passion: learning. Memorize the words and make sure you do your job the best you can. Evaluate the impact on all the four levels, including the financial impact. To demonstrate learning is indeed a rewarding enterprise, Donald Kirkpatrick gave you a clear road map with his four levels. This book is food for the head, the heart, and the hands. Just make sure your approach is practical, interesting, and enjoyable.

Diederick Stoel, M.A.
CEO and President
ProfitWise
Amsterdam, the Netherlands

Preface

In 1959, I wrote a series of four articles called "Techniques for Evaluating Training Programs," published in *Training and Development,* the journal of the American Society for Training and Development (ASTD). The articles described the four levels of evaluation that I had formulated. I am not sure where I got the idea for this model, but the concept originated with work on my Ph.D. dissertation at the University of Wisconsin, Madison.

The reason I developed this four-level model was to clarify the elusive term *evaluation.* Some training and development professionals believe that *evaluation* means measuring changes in behavior that occur as a result of training programs. Others maintain that the only real evaluation lies in determining what final results occurred because of training programs. Still others think only in terms of the comment sheets that participants complete at the end of a program. Others are concerned with the learning that takes place in the classroom, as measured by increased knowledge, improved skills, and changes in attitude. And they are all right—and yet wrong, in that they fail to recognize that all four approaches are parts of what we mean by *evaluating.*

These four levels are all important, and they should be understood by all professionals in the fields of education, training, and development, whether they plan, coordinate, or teach; whether the content of the program is technical or managerial; whether the participants are or are not managers; and whether the programs are conducted in education, business, or industry. In some cases, especially in academic institutions, there is no attempt to change behavior. The end result is simply to increase knowledge, improve skills, and change attitudes. In these cases, only the first two levels apply. But if the purpose of the training is to get better results by changing behavior, then all four levels apply.

The title of the book, *Evaluating Training Programs: The Four Levels,* is bold if not downright presumptuous, since other authors have described different approaches to the evaluation of training. However, in the field of training and development, these four levels are often quoted and used as the basic approach to evaluation all over the world, as evidenced by the fact that the second edition has been translated into Spanish, Polish, and Turkish.

I have used the word *training* in the title of this book, and I will use it throughout, to include development. Although a distinction is often made between these two terms, for simplicity I have chosen to speak of them both simply as *training* and to emphasize courses and programs designed to increase knowledge, improve skills, and change attitudes, whether for present job improvement or for development in the future. Because of my background, my primary focus will be on supervisory and management training, although the concepts, principles, and techniques can be applied to technical, sales, safety, and even academic courses.

This edition is divided into two parts. Part One describes concepts, principles, guidelines, and techniques for evaluating at all four levels. Part Two contains case studies written especially for this book. They represent different types and sizes of organizations. Three of them are from foreign countries. They have one thing in common. They describe how they have applied one or more of the four levels to evaluate their programs. Some case studies are quite simple. Others are comprehensive and technical. Nearly all of them include exhibits and figures to describe the forms and procedures they have used. Study the case studies that interest you, and look for designs, forms, procedures, and other details that you can use or adapt to your organization.

I wish to thank each of the authors who wrote the case studies. Many hours were spent in preparing the final drafts that would be of maximum interest and benefit to the readers. Thanks also to Jeevan Sivasubramanian, Jenny Williams, and Steve Piersanti of Berrett-Koehler for their encouragement and help.

And a very special thanks to Deborah Masi of Westchester Book Services and Estelle Silbermann, the copyeditor, for the thorough job she did in editing the original copy.

I also want to give special thanks to Bill Horton for his practical chapter on e-learning and to my son, Jim, for his helpful chapter on using Balanced Scorecards for helping to transfer Learning to Behavior.

Finally, I want to give special thanks to my wife, Fern, for her patience and encouragement during the many hours I spent on this book.

It is my sincere wish that this book will be of help to you, the reader, as you evaluate your programs.

Donald L. Kirkpatrick
April, 2005
Pewaukee, Wisconsin

PART ONE

CONCEPTS, PRINCIPLES, GUIDELINES, AND TECHNIQUES

Part One contains concepts, principles, guidelines, and techniques for understanding and implementing four levels with which to evaluate training programs. Most of the content is my own and results from my Ph.D. dissertation on evaluation and my studies and experience since that time. Some modifications were made from the input I received from reviewers that fit in with my objective in writing the book: to provide a simple, practical, four-level approach for evaluating training programs.

Chapter 1

Evaluating: Part of a Ten-Step Process

The reason for evaluating is to determine the effectiveness of a training program. When the evaluation is done, we can hope that the results are positive and gratifying, both for those responsible for the program and for upper-level managers who will make decisions based on their evaluation of the program. Therefore, much thought and planning need to be given to the program itself to make sure that it is effective. Later chapters discuss the reasons for evaluating and supply descriptions, guidelines, and techniques for evaluating at the four levels. This chapter is devoted to suggestions for planning and implementing the program to ensure its effectiveness. More details can be found in my book *Developing Managers and Team Leaders* (Woburn, MA: Butterworth Heinemann, 2001).

Each of the following factors should be carefully considered when planning and implementing an effective training program:

1. Determining needs
2. Setting objectives
3. Determining subject content
4. Selecting participants
5. Determining the best schedule
6. Selecting appropriate facilities
7. Selecting appropriate instructors
8. Selecting and preparing audiovisual aids
9. Coordinating the program
10. Evaluating the program

Suggestions for implementing each of these factors follow.

Determining Needs

If programs are going to be effective, they must meet the needs of participants. There are many ways to determine these needs. Here are some of the more common:

1. Ask the participants.
2. Ask the bosses of the participants.
3. Ask others who are familiar with the job and how it is being performed, including subordinates, peers, and customers.
4. Test the participants.
5. Analyze performance appraisal forms.

Participants, bosses, and others can be asked in interviews or by means of a survey. Interviews provide more detailed information, but they require much more time. A simple survey form can provide almost as much information and do it in a much more efficient manner.

A survey form, such as the one shown in Exhibit 1.1, can be readily developed to determine the needs seen both by participants and by their bosses. The topics to be considered can be determined by interviews or simply by answering the question, What are all the possible subjects that will help our people to do their best? The resulting list becomes the survey form.

As Exhibit 1.1 indicates, participants are asked to complete the survey by putting a check in one of three columns for each item. This is a much better process than having them list their needs in order of importance or simply writing down the topics that they feel will help them to do their job better. It is important to have them evaluate each topic so that the responses can be quantified.

After you tabulate their responses, the next step is to weight these sums to get a weighted score for each topic. The first column, *Of great need,* should be given a weight of 2; the second column, *Of some need,* should be given a weight of 1; and the last column, a weight of 0. The weighted score can then be used to arrive at a rank order for individual needs. If two topics are tied for third, the next rank is fifth, not

Exhibit 1.1. Survey of Training Needs

In order to determine which subjects will be of the greatest help to you in improving your job performance, we need your input. Please indicate your need for each subject by placing an X in the appropriate column.

Subject	Of great need	Of some need	Of no need
1. Diversity in the workforce—understanding employees			
2. How to motivate employees			
3. Interpersonal communications			
4. Written communication			
5. Oral communication			
6. How to manage time			
7. How to delegate effectively			
8. Planning and organizing			
9. Handling complaints and grievances			
10. How to manage change			
11. Decision making and empowerment			
12. Leadership styles—application			
13. Performance appraisal			
14. Coaching and counseling			
15. How to conduct productive meetings			
16. Building teamwork			
17. How to discipline			
18. Total quality improvement			
19. Safety			
20. Housekeeping			
21. How to build morale—quality of work life (QWL)			
22. How to reward performance			
23. How to train employees			
24. How to reduce absenteeism and tardiness			

25. Other topics of great need
    1.
    2.			

fourth, and if three needs have tied for seventh, the next rank is tenth. This rank order provides training professionals with data on which to determine priorities. Exhibit 1.2 illustrates the tabulations and the rank order.

The same form can be used to determine the needs seen by the bosses of the supervisors. The only change is in the instructions on the form, which should read: "In order to determine which subjects would be of greatest benefit to supervisors to help improve their performance, we need your input. Please put an X in one of the three columns after each subject to indicate the needs of your subordinates as you see them. Tabulations of this survey will be compared with the needs that they see to decide the priority of the subjects to be offered."

There will be a difference of opinion on some subjects. For example, in a manufacturing organization, the subject of housekeeping might be rated low by supervisors and high by their bosses. Other topics, such as motivation, will probably be given a high rating by both groups. In order to make the final decision on the priority of the subjects to be offered, it is wise to use an advisory committee of managers representing different departments and levels within the organization. The training professional can show the committee members the results of the survey and ask for their input. Their comments and suggestions should be considered to be advisory, and the training professional should make the final decision.

Participation by an advisory committee accomplishes four purposes:

1. Helps to determine subject content for training programs.
2. Informs committee members of the efforts of the training department to provide practical help.
3. Provides empathy regarding the needs seen by their subordinates.
4. Stimulates support of the programs by involving them in the planning.

The use of tests and inventories is another approach for determining needs. There are two practical ways of doing this. One way is to determine the knowledge, skills, and attitudes that a supervisor should have and develop the subject content accordingly. Then develop a test

Exhibit 1.2. Tabulating Responses to Survey of Training Needs

---

In order to determine which subjects will be of the greatest help to you in improving your job performance, we need your input. Please indicate your need for each subject by placing an X in the appropriate column.

Rank order	Subject	Weighted score	Of great need	Of some need	Of no need
13	1. Diversity in the workforce—understanding employees	40	15	10	5
4	2. How to motivate employees	51	22	7	1
6	3. Interpersonal communications	48	20	8	2
18	4. Written communication	33	11	11	8
23	5. Oral communication	19	6	7	17
10	6. How to manage time	44	17	10	3
20	7. How to delegate effectively	29	9	11	10
20	8. Planning and organizing	29	6	17	7
14	9. Handling complaints and grievances	39	13	13	4
1	10. How to manage change	56	26	4	0
3	11. Decision making and empowerment	53	24	5	1
6	12. Leadership styles—application	48	19	10	1
16	13. Performance appraisal	36	12	12	6
16	14. Coaching and counseling	36	8	20	2
20	15. How to conduct productive meetings	29	8	13	9
2	16. Building teamwork	55	25	5	0
9	17. How to discipline	47	18	11	1
14	18. Total quality improvement	39	13	13	4
11	19. Safety	43	15	13	2
23	20. Housekeeping	19	6	7	17
5	21. How to build morale—quality of work life (QWL)	50	22	6	2
12	22. How to reward performance	41	17	7	6
6	23. How to train employees	48	19	10	1
19	24. How to reduce absenteeism and tardiness	31	11	9	10
	25. Other topics of great need 1. 2.				

Note: Tabulated responses from thirty first-level supervisors.

that measures the knowledge, skills, and attitudes, and give it to participants as a pretest. An analysis of the results will provide information regarding subject content.

The other approach is to purchase a standardized instrument that relates closely to the subject matter being taught. The sixty-five-item Management Inventory on Managing Change (available from Donald L. Kirkpatrick, 842 Kirkland Ct., Pewaukee, WI 53072) is such an instrument. Here are some of the items in it:

1. If subordinates participate in the decision to make a change, they are usually more enthusiastic in carrying it out.
2. Some people are not anxious to be promoted to a job that has more responsibility.
3. Decisions to change should be based on opinions as well as on facts.
4. If a change is going to be unpopular with your subordinates, you should proceed slowly in order to obtain acceptance.
5. It is usually better to communicate with a group concerning a change than to talk to its members individually.
6. Empathy is one of the most important concepts in managing change.
7. It's a good idea to sell a change to the natural leader before trying to sell it to the others.
8. If you are promoted to a management job, you should make the job different from what it was under your predecessor.
9. Bosses and subordinates should have an understanding regarding the kinds of changes that the subordinate can implement without getting prior approval from the boss.
10. You should encourage your subordinates to try out any changes that they feel should be made.

Respondents are asked to agree or disagree with each statement. The "correct" answers were determined by the author to cover concepts, principles, and techniques for managing change. It is important to note that the possible answers are "agree" or "disagree" and not "true" or "false."

Five other standardized inventories are available from the source just named: Supervisory Inventory on Communication, Supervisory Inventory on Human Relations, Management Inventory on Time

Management, Management Inventory on Performance Appraisal and Coaching, and Management Inventory on Leadership, Motivation, and Decision Making.

Many other approaches are available for determining needs. Two of the most practical—surveying participants and their bosses and giving a pretest to participants before the program is run—have just been described.

Setting Objectives

Once the needs have been determined, it is necessary to set objectives. Objectives should be set for three different aspects of the program and in the following order:

1. What results are we trying to accomplish? These results can be stated in such terms as production, quality, turnover, absenteeism, morale, sales, profits, and return on investment (ROI).
2. What behaviors are needed to accomplish these desired results?
3. What knowledge, skills, and attitudes are necessary to achieve the desired behaviors?

The training program curriculum is then based on accomplishing no. 3. In some programs, only increased knowledge is needed. In others, new or improved skills are necessary. And in some, change in attitudes is what is needed. Diversity training is an example of a program whose objective it is to change attitudes.

Determining Subject Content

Needs and objectives are prime factors when determining subject content. Trainers should ask themselves the question, What topics should be presented to meet the needs and accomplish the objectives? The answers to this question establish the topics to be covered. Some modifications may be necessary depending on the qualifications of the trainers who will present the program and on the training budget.

For example, the subject of managing stress may be important, but the instructors available are not qualified, and there is no money to hire a qualified leader or buy videotapes and/or packaged programs on the subject. Other pertinent topics then become higher priorities.

Selecting Participants

When selecting participants for a program, four decisions need to be made:

1. Who can benefit from the training?
2. What programs are required by law or by government edict?
3. Should the training be voluntary or compulsory?
4. Should the participants be segregated by level in the organization, or should two or more levels be included in the same class?

In answer to the first question, all levels of management can benefit from training programs. Obviously, some levels can benefit more than others. The answer to the second question is obvious. Regarding the third question, I recommend that at least some basic programs be compulsory for first-level supervisors if not also for others. If a program is voluntary, many who need the training may not sign up, either because they feel they don't need it or because they don't want to admit that they need it. Those who are already good supervisors and have little need for the program can still benefit from it, and they can also help to train the others. This assumes, of course, that the program includes participatory activities on the part of attendees. To supplement the compulsory programs, other courses can be offered on a voluntary basis.

Some organizations have established a management institute that offers all courses on a voluntary basis. Training professionals may feel that this is the best approach. Or higher-level management may discourage compulsory programs. If possible, the needs of the supervisors, as determined by the procedures described in the preceding section, should become basic courses that should be compulsory. Others can be optional. The answer to the last question depends on the climate and on the rapport that exists among different levels of management within the organization. The basic question is whether subordinates will speak freely in a training class if their bosses are present. If the answer is yes, then it is a good idea to have different levels in the same program. They all get the same training at the same time. But if the answer is no, then bosses should not be included in the program for supervisors. Perhaps you can give the same or a similar program to upper-level managers before offering it to the first-level supervisors.

Determining the Best Schedule

The best schedule takes three things into consideration: the trainees, their bosses, and the best conditions for learning. Many times, training professionals consider only their own preferences and schedules. An important scheduling decision is whether to offer the program on a concentrated basis—for example, as a solid week of training—or to spread it out over weeks or months. My own preference is to spread it out as an ongoing program. One good schedule is to offer a three-hour session once a month. Three hours leave you time for participation as well as for the use of videotapes and other aids. The schedule should be set and communicated well in advance. The day of the program and the specific time should be established to meet the needs and desires of both the trainees and their bosses. Line managers should be consulted regarding the best time and schedule.

I recently conducted a week-long training program for all levels of management at a company in Racine, Wisconsin. Two groups of twenty each attended the program. The first session each day was scheduled from 7:00 to 10:30 A.M. The repeat session for the other group was scheduled from 3:00 to 6:30 P.M. Racine was too far away to go home each day, and what do you do in Racine from 10:30 A.M. to 3:00 P.M. each day for a week? This is the worst schedule I ever had, but it was the best schedule for all three shifts of supervisors who attended. The point is, the training schedule must meet the needs and desires of the participants instead of the convenience of the instructors.

Selecting Appropriate Facilities

The selection of facilities is another important decision. Facilities should be both comfortable and convenient. Negative factors to be avoided include rooms that are too small, uncomfortable furniture, noise or other distractions, inconvenience, long distances to the training room, and uncomfortable temperature, either too hot or too cold. A related consideration has to do with refreshments and breaks. I conducted a training program on managing change for a large Minneapolis company. They provided participants with coffee and sweet rolls in the morning, a nice lunch at noon, and a Coke and cookie break in the afternoon. Participants came from all over the country, including Seattle. In order to save money on transportation and hotel, the company decided to take the program to Seattle, where it had a large operation. In Seattle, no refreshments were offered, and participants were on their own for lunch. Unfortunately, some peers of the participants had attended the same program in Minneapolis. These factors caused negative attitudes on the part of those attending. And these attitudes could have affected their motivation to learn as well as their feeling toward the organization and the training department in particular. Incidentally, more and more companies are offering fruit instead of sweet rolls and cookies at breaks.

Selecting Appropriate Instructors

The selection of instructors is critical to the success of a program. Their qualifications should include a knowledge of the subject being taught, a desire to teach, the ability to communicate, and skill at getting people to participate. They should also be "learner oriented"— have a strong desire to meet learner needs.

Budgets may limit the possibilities. For example, some organizations limit the selection to present employees, including the training director, the Human Resources manager, and line and staff managers. There is no money to hire outside leaders. Therefore, subject content needs to be tailored to the available instructors, or else instructors need to receive special training. If budgets allow, outside instructors can be hired if internal expertise is not available. The selection of these instructors also requires care. Many organizations feel that they have been burned because they selected outside instructors who did a poor job. In order to be sure that a potential instructor will be effective, the best approach is to observe his or her performance in a similar situation. The next best approach is to rely on the recommendations of other training professionals who have already used the individual. A very unreliable method is to interview the person and make a decision based on your impressions.

I recently conducted a workshop for eighty supervisors and managers at St. Vincent Hospital in Indianapolis. I had been recommended to Frank Magliery, vice president of Operations, by Dave Neil of ServiceMaster. Dave had been in several of my sessions. In order to be sure that I was the right instructor, Frank attended another session that I did for ServiceMaster. He was able therefore not only to judge my effectiveness but also to offer suggestions about tailoring the training to his organization.

This is the kind of selection process that should be followed when you hire an outside consultant. It not only illustrates a process for selection but also emphasizes the importance of orienting an outside leader to the needs and desires of the specific organization.

Selecting and Preparing Audiovisual Aids

An audiovisual aid has two purposes: to help the leader maintain interest and to communicate. Some aids, hopefully only a few minutes long, are designed to attract interest and entertain. This is fine providing they develop a positive climate for learning. When renting or purchasing videotapes and packaged programs, take care to preview them first to be sure that the benefits for the program outweigh the cost. The extent to which such aids should become the main feature of a program depends on the instructor's knowledge and skills in developing his or her own subject content. Some organizations rely entirely on packaged programs because they have the budget but not the skills needed to develop and teach programs of their own. Other training professionals rely primarily on their own knowledge, skill, and materials, and rent or buy videos only as aids. Some organizations have a department that can make effective aids and provide the necessary

equipment. Other organizations have to rent or buy them. The important principle is that aids can be an important part of an effective program. Each organization should carefully make or buy the aids that will help it to maintain interest and communicate the message.

Coordinating the Program

Sometimes the instructor coordinates as well as teaches. In other situations a coordinator does not do the teaching. For those who coordinate and do not teach, there are two opposite approaches.

As an instructor, I have experienced two extremes in regard to coordination. At an eastern university offering continuing education, I had to introduce myself, find my way to the lunchroom at noon, tell participants where to go for breaks, conclude the program, and even ask participants to complete the reaction sheets. I couldn't believe that a university that prided itself on professional programming could do such a miserable job of coordinating.

The other extreme occurred in a program that I conducted for State Farm Insurance in Bloomington, Illinois. Steve Whittington and his wife took my wife, Fern, and me out to dinner the evening before the program. He picked me up at the hotel to take me to the training room in plenty of time to set the room up for the meeting. He made sure that I had everything I needed. He introduced me and stayed for the entire program, helping with handouts. He handled the breaks. He took me to lunch and, of course, paid for it. He concluded the meeting by thanking me and asking participants to complete reaction sheets. He took me back to the hotel and thanked me. In other words, he served as an effective coordinator who helped to make the meeting as effective as possible. Of course, the niceties that he included are not necessary for effective coordination, but they do illustrate that it is important to meet the needs of the instructor as well as of the participants.

Evaluating the Program

Details on evaluation are provided in the rest of the book.

As stated at the beginning of this chapter, to ensure the effectiveness of a training program, time and emphasis should be put on the planning and implementation of the program. These are critical if we are to be sure that, when the evaluation is done, the results are positive. Consideration of the concepts, principles, and techniques described in this chapter can help to ensure an effective program.

Chapter 2

Reasons for Evaluating

At a national conference of the National Society for Sales Training Executives (NSSTE), J. P. Huller of Hobart Corporation presented a paper on "evaluation." In the introduction, he says, "All managers, not just those of us in training, are concerned with their own and their department's credibility. I want to be accepted by my company. I want to be trusted by my company. I want to be respected by my company. I want my company and my fellow managers to say, 'We need you.'"

"When you are accepted, trusted, respected, and needed, lots and lots of wonderful things happen:

- Your budget requests are granted.
- You keep your job. (You might even be promoted.)
- Your staff keep their jobs.
- The quality of your work improves.
- Senior management listens to your advice.
- You're given more control.

"You sleep better, worry less, enjoy life more. . . . In short, it makes you happy."

"Wonderful! But just how do we become accepted, trusted, respected, and needed? We do so by proving that we deserve to be accepted, trusted, respected, and needed. We do so by evaluating and reporting upon the worth of our training."

This states in general terms why we need to evaluate training. Here are three specific reasons:

1. To justify the existence and budget of the training department by showing how it contributes to the organization's objectives and goals
2. To decide whether to continue or discontinue training programs → *has programme been with it ?*
3. To gain information on how to improve future training programs → *or their transfer into workplace*

There is an old saying among training directors: When there are cutbacks in an organization, training people are the first to go. Of course, this isn't always true. However, whenever downsizing occurs, top management looks for people and departments that can be eliminated with the fewest negative results. Early in their decision, they look at such "overhead" departments as Training, commonly called Corporate University, and Human Resources, which typically includes Employment, Salary Administration, Benefits, and Labor Relations (if there is a union). In some organizations, top management feels that all these functions except training are necessary. From this perspective, training is optional, and its value to the organization depends on top executives' view of its effectiveness. Huller is right when he states that training people must earn trust and respect if training is to be an important function that an organization will want to retain even in a downsizing situation. In other words, trainers must justify their existence. If they don't and downsizing occurs, they may be terminated, and the training function will be relegated to the Human Resources manager, who already has many other hats to wear.

The second reason for evaluating is to determine whether you should continue to offer a program. The content of some programs may become obsolete. For example, programs on Work Simplification, Transactional Analysis, and Management by Objectives were "hot" topics in past years. Most organizations have decided to replace these with programs on current hot topics such as Diversity, Empowerment, and Team Building. Also, some programs, such as computer training, are constantly subject to change. Some programs are offered on a pilot basis in hopes that they will bring about the results desired.

These programs should be evaluated to determine whether they should be continued. If the cost outweighs the benefits, the program should be discontinued or modified.

The most common reason for evaluation is to determine the effectiveness of a program and ways in which it can be improved. Usually, the decision to continue it has already been made. The question then is, How can it be improved? In looking for the answer to this question, you should consider these eight factors:

1. To what extent does the subject content meet the needs of those attending?
2. Is the leader the one best qualified to teach?
3. Does the leader use the most effective methods for maintaining interest and teaching the desired attitudes, knowledge, and skills?
4. Are the facilities satisfactory?
5. Is the schedule appropriate for the participants?
6. Are the aids effective in improving communication and maintaining interest?
7. Was the coordination of the program satisfactory?
8. What else can be done to improve the program?

A careful analysis of the answers to these questions can identify ways and means of improving future offerings of the program.

When I talked to Matt, a training director of a large bank, and asked him to write a case history on what his organization has done to evaluate its programs, here is what he said: "We haven't really done anything except the 'smile' sheets. We have been thinking a lot about it, and we are anxious to do something. I will be the first one to read your book!"

This is the situation in many companies. They use reaction sheets (or "smile" sheets, as Matt called them) of one kind or another. Most are thinking about doing more. They haven't gone any further for one or more of the following reasons:

- They don't consider it important or urgent.
- They don't know what to do or how to do it.
- There is no pressure from higher management to do more.
- They feel secure in their job and see no need to do more.

- They have too many other things that are more important or that they prefer to do.

In most organizations, both large and small, there is little pressure from top management to prove that the benefits of training outweigh the cost. Many managers at high levels are too busy worrying about profits, return on investment, stock prices, and other matters of concern to the board of directors, stockholders, and customers. They pay little or no attention to training unless they hear bad things about it. As long as trainees are happy and do not complain, trainers feel comfortable, relaxed, and secure.

However, if trainees react negatively to programs, trainers begin to worry, because the word might get to higher-level managers that the program is a waste of time or even worse. And higher-level managers might make decisions based on this information.

In a few organizations, upper-level managers are putting pressure on trainers to justify their existence by proving their worth. Some have even demanded to see tangible results as measured by improvements in sales, productivity, quality, morale, turnover, safety records, and profits. In these situations, training professionals need to have guidelines for evaluating programs at all four levels. And they need to use more than reaction sheets at the end of their programs.

What about trainers who do not feel pressure from above to justify their existence? I suggest that they operate as if there were going to be pressure and be ready for it. Even if the pressure for results never comes, trainers will benefit by becoming accepted, respected, and self-satisfied.

Summary

There are three reasons for evaluating training programs. The most common reason is that evaluation can tell us how to improve future programs. The second reason is to determine whether a program should be continued or dropped. The third reason is to justify the existence of the training department (Corporate University) and its budget. By demonstrating to top management that training has tangible, positive results, trainers will find that their job is more secure, even if and when downsizing occurs. If top-level managers need to cut back, their impression of the need for a training department will determine whether they say, "That's one department we need to keep" or "That's a department that we can eliminate or reduce without hurting us." And their impression will be be greatly influenced by trainers who evaluate at all levels and communicate the results to them.

Chapter 3

The Four Levels: An Overview

The four levels represent a sequence of ways to evaluate programs. Each level is important and has an impact on the next level. As you move from one level to the next, the process becomes more difficult and time-consuming, but it also provides more valuable information. None of the levels should be bypassed simply to get to the level that the trainer considers the most important. These are the four levels:

Level 1—Reaction
Level 2—Learning
Level 3—Behavior
Level 4—Results

Reaction

As the word *reaction* implies, evaluation on this level measures how those who participate in the program react to it. I call it a measure of customer satisfaction. For many years, I conducted seminars, institutes, and conferences at the University of Wisconsin Management Institute. Organizations paid a fee to send their people to these public programs. It is obvious that the reaction of participants was a measure of customer satisfaction. It is also obvious that reaction had to be favorable if we were to stay in business and attract new customers as well as get present customers to return to future programs.

It isn't quite so obvious that reaction to in-house programs is also a measure of customer satisfaction. In many in-house programs, participants are required to attend whether they want to or not. However, they still are customers even if they don't pay, and their reactions can make or break a training program. What they say to their bosses often gets to higher-level managers, who make decisions about the future of training programs. So, positive reactions are just as important for trainers who run in-house programs as they are for those who offer public programs.

It is important not only to get a reaction but to get a positive reaction. As just described, the future of a program depends on positive reaction. In addition, if participants do not react favorably, they probably will not be motivated to learn. Positive reaction may not ensure learning, but negative reaction almost certainly reduces the possibility of its occurring.

Learning

Learning can be defined as the extent to which participants change attitudes, improve knowledge, and/or increase skill as a result of attending the program.

Those are the three things that a training program can accomplish. Programs dealing with topics like diversity in the workforce aim primarily at changing attitudes. Technical programs aim at improving skills. Programs on topics like leadership, motivation, and communication can aim at all three objectives. In order to evaluate learning, the specific objectives must be determined.

Some trainers say that no learning has taken place unless change in behavior occurs. In the four levels described in this book, learning has taken place when one or more of the following occurs: Attitudes are changed. Knowledge is increased. Skill is improved. One or more of these changes must take place if a change in behavior is to occur.

Behavior

Behavior can be defined as the extent to which change in behavior has occurred because the participant attended the training program.

Some trainers want to bypass levels 1 and 2—reaction and learning—in order to measure changes in behavior. This is a serious mistake. For example, suppose that no change in behavior is discovered. The obvious conclusion is that the program was ineffective and that it should be discontinued. This conclusion may or may not be accurate. Reaction may have been favorable, and the learning objectives may have been accomplished, but the level 3 or 4 conditions may not have been present.

In order for change to occur, four conditions are necessary:

1. The person must have a desire to change.
2. The person must know what to do and how to do it.
3. The person must work in the right climate.
4. The person must be rewarded for changing.

The training program can accomplish the first two requirements by creating a positive attitude toward the desired change and by teaching the necessary knowledge and skills. The third condition, right climate, refers to the participant's immediate supervisor. Five different kinds of climate can be described:

1. *Preventing:* The boss forbids the participant from doing what he or she has been taught to do in the training program. The boss may be influenced by the organizational culture established by top management. Or the boss's leadership style may conflict with what was taught.

2. *Discouraging:* The boss doesn't say, "You can't do it," but he or she makes it clear that the participant should not change behavior because it would make the boss unhappy. Or the boss doesn't model the behavior taught in the program, and this negative example discourages the subordinate from changing.

3. *Neutral:* The boss ignores the fact that the participant has attended a training program. It is business as usual. If the subordinate wants to change, the boss has no objection as long as the job gets done. If negative results occur because behavior has changed, then the boss may turn into a discouraging or even preventing climate.

4. *Encouraging:* The boss encourages the participant to learn and apply his or her learning on the job. Ideally, the boss discussed the program with the subordinate beforehand and stated that the two would discuss application as soon as the program was over. The boss

basically says, "I am interested in knowing what you learned and how I can help you transfer the learning to the job."

5. *Requiring:* The boss knows what the subordinate learns and makes sure that the learning transfers to the job. In some cases, a learning contract is prepared that states what the subordinate agrees to do. This contract can be prepared at the end of the training session, and a copy can be given to the boss. The boss sees to it that the contract is implemented. Malcolm Knowles's book *Using Learning Contracts* (San Francisco: Jossey-Bass, 1986) describes this process.

The fourth condition, rewards, can be intrinsic (from within), extrinsic (from without), or both. Intrinsic rewards include the feelings of satisfaction, pride, and achievement that can occur when change in behavior has positive results. Extrinsic rewards include praise from the boss, recognition by others, and monetary rewards, such as merit pay increases and bonuses.

It becomes obvious that there is little or no chance that training will transfer to job behavior if the climate is preventing or discouraging. If the climate is neutral, change in behavior will depend on the other three conditions just described. If the climate is encouraging or requiring, then the amount of change that occurs depends on the first and second conditions.

As stated earlier, it is important to evaluate both reaction and learning in case no change in behavior occurs. Then it can be determined whether the fact that there was no change was the result of an ineffective training program or of the wrong job climate and lack of rewards.

It is important for trainers to know the type of climate that participants will face when they return from the training program. It is also important for them to do everything that they can to see to it that the climate is neutral or better. Otherwise there is little or no chance that the program will accomplish the behavior and results objectives, because participants will not even try to use what they have learned. Not only will no change occur, but those who attended the program will be frustrated with the boss, the training program, or both for teaching them things that they can't apply.

One way to create a positive job climate is to involve bosses in the development of the program. Chapter 1 suggested asking bosses to help to determine the needs of subordinates. Such involvement helps to ensure that a program teaches practical concepts, principles, and techniques. Another approach is to present the training program, or at least a condensed version of it, to the bosses before the supervisors are trained.

A number of years ago, I was asked by Dave Harris, personnel manager, to present an eighteen-hour training program to 240 supervisors at A. O. Smith Corporation in Milwaukee. I asked Dave if he could arrange for me to present a condensed, three- to six-hour version to the company's top management. He arranged for the condensed version to be offered at the Milwaukee Athletic Club. After the six-hour program, the eight upper-level managers were asked for their opinions and suggestions. They not only liked the program but told us to present the entire program first to the thirty-five general foremen and superintendents who were the bosses of the 240 supervisors. We did what they suggested. We asked these bosses for their comments and encouraged them to provide an encouraging climate when the supervisors had completed the program. I am not sure to what extent this increased change in behavior over the level that we would have seen if top managers had not attended or even known the content of the program, but I am confident that it made a big difference. We told the supervisors that their bosses had already attended the program. This increased their motivation to learn and their desire to apply their learning on the job.

Results

Results can be defined as the final results that occurred because the participants attended the program. The final results can include increased production, improved quality, decreased costs, reduced frequency and/or severity of accidents, increased sales, reduced turnover, and higher profits. It is important to recognize that results like these are the reason for having some training programs. Therefore, the final objectives of the training program need to be stated in these terms.

Some programs have these in mind on a long-term basis. For example, one major objective of the popular program on diversity in the workforce is to change the attitudes of supervisors and managers toward minorities in their departments. We want supervisors to treat all people fairly, show no discrimination, and so on. These are not tangible results that can be measured in terms of dollars and cents. But it is hoped that tangible results will follow. Likewise, it is difficult if not impossible to measure final results for programs on such topics as leadership, communication, motivation, time management, empowerment, decision making, or managing change. We can state and evaluate desired behaviors, but the final results have to be measured in terms of improved morale or other nonfinancial terms. It is hoped that such things as higher morale or improved quality of work life will result in the tangible results just described.

Summary

Trainers should begin to plan by considering the desired results. These results should be determined in cooperation with managers at various levels. Surveys and/or interviews can be used. A desirable and practical approach is to use an advisory committee consisting of managers from different departments. Their participation will give them a feeling of ownership and will probably increase the chances of their creating a climate that encourages change in behavior. The next step is to determine what behaviors will produce the desired results. Then trainers need to determine what knowledge, skills, and attitudes will produce the desired behavior.

The final challenge is to present the training program in a way that enables the participants not only to learn what they need to know but also to react favorably to the program. This is the sequence in which programs should be planned. The four levels of evaluation are considered in reverse. First, we evaluate reaction. Then, we evaluate learning, behavior, and results—in that order. Each of the four levels is important, and we should not bypass the first two in order to get to levels 3 and 4. Reaction is easy to do, and we should measure it for every program. Trainers should proceed to the other three levels as staff, time, and money are available. The next four chapters provide guidelines, suggested forms, and procedures for each level. The case studies in Part Two of the book describe how the levels were applied in different types of programs and organizations.

Chapter 4

Evaluating Reaction

Evaluating reaction is the same thing as measuring customer satisfaction. If training is going to be effective, it is important that trainees react favorably to it. Otherwise, they will not be motivated to learn. Also, they will tell others of their reactions, and decisions to reduce or eliminate the program may be based on what they say. Some trainers call the forms that are used for the evaluation of reaction *happiness sheets*. Although they say this in a critical or even cynical way, they are correct. These forms really are happiness sheets. But they are not worthless. They help us to determine how effective the program is and learn how it can be improved.

Measuring reaction is important for several reasons. First, it gives us valuable feedback that helps us to evaluate the program as well as comments and suggestions for improving future programs. Second, it tells trainees that the trainers are there to help them do their job better and that they need feedback to determine how effective they are. If we do not ask for reaction, we tell trainees that we know what they want and need and that we can judge the effectiveness of the program without getting feedback from them. Third, reaction sheets can provide quantitative information that you can give to managers and others concerned about the program. Finally, reaction sheets can provide trainers with quantitative information that can be used to establish standards of performance for future programs.

Evaluating reaction is not only important but also easy to do and do effectively. Most trainers use reaction sheets. I have seen dozens of forms and various ways of using them. Some are effective, and some are not. Here are some guidelines that will help trainers to get maximum benefit from reaction sheets:

Guidelines for Evaluating Reaction

1. Determine what you want to find out.
2. Design a form that will quantify reactions.
3. Encourage written comments and suggestions.
4. Get 100 percent immediate response.
5. Get honest responses.
6. Develop acceptable standards.
7. Measure reactions against standards and take appropriate action.
8. Communicate reactions as appropriate.

The next eight sections contain suggestions for implementing each of these guidelines.

Determine What You Want to Find Out

In every program, it is imperative to get reactions both to the subject and to the leader. And it is important to separate these two ingredients of every program. In addition, trainers may want to get trainees' reactions to one or more of the following: the facilities (location, comfort, convenience, and so forth); the schedule (time, length of program, breaks, convenience, and so forth); meals (amount and quality of food and so forth); case studies, exercises, and so forth; audiovisual aids (how appropriate, effective, and so forth); handouts (how helpful, amount, and so forth); the value that participants place on individual aspects of the program.

Design a Form That Will Quantify Reactions

Trainers have their own philosophy about the forms that should be used. Some like open questions that require a lot of writing. They feel that checking boxes does not provide enough feedback. Some even feel that it amounts to telling trainees what to do. Others keep it as simple as possible and just ask trainees to check a few boxes.

The ideal form provides the maximum amount of information and requires the minimum amount of time. When a program is over, most trainees are anxious to leave, and they don't want to spend a lot of time completing evaluation forms. Some even feel that trainers do not consider their comments anyway.

There are a number of different forms that can provide the maximum information and require a minimum amount of time to complete. Exhibits 4.1, 4.2, 4.3, and 4.4 show forms that can be used

Exhibit 4.1. Reaction Sheet

Please give us your frank reactions and comments. They will help us to evaluate this program and improve future programs.

Leader _____   Subject _____

1. How do you rate the subject? (interest, benefit, etc.)

    _____ Excellent   Comments and suggestions:

    _____ Very good

    _____ Good

    _____ Fair

    _____ Poor

2. How do you rate the conference leader? (knowledge of subject matter, ability to communicate,etc.)

    _____ Excellent   Comments and suggestions:

    _____ Very good

    _____ Good

    _____ Fair

    _____ Poor

3. How do you rate the facilities? (comfort, convenience, etc.)

    _____ Excellent   Comments and suggestions:

    _____ Very good

    _____ Good

    _____ Fair

    _____ Poor

4. How do you rate the schedule?

    _____ Excellent   Comments and suggestions:

    _____ Very good

    _____ Good

    _____ Fair

    _____ Poor

5. What would have improved the program?

Exhibit 4.2. Reaction Sheet

Leader _____ Subject _____

1. How pertinent was the subject to your needs and interests?

    _____ Not at all _____ To some extent _____ Very much

2. How was the ratio of presentation to discussion?

    _____ Too much presentation _____ Okay _____ Too much discussion

3. How do you rate the instructor?

	Excellent	Very good	Good	Fair	Poor
a. In stating objectives					
b. In keeping the session alive and interesting					
c. In communicating					
d. In using aids					
e. In maintaining a friendly and helpful attitude					

4. What is your overall rating of the leader?

    _____ Excellent   Comments and suggestions:

    _____ Very good

    _____ Good

    _____ Fair

    _____ Poor

5. What would have made the session more effective?

---

effectively when one leader conducts the entire program. Exhibit 4.5 is unusual because it is truly a "smile" sheet, as many reaction sheets are called. I found it in a hotel in Geneva, Switzerland. The original form was written in French. Exhibits 4.5 and 4.6 show forms that can be used when more than one leader conducts the program and it is not desirable to have trainees complete a separate form for each. All

Exhibit 4.3. Reaction Sheet

In order to determine the effectiveness of the program in meeting your needs and interests, we need your input. Please give us your reactions, and make any comments or suggestions that will help us to serve you.

Instructions: Please circle the appropriate response after each statement.

	Strongly disagree		*Agree*		*Strongly agree*
1. The material covered in the program was relevant to my job.	1 2 3 4 5 6 7 8				
2. The material was presented in an interesting way.	1 2 3 4 5 6 7 8				
3. The instructor was an effective communicator.	1 2 3 4 5 6 7 8				
4. The instructor was well prepared.	1 2 3 4 5 6 7 8				
5. The audiovisual aids were effective.	1 2 3 4 5 6 7 8				
6. The handouts will be of help to me.	1 2 3 4 5 6 7 8				
7. I will be able to apply much of the material to my job.	1 2 3 4 5 6 7 8				
8. The facilities were suitable.	1 2 3 4 5 6 7 8				
9. The schedule was suitable.	1 2 3 4 5 6 7 8				
10. There was a good balance between presentation and group involvement.	1 2 3 4 5 6 7 8				
11. I feel that the workshop will help me do my job better.	1 2 3 4 5 6 7 8				

What would have improved the program?

---

forms can be quantified and used to establish standards for future evaluations. It would be worthwhile to try a form with several groups to see whether trainees understand it and whether it serves the purpose for which it was designed. All the forms illustrated in this chapter need to be tabulated by hand. They can be readily adapted so that they can be tabulated and analyzed by computer if that is easier.

Exhibit 4.4. Reaction Sheet

Please complete this form to let us know your reaction to the program. Your input will help us to evaluate our efforts, and your comments and suggestions will help us to plan future programs that meet your needs and interests.

Instructions: Please circle the appropriate number after each statement and then add your comments.

	High				*Low*
1. How do you rate the subject content? (interesting, helpful, etc.) Comments:	5	4	3	2	1
2. How do you rate the instructor? (preparation, communication, etc.) Comments:	5	4	3	2	1
3. How do you rate the facilities? (comfort, convenience, etc.) Comments:	5	4	3	2	1
4. How do you rate the schedule? (time, length, etc.) Comments:	5	4	3	2	1
5. How would you rate the program as an educational experience to help you do your job better?	5	4	3	2	1

6. What topics were most beneficial?

7. What would have improved the program?

Exhibit 4.5. Reaction Sheet

Dear Client,

We would like to have your comments and suggestions to enable us to offer you the kind of service you would like.

Would you help us by ticking the face that is most indicative of your feelings:

☐ **breakfast**   ☐ **lunch**   *Very good*   *Good*   *Average*

1. Are you satisfied with the quality of the meals?

2. Are you satisfied with the variety of dishes available?

3. Do you find our prices competitive?

4. What do you think of the service?

5. How do you find the atmosphere in the restaurant?

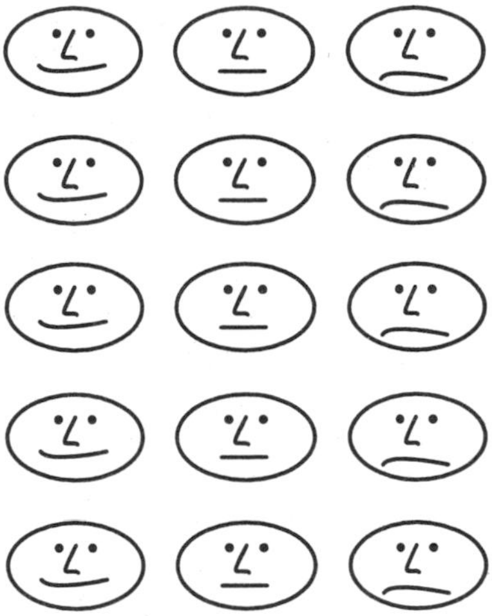

6. Suggestions:

Name: _____

Address: _____

Exhibit 4.6. Reaction Sheet

Please give your frank and honest reactions. Insert the appropriate number.

Scale: 5 = Excellent   4 = Very good   3 = Good   2 = Fair   1 = Poor

Leader	*Subject*	*Presentation*	*Discussion*	*Audiovisual aids*	*Overall*
Tom Jones					
Gerald Ford					
Luis Aparicio					
Simon Bolivar					
Muhammad Ali					
Chris Columbus					
Bart Starr					

Facilities   Rating _____   Meals   Rating _____

Comments: Comments:

Schedule   Rating _____   Overall program   Rating _____

Comments: Comments:

What would have improved the program?

Encourage Written Comments and Suggestions

The ratings that you tabulate provide only part of the participants' reactions. They do not provide the reasons for those reactions or suggest what can be done to improve the program. Therefore, it is important to get additional comments. All the forms shown in this chapter give participants opportunities to comment.

Typically, reaction sheets are passed out at the end of a program. Participants are encouraged to complete the forms and leave them on the back table on their way out. If they are anxious to leave, most will not take time to write in their comments. You can prevent this by making the completion of reaction sheets part of the program. For example, five minutes before the program is scheduled to end, the instructor can say, "Please take time to complete the reaction sheet, including your comments. Then I have a final announcement." This simple approach will ensure that you receive comments from all or nearly all the participants.

Another approach is to pass the forms out at the beginning of the program and stress the importance of comments and suggestions.

Get a 100 Percent Immediate Response

I have attended many programs at which reaction sheets are distributed to participants with instructions to send them back after they have a chance to complete them. This reduces the value of the reaction sheets for two reasons. First, some, perhaps even most, of the participants will not do it. Second, the forms that are returned may not be a good indication of the reaction of the group as a whole. Therefore, have participants turn in their reaction sheets before they leave the room. If you feel that reactions would be more meaningful if participants took more time to complete them, you can send out a follow-up reaction sheet after the training together with a cover memo that says something like this: "Thanks for the reaction sheet you completed at the end of the training meeting. As you think back on the program, you may have different or additional reactions and comments. Please complete the enclosed form, and return it within the next three days. We want to provide the most practical training possible. Your feedback will help us."

Get Honest Responses

Getting honest responses may seem to be an unnecessary requirement, but it is important. Some trainers like to know who said what. And they use an approach that lets them do just that. For example, they have the participants sign the forms. Or they tell them to complete the form and leave it at their place. In one program, the trainers used a two-sided form. One side was the reaction sheet. The other side sought attendance information: Participants were asked to give their name, department, and so on. I don't know whether the trainers were being clever or stupid.

In some programs, like those at the University of Wisconsin Management Institute, there is space at the bottom of the reaction sheets labeled *signature (optional)*. It is often meaningful to know who made a comment for two reasons: if the comment is positive, so that you can quote that person in future program brochures, or so that you can contact that person relative to the comment or suggestion.

Where people attend outside programs, they are usually free to give their honest opinion even if it is critical. They see little or no possibility of negative repercussions. The situation can be different in an in-house program. Some participants may be reluctant to make a critical reaction or comment because they fear repercussions. They may be afraid that the instructor or training department staff will feel that the reaction is not justified and that there is something wrong with the participant, even that trainers might tell the participant's boss about the negative reaction and that it could affect their future. Therefore, to be sure that reactions are honest, you should not ask participants to sign the forms. Also, you should ask that completed forms be put in a pile on a table so there is no way to identify the person who completed an individual form. In cases where it would be beneficial to identify the individual, the bottom of the form can have a space for a signature that is clearly labeled as *optional*.

Develop Acceptable Standards

A numerical tabulation can be made of all the forms discussed and shown in this chapter. Exhibit 4.7 shows a tabulation of the reactions of twenty supervisors to the form shown in Exhibit 4.1. The following five-point scale can be used to rate the responses on a form.

Excellent = 5 Very good = 4 Good = 3 Fair = 2 Poor = 1

You tally the responses in each category for all items. For each item, you multiply the number of responses by the corresponding weighting and add the products together. Then you divide by the total number of responses received. For example, you calculate the rating for item 1, subject, as follows:

Exhibit 4.7. Tabulating Responses to Reaction Sheets

Please give us your frank reactions and comments. They will help us to evaluate this program and improve future programs.

Leader __Tom Jones__   Subject __Leadership__

1. How do you rate the subject? (interest, benefit, etc.)

    __10__ Excellent   Comments and suggestions:

    __5__ Very good

    __3__ Good   Rating = *4.1*

    __1__ Fair

    __1__ Poor

2. How do you rate the conference leader? (knowledge of subject matter, ability to communicate, etc.)

    __8__ Excellent   Comments and suggestions:

    __4__ Very good

    __5__ Good   Rating = *3.8*

    __2__ Fair

    __1__ Poor

3. How do you rate the facilities? (comfort, convenience, etc.)

    __7__ Excellent   Comments and suggestions:

    __7__ Very good

    __5__ Good   Rating = *4.0*

    __1__ Fair

    __0__ Poor

4. What would have improved the program?

Note: Ratings are on a five-point scale.

$$(10 \times 5 = 50) + (5 \times 4 = 20) + (3 \times 3 = 9)$$
$$+ (1 \times 2 = 2) + (1 \times 1 = 1) = 82$$

The rating is 82/20 or 4.1.

You can use these ratings to establish a standard of acceptable performance. This standard can be based on a realistic analysis of what can be expected considering such conditions as budgets, facilities available, skilled instructors available, and so on. For example, at the University of Wisconsin Management Institute, the standard of subjects and leaders was placed at 4.7 on a five-point scale. This standard was based on past ratings. In this situation, budgets were favorable, and most of the instructors were full-time, professional trainers operating in nice facilities. In many organizations, limitations would lower the standard. You can have different standards for different aspects of the program. For example, the standard for instructors could be higher than the standard for facilities. The standards should be based on past experience, considering the ratings that effective instructors have received.

Measure Reactions Against Standards and Take Appropriate Action

Once realistic standards have been established, you should evaluate the various aspects of the program and compare your findings with the standards. Your evaluation should include impressions of the coordinator as well as an analysis of the reaction sheets of participants. Several approaches are possible if the standard is not met.

1. Make a change—in leaders, facilities, subject, or something else.
2. Modify the situation. If the instructor does not meet the standard, help by providing advice, new audiovisual aids, or something else.
3. Live with an unsatisfactory situation.
4. Change the standard if conditions change.

In regard to the evaluation of instructors, I once faced a situation that I'll never forget. At the Management Institute, I selected and hired an instructor from General Electric to conduct a seminar for top management. He had a lot of experience, both of the subject and in conducting seminars both inside and outside the company. His rating was 3.3, far below our standard of 4.7. He saw that we used reaction sheets and asked me to send him a summary. He also said, "Don, I know that you conduct and coordinate a lot of seminars. I would appreciate your personal comments and any suggestions for improvement." I agreed to do it.

I enclosed a thank-you letter with a summary of the comment sheets. My thank-you tactfully offered the following suggestions, which, I indicated, were based on the reaction sheets and on my own observations: "Use more examples to illustrate your points. Give the group more opportunity to ask questions. Ask your audiovisual department to prepare some professional slides and/or transparencies that will help to maintain interest and communicate."

I waited for a thank-you for my constructive suggestions. I am still waiting, and this happened in 1969. I did hear through a mutual friend that the instructor was very unhappy with my letter. He complained that he had taken time from a busy schedule to speak at the University of Wisconsin, he didn't take any fee or expenses, and the only thanks he had gotten was my letter. That was the last time he'd agree to be on our programs.

This example suggests that program coordinators should be very tactful in "helping" instructors by offering suggestions, especially if the instructors are members of top management within their own organization. One practical approach is to let instructors know ahead of time that reaction sheets will be used and that ratings will be compared with a standard. Instructors are usually eager to meet or beat the standard. If they don't, most will either ask for helpful suggestions or decide that someone else should probably do the teaching in the future. This is usually good news for the training staff, who may want to make a change anyway.

Obviously, all reactions that can be tabulated should be tabulated and the ratings calculated. In regard to comments, trainers can either record all comments on a summary sheet or summarize the comments that are pertinent. Tabulations can even be made of similar comments.

Communicate Reactions as Appropriate

Trainers are always faced with decisions regarding the communication of reactions to programs. Obviously, if instructors want to see their reaction sheets, they should be shown them or at least a summary of the responses. Other members of the training department should certainly have access to them. The person to whom the training department reports, usually the manager of Human Resources, should be able to see them. Communicating the reactions to others depends on two factors: who wants to see them and with whom training staff want to communicate.

Regarding who wants to see them, training staff must decide whether it is appropriate. Is it only out of curiosity, or does the requester have legitimate reasons?

Regarding the desire of training staff to communicate the reactions, the question is how often the information should be communicated and in what detail. Those who make decisions about staffing, budgets, salary increases, promotions, layoffs, and so on should be informed. Also, as I suggested in Chapter 1, if there is an advisory committee, its members should be informed. If the concepts and principles described in Chapter 1 have been implemented, the reactions will be favorable, and top management will respect the training department and realize how much the organization needs it in good and bad times.

Summary

Measuring reaction is important and easy to do. It is important because the decisions of top management may be based on what they have heard about the training program. It is important to have tangible data that reactions are favorable. It is important also because the interest, attention, and motivation of participants has much to do with the learning that occurs. Still another reason it is important is that trainees are customers, and customer satisfaction has a lot to do with repeat business.

This chapter has provided guidelines, forms, procedures, and techniques for measuring reaction effectively. Reaction is the first level in the evaluation process. It should be evaluated for all training programs.

The responses to reaction sheets should be tabulated, and the results should be analyzed. The comments received from participants should be considered carefully, and programs should be modified accordingly. This measure of customer satisfaction can make or break a training department. It is only the first step, but it is an important one.

P.S. If you refer to reaction sheets as "smile" sheets, smile when you do so and hope that participants are smiling when they leave the program!

Chapter 5

Evaluating Learning

There are three things that instructors in a training program can teach: knowledge, skills, and attitudes. Measuring learning, therefore, means determining one or more of the following:

> What knowledge was learned?
> What skills were developed or improved?
> What attitudes were changed?

It is important to measure learning because no change in behavior can be expected unless one or more of these learning objectives have been accomplished. Moreover, if we were to measure behavior change (level 3) and not learning and if we found no change in behavior, the likely conclusion would be that no learning took place. This conclusion may be very erroneous. The reason no change in behavior was observed may be that the climate was preventing or discouraging, as described in Chapter 3. In these situations, learning may have taken place, and the learner may even have been anxious to change his or her behavior. But because his or her boss either prevented or discouraged the trainee from applying his or her learning on the job, no change in behavior took place.

Note: In the guidelines for levels 2, 3, and 4, no information has been given on how to use statistics. This subject is too complex to be included here. I encourage readers to consider statistical analysis. Consult people within your organization who are knowledgeable and ask them to help you apply statistics to level 2 as well as to levels 3 and 4.

42

The measurement of learning is more difficult and time-consuming than the measurement of reaction. These guidelines will be helpful:

Guidelines for Evaluating Learning

1. Use a control group if practical.
2. Evaluate knowledge, skills, and/or attitudes both before and after the program.
3. Use a paper-and-pencil test to measure knowledge and attitudes.
4. Use a performance test to measure skills.
5. Get a 100 percent response.
6. Use the results of the evaluation to take appropriate action.

The remainder of this chapter suggests ways of implementing these guidelines.

Use a Control Group If Practical

The term *control group* will be used in levels 3 and 4 as well as here in level 2. It refers to a group that does not receive the training. The group that receives the training is called the *experimental group*. The purpose of using a control group is to provide better evidence that change has taken place. Any difference between the control group and the experimental group can be explained by the learning that took place because of the training program.

The phrase *whenever practical* is important for several reasons. For example, in smaller organizations there will be a single training program in which all the supervisors are trained. In larger organizations, there are enough supervisors that you can have a control group as well as an experimental group. In this case, you must take care to be sure that the groups are equal in all significant characteristics. Otherwise, comparisons are not valid. It could be done by giving the training program only to the experimental group and comparing scores before training with scores after training for both the experimental and control groups. The control group would receive the training at a later time. The example of test scores later in this chapter will illustrate this.

Evaluate Knowledge, Skills, and/or Attitudes

The second guideline is to measure attitudes, knowledge, and/or attitudes before and after the program. The difference indicates what learning has taken place.

Evaluating Increase in Knowledge and Changes in Attitudes

If increased knowledge and/or changed attitudes is being measured, a paper-and-pencil test can be used. (This term must have been coined before ballpoint pens were invented.) I'll use the Management Inventory on Managing Change (MIMC) described in Chapter 1 to illustrate.

Example 1 in Table 5.1 shows that the average score of the experimental group on the pretest (that is, on the test given before the program started) was 45.5 on a possible score of 65. The average score of the experimental group on the posttest (the same test given at the conclusion of the program) was 55.4—a net gain of 9.9.

Example 1 also shows that the average score of the control group on the pretest was 46.7 and that the score of the control group on the posttest was 48.2. This means that factors other than the training pro-

Table 5.1. Pretest and Posttest Scores
on the Management Inventory on Managing Change

		Experimental group	*Control group*
Example 1	Pretest	45.5	46.7
	Posttest	55.4	48.2
	Gain	+9.9	+1.5
		Net Gain 9.9 − 1.5 = 8.4	
		Experimental group	*Control group*
Example 2	Pretest	45.5	46.7
	Posttest	55.4	54.4
	Gain	+9.9	+7.7
		Net Gain 9.9 − 7.7 = 2.2	

gram caused the change. Therefore, the gain of 1.5 must be deducted from the 9.9 gain of the experimental group to show the gain resulting from the training program. The result is 8.4.

Example 2 in Table 5.1 shows a different story. The net gain for the control group between the pretest score of 46.7 and the posttest score of 54.4 is 7.7. When this difference is deducted from the 9.9 registered for the experimental group, the gain that can be attributed to the training program is only 2.2.

This comparison of total scores on the pretest and posttest is one method of measuring increased knowledge and/or changes in attitude. Another important measure involves the comparison of pretest and posttest answers to each item on the inventory or test. For example, this is item 4 of the MIMC described in Chapter 1: "If a change is going to be unpopular with your subordinates, you should proceed slowly in order to obtain acceptance."

Table 5.2 shows that seven of the twenty-five supervisors in the

Table 5.2. Responses to Two Items
on the Management Inventory on Managing Change

Item 4. "If a change is going to be unpopular with your subordinates, you should proceed slowly in order to obtain acceptance." (The correct answer is *Agree*.)

| | Experimental group | | Control group | |
	Agree	Disagree	Agree	Disagree
Pretest	7	18	6	19
Posttest	20	5	7	18
Gain	+13		+1	
	Net Gain 13 − 1 = 12			

Item 8. "If you are promoted to a management job, you should make the job different than it was under your predecessor." (The correct answer is *Agree*.)

| | Experimental group | | Control group | |
	Agree	Disagree	Agree	Disagree
Pretest	5	20	5	20
Posttest	6	19	6	19
Gain	+1		+1	
	Net Gain 1 − 1 = 0			

experimental group agreed with item 4 on the pretest, and eighteen disagreed. It also shows that twenty agreed with it on the posttest, and five disagreed. The correct answer is *Agree,* so the positive gain was 11. Table 5.2 also shows the pretest and posttest responses from the control group. For it, the gain was 1. Therefore, the net gain due to the training program was 10.

Item 8 in Table 5.2 shows a different story. Item 8 states: "If you are promoted to a management job, you should make the job different than it was under your predecessor."

Five of those in the experimental group agreed on the pretest, and twenty disagreed. On the posttest, six agreed, and nineteen disagreed. The correct answer is *Agree.* The net gain was 1. The figures for the control group were the same. So there was no change in attitude and/or knowledge on this item.

This evaluation of learning is important for two reasons. First, it measures the effectiveness of the instructor in increasing knowledge and/or changing attitudes. It shows how effective he or she is. If little or no learning has taken place, little or no change in behavior can be expected.

Just as important is the specific information that evaluation of learning provides. By analyzing the change in answers to individual items, the instructor can see where he or she has succeeded and where he or she has failed. If the program is going to be repeated, the instructor can plan other techniques and/or aids to increase the chances that learning will take place. Moreover, if follow-up sessions can be held with the same group, the things that have not been learned can become the objectives of these sessions.

These examples have illustrated how a control group can be used. In most organizations, it is not practical to have a control group, and the evaluation will include only figures for those who attended the training program.

It almost goes without saying that a standardized test can be used only to the extent that it covers the subject matter taught in the training program. When I teach, I use the various inventories that I have developed as teaching tools. Each inventory includes much of the content of the corresponding program. The same principles and techniques can and should be used with a test developed specifically for the organization. For example, MGIC, a mortgage insurer in Milwaukee, has developed an extensive test covering information that its supervisors need to know. Much of this information is related to the specific policies, procedures, and facts of the business and organization. Some of the items are true or false, while others are multiple choice, as Exhibit 5.1 shows.

The training people have determined what the supervisors need to know. Then they have written a test covering that information.

Exhibit 5.1. Sample Items from a MGIC Test to Evaluate Supervisor Knowledge

---

1. T or F When preparing a truth-in-lending disclosure with a financed single premium, mortgage insurance should always be disclosed for the life of the loan.

2. T or F GE and MGIC have the same refund policy for refundable single premiums.

3. T or F MGIC, GE, and PMI are the only mortgage insurers offering a non-refundable single premium.

4. _____ Which of the following is not a category in the loan progress reports?

  a. Loans approved

  b. Loans-in-suspense

  c. Loans denied

  d. Loans received

5. _____ Which of the following do not affect the MGIC Plus buying decision?

  a. Consumer

  b. Realtor

  c. MGIC underwriter

  d. Secondary market manager

  e. Servicing manager

  f. All the above

  g. None of the above

  h. Both b and c

  i. Both c and e

6. _____ The new risk-based capital regulations for savings and loans have caused many of them to

  a. Convert whole loans into securities

  b. Begin originating home equity loans

  c. Put MI on their uninsured 90s

  d. All the above

  e. Both e and c

  f. Both b and c

They have combined true-or-false statements with multiple-choice items to make the test interesting. A tabulation of the pretest responses to each item will tell the instructors what the supervisors do and do not know before they participate in the program. It will help them to determine the need for training. If everyone knows the answer to an item before the program takes place, there is no need to cover the item in the program. A tabulation of posttest responses will tell the instructor where he or she has succeeded and where he or she has failed in getting the participants to learn the information that the test covers. It will help instructors to know what they need to emphasize and whether they need to use more aids in future programs. It will also tell them what follow-up programs are needed.

This type of test is different from the inventories described earlier. Participants must know the answers to the questions in Exhibit 5.1. Therefore, those who take the posttest put their name on it, and they are graded. Those who do not pass must take further training until they pass the test.

In regard to the inventories, there is no need to identify the responses and scores of individual persons. The scoring sheet shown in Exhibit 5.2 is given to supervisors. They score their own inventory and circle the number of each item that they answered incorrectly. They keep their inventory and turn in the scoring sheet. These can be tabulated to determine both the total score and the responses to individual items. You can then use the resulting numbers as shown in Tables 5.1 and 5.2.

Exhibit 5.2. Scoring Sheet for the Management Inventory on Managing Change

---

Management Inventory on Managing Change   Date _____

Please circle by number those items you answered incorrectly according to the scoring key. Then determine your score by subtracting the number wrong from 65.

1	2	3	4	5	6	7	8	9	10	11	12	13	14	15	16	17	18
19	20	21	22	23	24	25	26	27	28	29	30	31	32	33	34
35	36	37	38	39	40	41	42	43	44	45	46	47	48	49	50
51	52	53	54	55	56	57	58	59	60	61	62	63	64	65

Score 65 –   =

Both the MIMC and the MGIC examples are typical of efforts to measure increase in knowledge and/or changes in attitudes.

Evaluating Increase in Skills

If the objective of a program is to increase the skills of participants, then a performance test is needed. For example, some programs aim at improving oral communication skills. A trained instructor can evaluate the level of proficiency. Other participants may also be qualified if they have been given standards of performance. For the pretest, you can have each person give a short talk before any training has been given. The instructor can measure these talks and assign them a grade. During the program, the instructor provides principles and techniques for making an effective talk. The increase in skills can be measured for each succeeding talk that participants give. The same approach can be used to measure such skills as speaking, writing, conducting meetings, and conducting performance appraisal interviews.

The same principles and techniques apply when technical skills, such as using a computer, making out forms, and selling, are taught. Of course, the before-and-after approach is not necessary where the learner has no previous skill. An evaluation of the skill after instruction measures the learning that has taken place.

Get a 100 Percent Response

Anything less than a 100 percent response requires a carefully designed approach to select a sample group and analyze the results statistically. It is not difficult to get everyone in the group to participate, and tabulations become simple. Tables 5.1 and 5.2 show how this can be done. It is desirable to analyze the tabulations shown in Tables 5.1 and 5.2 statistically, but in most organizations it is not necessary.

Take Appropriate Action

There is an old saying that, if the learner hasn't learned, the teacher hasn't taught. This is a good philosophy for each instructor to have. It is only too easy to blame a learner for not learning. How many times have we trainers said (or perhaps only thought) to someone whom we are teaching, "How many times do I have to tell you before you catch on?" And usually the tone makes it clear that we are criticizing the learner, not simply asking a question. Another old saying applies pretty well to the same situation: When you point a finger at another person, you are pointing three fingers at yourself! This saying, too, can be applied in many teaching situations.

The important point is that we are measuring our own effectiveness as instructors when we evaluate participants' learning. If we haven't succeeded, let's look at ourselves and ask where we have failed, not what is the matter with the learners. And if we discover that we have not been successful instructors, let's figure out how we can be more effective in the future. Sometimes the answer is simply better preparation. Sometimes it's the use of aids that help us to maintain interest and communicate more effectively. And sometimes the answer is to replace the instructor.

Summary

Evaluating learning is important. Without learning, no change in behavior will occur. Sometimes, the learning objective is to increase knowledge. Increased knowledge is relatively easy to measure by means of a test related to the content of the program that we administer before and after the training. If the knowledge is new, there is no need for a pretest. But if we are teaching concepts, principles, and techniques that trainees may already know, a pretest that we can compare with a posttest is necessary.

We can measure attitudes with a paper-and-pencil test. For example, programs on diversity in the workforce aim primarily at changing attitudes. We can design an attitude survey that covers the attitudes we want participants to have after taking part in the program. A comparison of the results from before and after training can indicate what changes have taken place. In such cases, it is important not to identify learners so we can be sure that they will give honest answers, not the answers that we want them to give.

The third thing that can be learned is skills. In these situations, a performance test is necessary. A pretest will be necessary if it is possible that they already possess some of the skills taught. If you are teaching something entirely new, then the posttest alone will measure the extent to which they have learned the skill.

Chapter 6

Evaluating Behavior

What happens when trainees leave the classroom and return to their jobs? How much transfer of knowledge, skills, and attitudes occurs? That is what level 3 attempts to evaluate. In other words, what change in job behavior occurred because people attended a training program?

It is obvious that this question is more complicated and difficult to answer than evaluating at the first two levels. First, trainees cannot change their behavior until they have an opportunity to do so. For example, if you, the reader of this book, decide to use some of the principles and techniques that I have described, you must wait until you have a training program to evaluate. Likewise, if the training program is designed to teach a person how to conduct an effective performance appraisal interview, the trainee cannot apply the learning until an interview is held.

Second, it is impossible to predict when a change in behavior will occur. Even if a trainee has an opportunity to apply the learning, he or she may not do it immediately. In fact, change in behavior may occur at any time after the first opportunity, or it may never occur.

Third, the trainee may apply the learning to the job and come to one of the following conclusions: "I like what happened, and I plan to continue to use the new behavior." "I don't like what happened, and I will go back to my old behavior." "I like what happened, but the boss and/or time restraints prevent me from continuing it." We all hope that the rewards for changing behavior will cause the trainee to come

[handwritten: self minor use / pay scale]

to the first of these conclusions. It is important, therefore, to provide help, encouragement, and rewards when the trainee returns to the job from the training class. One type of reward is intrinsic. This term refers to the inward feelings of satisfaction, pride, achievement, and happiness that can occur when the new behavior is used. Extrinsic rewards are also important. These are the rewards that come from the outside. They include praise, increased freedom and empowerment, merit pay increases, and other forms of recognition that come as the result of the change in behavior.

In regard to reaction and learning, the evaluation can and should take place immediately. When you evaluate change in behavior, you have to make some important decisions: when to evaluate, how often to evaluate, and how to evaluate. This makes it more time-consuming and difficult to do than levels 1 and 2. Here are some guidelines to follow when evaluating at level 3.

[handwritten: Good to make comparison]

Guidelines for Evaluating Behavior

[handwritten: on how long qualified e extent behaviour change y any has sustained]

1. Use a control group if practical.
2. Allow time for behavior change to take place.
3. Evaluate both before and after the program if practical.
4. Survey and/or interview one or more of the following: trainees, their immediate supervisor, their subordinates, and others who often observe their behavior. *[handwritten: L e 72s]*
5. Get 100 percent response or a sampling.
6. Repeat the evaluation at appropriate times.
7. Consider cost versus benefits.

The remainder of this chapter suggests ways of implementing these guidelines.

[handwritten: ✓ not students as can be in college for 4 car]

Use a Control Group If Practical

Chapter 5 described the use of control groups in detail. A comparison of the change in behavior of a control group with the change experienced by the experimental group can add evidence that the change in behavior occurred because of the training program and not for other reasons. However, caution must be taken to be sure the two groups

[handwritten: Difficult to compare 2 groups that are equal in all factors - maybe able to for some aspects eg. confidence]

are equal in all factors that could have an effect on behavior. This may be difficult if not impossible to do.

Allow Time for Behavior Change to Take Place

As already indicated, no evaluation should be attempted until trainees have had an opportunity to use the new behavior. Sometimes, there is an immediate opportunity for applying it on the job. For example, if the training program is trying to change attitudes toward certain subordinates by teaching about diversity in the workforce, participants have an immediate opportunity to change attitudes and behavior as soon as they return to the job. Or if the program teaches management by walking around (MBWA), as encouraged by United Airlines and Hewlett-Packard, participants have an opportunity to use the technique right away. However, if the purpose of the training is to teach a foreman how to handle a grievance, no change in behavior is possible until a grievance has been filed.

Even if a participant has an immediate opportunity to transfer the training to the job, you should still allow some time for this transfer to occur. For some programs, two or three months after training is a good rule of thumb. For others, six months is more realistic. Be sure to give trainees time to get back to the job, consider the new suggested behavior, and try it out.

Question: how quickly behavior changed, if it did, + sustained over time.

Evaluate Both Before and After the Program If Practical

Sometimes evaluation before and after a program is practical, and sometimes it is not even possible. For example, supervisors who attend the University of Wisconsin Management Institute training programs sometimes do not enroll until a day or two before the program starts. It would not be possible for the instructors or designated research students to measure their behavior before the program. In an in-house program, it would be possible, but it might not be practical because of time and budget constraints.

It is important when planning a supervisory training program to determine the kind of behavior that supervisors should have in order to be most effective. Before the training program, you measure the

Prob. period but no universally used. No apart from student survey or attainment

behavior of the supervisors. After the program, at a time to be determined as just outlined, you measure the behavior of the supervisors again to see whether any change has taken place in relation to the knowledge, skills, and/or attitudes that the training program taught. By comparing the behaviors observed before and after the program, you can determine any change that has taken place.

An alternative approach can also be effective. Under this approach, you measure behavior after the program only. Those whom you interview or survey are asked to identify any behavior that was different than it had been before the program. This was the approach that we used at the Management Institute to evaluate the three-day supervisory training program called Developing Supervisory Skills. Chapter 14 describes this evaluation.

In some cases, the training professionals and/or persons whom they select can observe the behavior personally.

Survey and/or Interview Persons Who Know the Behavior

As the guideline suggests, evaluators should survey and/or interview one or more of the following: trainees, their immediate supervisor, their subordinates, and others who are knowledgeable about their behavior.

Four questions need to be answered: Who is best qualified? Who is most reliable? Who is most available? Are there any reasons why one or more of the possible candidates should not be used?

If we try to determine who is best qualified, the answer is probably the subordinates who see the behavior of the trainee on a regular basis. In some cases, others who are neither boss nor subordinate have regular contact with the trainee. And, of course, the trainee knows (or should know) his or her own behavior. Therefore, of the four candidates just named, the immediate supervisor may be the person least qualified to evaluate the trainee unless he or she spends a great deal of time with the trainee.

Who is the most reliable? The trainee may not admit that behavior has not changed. Subordinates can be biased in favor of or against the trainee and therefore give a distorted picture. In fact, anyone can give a distorted picture, depending on his or her attitude toward the trainee or the program. This is why more than one source should be used.

Who is the most available? The answer depends on the particular situation. If interviews are to be conducted, then availability is critical. If a survey questionnaire is used, it is not important. In this case, the answer depends on who is willing to spend the time needed to complete the survey.

Are there any reasons why one or more of the possible candidates should not be used? The answer is yes. For example, asking subordinates for information on the behavior of their supervisor may not set well with the supervisor. However, if the trainee is willing to have subordinates questioned, this may be the best approach of all.

A significant decision is whether to use a questionnaire or an interview. Both have their advantages and disadvantages. The interview gives you an opportunity to get more information. The best approach is to use a patterned interview in which all interviewees are asked the same questions. Then you can tabulate the responses and gather quantitative data on behavior change.

But interviews are very time-consuming, and only a few can be conducted if the availability of the person doing the interviewing is limited. Therefore, a small sample of those trained can be interviewed. However, the sample may not be representative of the behavior change that took place in trainees. And you cannot draw conclusions about the overall change in behavior. Exhibit 6.1 shows a patterned interview that can be used as is or adapted to your particular situation.

A survey questionnaire is usually more practical. If it is designed properly, it can provide the data that you need to evaluate change in behavior. The usual problem of getting people to take the time to complete it is always present. However, you can overcome this problem by motivating the people whom you ask to complete the survey. Perhaps there can be some reward, either intrinsic or extrinsic, for doing it. Or a person can be motivated to do it as a favor to the person doing the research. Producing information for top management as the reason for doing it may convince some. If the instructor, the person doing the evaluation, or both have built a rapport with those who are asked to complete the survey, they usually will cooperate. Exhibit 6.2 shows a survey questionnaire that you can use as is or adapt to your organization.

Need to know what programme promised to deliver — what College / Managers expected

Exhibit 6.1. Patterned Interview.

The interviewer reviews the program with the interviewee and highlights the behaviors that the program encouraged. The interviewer then clarifies the purpose of the interview, which is to evaluate the effectiveness of the course so that improvements can be made in the future. Specifically, the interview will determine the extent to which the suggested behaviors have been applied on the job. If they have not been applied, the interview will seek to learn why not. The interviewer makes it clear that all information will be held confidential so that the answers given can be frank and honest.

1. What specific behaviors were you taught and encouraged to use?

2. When you left the program, how eager were you to change your behavior on the job?

_____ Very eager   _____ Quite eager   _____ Not eager

Comments:

3. How well equipped were you to do what was suggested?

_____ Very   _____ Quite   _____ Little   _____ None

4. If you are <u>not doing</u> some of the things that you were encouraged and taught to do, why not?

	How Significant?		
	Very	*To some extent*	*Not*
a. It wasn't practical for my situation.			
b. My boss discourages me from changing.			
c. I haven't found the time.			
d. I tried it, and it didn't work.			
e. Other reasons.			

5. To what extent do you plan to do things differently in the future?

_____ Large extent   _____ Some extent   _____ No extent

6. What suggestions do you have for making the program more helpful?

Exhibit 6.2. Survey Questionnaire

Instructions: The purpose of this questionnaire is to determine the extent to which those who attended the recent program on leadership methods have applied the principles and techniques that they learned there to the job. The results of the survey will help us to assess the effectiveness of the program and identify ways in which it can be made more practical for those who attend. Please be frank and honest in your answers. Your name is strictly optional. The only reason we ask is that we might want to follow up on your answers to get more comments and suggestions from you.

Please circle the appropriate response after each question.

5 = Much more   4 = Some more   3 = The same   2 = Some less   1 = Much less

Understanding and Motivating	*Time and energy spent after the program compared to time and energy spent before the program*				
1. Getting to know my employees	5	4	3	2	1
2. Listening to my subordinates	5	4	3	2	1
3. Praising good work	5	4	3	2	1
4. Talking with employees about their families and other personal interests	5	4	3	2	1
5. Asking subordinates for their ideas	5	4	3	2	1
6. Managing by walking around	5	4	3	2	1
Orienting and Training					
7. Asking new employees about their families, past experience, etc.	5	4	3	2	1
8. Taking new employees on a tour of the department and other facilities	5	4	3	2	1
9. Introducing new employees to their coworkers	5	4	3	2	1
10. Using the four-step method when training new and present employees	5	4	3	2	1
11. Being patient when employees don't learn as fast as I think they should	5	4	3	2	1
12. Tactfully correcting mistakes and making suggestions	5	4	3	2	1
13. Using the training inventory and timetable concept	5	4	3	2	1

What would have made the program more practical and helpful to you?

Name (optional) _____

Get 100 Percent Response or a Sampling

The dictum that something beats nothing can apply when you evaluate change in behavior. The person doing the evaluation can pick out a few "typical" trainees at random and interview or survey them. Or you can interview or survey the persons most likely not to change. The conclusion might be that, if Joe and Charlie have changed their behavior, then everyone has. This conclusion may or may not be true, but the approach can be practical. Obviously, the best approach is to measure the behavior change in all trainees. In most cases, this is not practical. Each organization must determine the amount of time and money that it can spend on level 3 evaluation and proceed accordingly.

Repeat the Evaluation at Appropriate Times

Some trainees may change their behavior as soon as they return to their job. Others may wait six months or a year or never change. And those who change immediately may revert to the old behavior after trying out the new behavior for a period of time. Therefore, it is important to repeat the evaluation at an appropriate time.

I wish I could describe what an appropriate time is. Each organization has to make the decision on its own, taking into account the kind of behavior, the job climate, and other significant factors unique to the situation. I would suggest waiting two or three months before conducting the first evaluation, the exact number depending on the opportunity that trainees have to use the new behavior. Perhaps another six months should elapse before the evaluation is repeated. And, depending on circumstances and the time available, a third evaluation could be made three to six months later.

Consider Cost Versus Benefits

need to acknowledge on some it'll be years— years

Just as with other investments, you should compare the cost of evaluating change in behavior with the benefits that could result from the evaluation. In many organizations, much of the cost of evaluation at level 3 is in the staff time that it takes to do. And time is money. Other costs of evaluation can include the hiring of an outside expert to guide or even conduct the evaluation. For example, I have recently been hired by Kemper Insurance, Ford, GE, Blockbuster, and Northern States Power to present and discuss the four levels of evaluation with their training staff. At Kemper, I was asked to offer specific suggestions and return three months later to comment on the evaluations that they had done. In these instances, I was called in not to evaluate a specific program but to provide guidelines and specific suggestions on how programs could be evaluated at all four levels. Other consultants can be called in to evaluate the changes in behavior that result from a specific program. You should consider such costs as these when you decide whether to evaluate changes in behavior.

The other factor to consider is the benefits that can be derived from evaluation, including changes in behavior and final results. The greater the potential benefits, the more time and money can be spent on the evaluation not only of behavior change but in level 4 also. Another important consideration is the number of times the program will be offered. If it is run only once and it will not be repeated, there is little justification for spending time and money to evaluate possible changes in behavior. However, if a program is going to be repeated, the time and money spent evaluating it can be justified by the possible improvements in future programs.

It is important to understand that change in behavior is not an end in itself. Rather, it is a means to an end: the final results that can be achieved if change in behavior occurs. If no change in behavior occurs, then no improved results can occur. At the same time, even if change in behavior does occur, positive results may not be achieved. A good example is the principle and technique of managing by walking around (MBWA). Some organizations, including United Airlines and Hewlett-Packard, have found that higher morale and increased productivity can result. These organizations therefore encourage managers at all levels to walk among the lowest-level employees to show that they care. Picture a manager who has never shown concern for people. He attends a seminar at which he is told to change his behavior by walking around among lower-level employees to show that he cares. So the manager—for the first time—changes his behavior. He asks one employee about the kids. He comments to another employee regarding a vacation trip that the employee's family is planning. And he asks another employee about Sam, the pet dog. (The manager has learned about these things before talking to the three employees.) What are the chances that the three employees are now going to be motivated to increase their productivity because the manager really cares? Or will they look with suspicion on the new behavior and wonder what the boss is up to? The manager's change in behavior could even have negative results. This possibility underlines the fact that some behavior encouraged in the classroom is not appropriate for all participants. Encouraging supervisors to empower employees is a behavior that would not be appropriate in departments that had a lot of new employees, employees with negative attitudes, or employees with limited knowledge.

Summary

Level 3 evaluation determines the extent to which change in behavior occurs because of the training program. No final results can be expected unless a positive change in behavior occurs. Therefore, it is important to see whether the knowledge, skills, and/or attitudes learned in the program transfer to the job. The process of evaluating is complicated and often difficult to do. You have to decide whether to use interviews, survey questionnaires, or both. You must also decide whom to contact for the evaluation.

Two other difficult decisions are when and how often to conduct the evaluation. Whether to use a control group is still another important consideration. The sum of these factors discourages most trainers from even making an attempt to evaluate at level 3. But something beats nothing, and I encourage trainers to do some evaluating of behavior even if it isn't elaborate or scientific. Simply ask a few people, Are you doing anything different on the job because you attended the training program?

If the answer is yes, ask, Can you briefly describe what you are doing and how it is working out? If you are not doing anything different, can you tell me why? Is it because you didn't learn anything that you can use on the job? Does your boss encourage you to try out new things, or does your boss discourage any change in your behavior? Do you plan to change some of your behavior in the future? If the answer is yes, ask, What do you plan to do differently?

Questions like these can be asked on a questionnaire or in an interview. A tabulation of the responses can provide a good indication of changes in behavior.

If the program is going to be offered a number of times in the future and the potential results of behavior changes are significant, then a more systematic and extensive approach should be used. The guidelines in this chapter will prove helpful.

Chapter 7

Evaluating Results

Now comes the most important and perhaps the most difficult part of the process, you decide—determining what final results occurred because of attendance and participation in a training program. Trainers consider questions like these:

How much did quality improve because of the training program on total quality improvement that we have presented to all supervisors and managers? How much has it contributed to profits?

How much did productivity increase because we conducted a program on diversity in the workforce for all supervisors and managers?

What reduction did we get in turnover and scrap rate because we taught our foremen and supervisors to orient and train new employees?

How much has "management by walking around" improved the quality of work life?

What has been the result of all our programs on interpersonal communications and human relations?

How much has productivity increased and how much have costs been reduced because we have trained our employees to work in self-directed work teams?

What tangible benefits have we received for all the money we have spent on programs on leadership, time management, and decision making?

> How much have sales increased as the result of teaching our salespeople such things as market research, overcoming objections, and closing a sale?
>
> What is the return on investment for all the money we spend on training?

All these and many more questions usually remain unanswered for two reasons: First, trainers don't know how to measure the results and compare them with the cost of the program. Second, even if they do know how, the findings probably provide evidence at best and not clear proof that the positive results come from the training program. There are exceptions, of course. Increases in sales may be found to be directly related to a sales training program, and a program aimed specifically at reducing accidents or improving quality can be evaluated to show direct results from the training program.

A number of years ago, Jack Jenness, a friend of mine at Consolidated Edison in New York, was asked by his boss to show results in terms of dollars and cents from an expensive program on leadership that they were giving to middle- and upper-level managers. The company had hired consultants from St. Louis at a very high fee to conduct the program. I told Jack, "There is no way it can be done!" He said, "That's what I told my boss." Jack then asked me to come out to his organization to do two things: Conduct a workshop with their trainers on the four levels of evaluation, and tell his boss that it couldn't be done. I did the first. I didn't get a chance to do the second because the boss had either been convinced and didn't see the need, or he didn't have the time or desire to hear what I had to say.

This example is unusual at this point in history, but it might not be too unusual in the future. Whenever I get together with trainers, I ask, "How much pressure are you getting from top management to prove the value of your training programs in results, such as dollars and cents?" Only a few times have they said they were feeling such pressure. But many trainers have told me that the day isn't too far off when they expect to be asked to provide such proof.

When we look at the objectives of training programs, we find that almost all aim at accomplishing some worthy result. Often, it is improved quality, productivity, or safety. In other programs, the objective is improved morale or better teamwork, which, it is hoped, will lead to better quality, productivity, safety, and profits. Therefore, trainers look at the desired end result and say to themselves and others, "What behavior on the part of supervisors and managers will achieve these results?" Then they decide what knowledge, skills, and attitudes supervisors need in order to behave in that way. Finally, they determine the training needs and proceed to do the things described in Chapter 1. In so doing, they hope (and sometimes pray) that the trainees will like the program; learn the knowledge, skills, and attitudes taught; and transfer them to the job. The first three levels of evaluation attempt to determine the degree to which these three things have been accomplished.

So now we have arrived at the final level, What final results were accomplished because of the training program? Here are some guidelines that will be helpful:

Guidelines for Evaluating Results

1. Use a control group if practical.
2. Allow time for results to be achieved.
3. Measure both before and after the program if practical.
4. Repeat the measurement at appropriate times.
5. Consider cost versus benefits.
6. Be satisfied with evidence if proof is not possible.

Do these guidelines look familiar? They are almost the same ones that were listed in Chapter 6 for evaluating change in behavior. Some have the same principles and difficulty. At least one (no. 3) is much easier.

Use a Control Group If Practical

Enough has been said about control groups in Chapters 5 and 6 that I do not need to dwell on them here. The reason for control groups is always the same: to eliminate the factors other than training that could have caused the changes observed to take place. In a sales training program, for example, it might be quite easy to use control groups. If salespeople in different parts of the country are selling the same products, then a new sales training program can be conducted in some areas and not in others. By measuring the sales figures at various times after the program and comparing them with sales before the program, you can readily see differences. The increase (or decrease) in sales in the regions where the new sales program has been presented can easily be compared to the increase (or decrease) in areas where the program has not been presented. This does not prove that the difference resulted from the training program, even if the control and experimental groups were equal. Other factors may have influenced the sales. These factors can include such things as these: a new competitor has entered the marketplace, a good customer has gone out of business, the economy in a region has gone bad, a competitor has gone out of business, a new customer has moved into the region, or a present customer got a new order that requires your product. These and other factors force us to use the term *evidence* in place of *proof*.

Allow Time for Results to Be Achieved

In the sales example just cited, time has to elapse before the evaluation can be done. How long does it take for a customer to increase orders? There is no sure answer to the question because each situation is different. Likewise, if a program aims to teach such subjects as leadership, communication, motivation, and team building, the time between training and application on the job may be different for each individual. And improved results, if they occur, will lag behind the changes in behavior. In deciding on the time lapse before evaluating, a trainer must consider all the factors that are involved.

Measure Both Before and After the Program If Practical

This is easier to do when you are evaluating results than when you are evaluating changes in behavior. Records are usually available to determine the situation before the program. If a program aims at reducing the frequency and severity of accidents, figures are readily available. Figures are also available for the sales example just used. The same is true for quality, production, turnover, number of grievances, and absenteeism. For morale and attitudes, preprogram figures may also be available from attitude surveys and performance appraisal forms.

Repeat the Measurement at Appropriate Times

Each organization must decide how often and when to evaluate. Results can change at any time in either a positive or negative direction. It is up to the training professional to determine the influence of training on these results. For example, sales may have increased because of a big push and close supervision to use a new technique. When the push is over and the boss has other things to do, the salesperson may go back to the old way, and negative results may occur.

because of different students

Consider Cost Versus Benefits

How much does it cost to evaluate at this level? Generally, it isn't nearly as costly as it is to evaluate change in behavior. The figures you need are usually available. The difficulty is to determine just what figures are meaningful and to what extent they are related, directly or otherwise, to the training. I almost laugh when I hear people say that training professionals should be able to show benefits in terms of return on investment (ROI) from a company standpoint. The same thought occurs to me when they expect trainers to relate training programs directly to profits. Just think of all the factors that affect profits. And you can add to the list when you consider all the things that affect ROI. *Return on expectation:*

The amount of money that should be spent on level 4 evaluation should be determined by the amount of money that the training program costs, the potential results that can accrue because of the program, and the number of times that the program will be offered. The higher the value of potential results and the more times the program will be offered, the more time and money should be spent. The value of the actual results (if it can be determined accurately) should then be compared to the cost of the program. The results of this evaluation should determine whether the program should be continued.

How Much Evidence Is Needed?

How much evidence does your top management expect from you? The two O. J. Simpson trials illustrate the difference that exists in different organizations. In the first trial (for murder), the jury had to be unanimous in finding Simpson guilty "beyond a reasonable doubt." They arrived at a "not guilty" verdict. In the second trial (for money), only nine members of the jury had to agree that the "preponderance of evidence" proved him guilty. They agreed unanimously that over 50 percent of the evidence pointed to his guilt, so they reached a verdict of "guilty."

The top management of some organizations requires "evidence beyond a reasonable doubt," whereas others only require "preponderance of evidence," which can be just what they have heard about the program from those who have attended and/or their bosses. Human resource professionals need to know what their top management expects and/or demands and evaluate accordingly. Following is an example that would probably be sufficient evidence for most top executives.

Turnover in a certain company was far too high. The main reason for the turnover, as determined by the training department, was that supervisors and foremen were doing a poor job of orienting and training new employees. Therefore, a training program on how to orient and train employees was conducted in April for all supervisors and foremen. Here are the turnover figures before and after the April training.

Oct.	Nov.	Dec.	Jan.	Feb.	Mar.	Apr.	May	June	July	Aug.	Sept.
6%	7%	5%	7%	6%	7%	6%	4%	2%	2%	2%	3%

It seems obvious that the training program caused the positive results. After all, the objective of the training program was to reduce turnover, and turnover certainly dropped. But some wise guy asks, "Are you sure that some other factor didn't cause the reduction?" And the trainer says, "Like what?" And the wise guy says, "The unemployment figures in your city went way up, and new employees got a nice raise, and the figures for last year were about the same, and I understand that your employment department is hiring more mature people instead of kids right out of high school." I would consider this to be a "preponderance of evidence" but not "evidence beyond a reasonable doubt." But this is an objective way to measure results and show that the objective of reducing turnover was reached.

Summary

Evaluating results, level 4, provides the greatest challenge to training professionals. After all, that is why we train, and we ought to be able to show tangible results that more than pay for the cost of the training. In some cases, such evaluation can be done and quite easily. Programs that aim at increasing sales, reducing accidents, reducing turnover, and reducing scrap rates can often be evaluated in terms of results. And the cost of the program isn't too difficult to determine. A comparison can readily show that training pays off.

Most of the programs that I teach have results in mind. When I conduct a management workshop on how to manage change, I certainly hope that those who attend will make better changes in the future and that the changes will be accepted and implemented enthusiastically. The results will be such things as better quality of work, more productivity, more job satisfaction, and fewer mistakes. When I teach how to improve communication effectiveness, I expect participating supervisors to communicate better on the job afterward and the result to be fewer misunderstandings, fewer mistakes, improved rapport between supervisor and subordinate, and other positive results. When I teach leadership, motivation, and decision making, I expect participants to understand what I teach, accept my ideas, and use them on the job. This will, of course, end up with tangible results. But how can I tell? Can I prove or even find evidence beyond a reasonable doubt that the final results occur? The answer is a resounding no. There are too many other factors that affect results.

So what should a trainer do when top management asks for tangible evidence that training programs are paying off? Sometimes, you can find evidence that positive results have occurred. In other situations, you will have to go back a level or two and evaluate changes in behavior, learning, or both. In many cases, positive reaction sheets from supervisors and managers will convince top management. After all, if top management has any confidence in the management team, isn't it enough to know that the supervisors and managers feel the training is worthwhile?

If your programs aim at tangible results rather than teaching management concepts, theories, and principles, then it is desirable to evaluate in terms of results. Consider the guidelines given in this chapter.

And most important, be satisfied with evidence, because proof is usually impossible to get.

P.S. The most frequent question I am asked is, How do you evaluate level 4? Be prepared for my answer if you ask this question. I will probably describe at length all four levels, beginning with level 1.

Chapter 8

Implementing the Four Levels

"Everybody talks about it, but nobody does anything about it." When Mark Twain said this, he was talking about the weather. It also applies to evaluation—well, almost. My contacts with training professionals indicate that most use some form of reaction, "smile," or "happiness" sheets. Some of these sheets are, in my opinion, very good and provide helpful information that measures customer satisfaction. Others do not meet the guidelines that I listed in Chapter 4. And many trainers ignore critical comments by saying, "Well, you can't please everybody" or "I know who said that, and I am not surprised."

Where do I start? What do I do first? These are typical questions from trainers who are convinced that evaluation is important but have done little about it.

My suggestion is to start at level 1 and proceed through the other levels as time and opportunity allow. Some trainers are anxious to get to level 3 or 4 right away because they think the first two aren't as important. Don't do it. Suppose, for example, that you evaluate at level 3 and discover that little or no change in behavior has occurred. What conclusions can you draw? The first conclusion is probably that the training program was no good and we had better discontinue it or at least modify it. This conclusion may be entirely wrong. As I described in Chapter 3, the reason for no change in job behavior may be that the climate prevents it. Supervisors may have gone back to the job with the necessary knowledge, skills, and attitudes, but the boss wouldn't allow change to take place. Therefore, it is important to eval-

*or change them
because
of untrue*

uate at level 2 so you can determine whether the reason for no change in behavior was lack of learning or negative job climate.

The first step for you to take in implementing the evaluation concepts, theories, and techniques described in the preceding chapters is to understand the guidelines of level 1 and apply them in every program. Use a philosophy that states, "If my customers are unhappy, it is my fault, and my challenge is to please them." If you don't, your entire training program is in trouble. It is probably true that you seldom please everyone. For example, it is a rare occasion when everyone in my training classes grades me excellent. Nearly always some participants are critical of my sense of humor, some content that I presented, or the quality of the audiovisual aids. I often find myself justifying what I did and ignoring their comments, but I shouldn't do that. My style of humor, for example, is to embarrass participants, I hope in a pleasant way so that they don't resent it. That happens to be my style, and most people enjoy and appreciate it. If I get only one critical comment from a group of twenty-five, I will ignore it and continue as I did in the past. However, if the reaction is fairly common because I have overdone it, then I will take the comment seriously and change my approach.

I used to tell a funny story in class. It was neither dirty nor ethnic. Nearly everyone else thought it was funny, too, and I had heard no objections to it. One day, I conducted a training class with social workers. I told the story at the beginning of the class and proceeded to do the training. After forty minutes, I asked whether anyone had a comment or question. One lady raised her hand and said, "I was offended by the joke you told at the beginning of the session, and I didn't listen to anything you said after that!"

I couldn't believe it. I was sure she was the only one who felt that way, so I asked the question, "Did any others feel the same way?" Seven other women raised their hands. There were about forty-five people in the class, so the percentage was very much in my favor. But I decided that that particular joke had no place in future meetings. If she had been the only one, I probably would still be telling it.

The point is this: Look over all the reaction sheets and read the comments. Consider each one. Is there a suggestion that will improve future programs? If yes, use it. If it is an isolated comment that will not improve future programs, appreciate it, but ignore it.

Evaluating at level 2 isn't that difficult. All you need to do is to decide what knowledge, skills, and attitudes you want participants to have at the end of the program. If there is a possibility that one or more of these three things already exist, then a pretest is necessary. If you are presenting something entirely new, then no pretest is necessary. You can use a standardized test if you can find one that covers the things you are teaching. Several examples were given in Chapter 5. Or you can develop your own test to cover the knowledge and attitudes that you are teaching. An example from MGIC was also given in Chapter 5. Study the guidelines and suggestions from Chapter 5 and then do it!

Levels 3 and 4 are not easy. A lot of time will be required to decide on an evaluation design. A knowledge of statistics to determine the level of significance may be desirable. Check with the research people in your organization for help in the design. If necessary, you may have to call in an outside consultant to help you or even do the evaluation for you. Remember the principle that the possible benefits from an evaluation should exceed the cost of doing the evaluation, and be satisfied with evidence if proof is not possible.

There is an important principle that applies to all four levels: You can borrow evaluation forms, designs, and procedures from others, but you cannot borrow evaluation results. If another organization offers the same program as you do and they evaluate it, you can borrow their evaluation methods and procedures, but you can't say, "They evaluated it and found these results. Therefore, we don't have to do it, because we know the results we would get."

Learn more about all aspects of "evaluation." As a start, read the case studies in Part Two of this book and look for forms, methods, techniques, and designs that you can copy or adapt. An excellent source for further reading is the American Society For Training and Development (ASTD) in Alexandria, VA. They have many books and pamphlets on evaluation. If you do a lot of e-learning, study William Horton's Chapter 11, "So, How Is E-Learning Different?" If you are not sure how to manage the changes that need to take place, study Chapter 9, "Managing Change." If you are concerned with the problems and solutions for transferring learning to behavior, study Jim Kirkpatrick's Chapter 10 on the subject.

In teaching management courses, I usually start by telling the group about a study made by the Society for Advancement of Management, a branch of the American Management Association. A special task force was assigned the job of deciding on a definition of management. The task force decided that management is a science and an art. It defined these two words as follows: "As a science, it is organized knowledge—concepts, theory, principles, and techniques. As an art, it is the application of the organized knowledge to realities in a situation, usually with blend or compromise, to obtain desired practical results."

I would like to use the same definition for *evaluation*. It is a science and an art. This book provides the organized knowledge—concepts, theory, principles, and techniques. It is up to you to do the application. May you be successful in doing it.

Chapter 9

Managing Change

There is one important ingredient that is basic to all evaluation approaches. There must be a realization that managing change is that ingredient. It starts with the determination of what changes are needed. We call it "determining needs." We need to determine what knowledge, skills, and/or attitudes are needed to achieve the desired behavior and results. This means that training and development professionals must know the concepts, principles and techniques required for "managing" change. I have put "managing" in quotes because it has a twofold meaning. It not only means to decide on the changes to be made but also to get the acceptance of those involved in the change.

This chapter is written not only for training and development professionals but also for line managers. It is important to emphasize that the training and development professionals can control the determining of needs and the learning content. But it is also important to emphasize that changing behavior is under the control of the manager whose subordinates were trained. Therefore, these concepts, principles, and techniques are equally important to trainers and managers.

Following are ten statements concerning "managing change." Before I describe the concepts, principles, and techniques that I think are important, I would like you to agree (A) or disagree (DA) with the following statements. Then I will give you my answers and the rationale behind them.

Please circle the A or DA in front of each statement.

A DA   1. Everyone is resistant to change.
A DA   2. People will always accept changes that have been decided on by "experts."
A DA   3. If you want people to accept or welcome a change, give them a feeling of "ownership."
A DA   4. People who don't understand the reason for a change will always resent and/or resist it.
A DA   5. Empathy is one of the most important concepts in managing change.
A DA   6. Persons who have no control over the people affected by a change can have little or no effect on their acceptance of the change.
A DA   7. Managers should encourage and accept suggestions from all employees.
A DA   8. If changes are going to be resisted by subordinates, managers should move slowly in order to gain acceptance of the changes.
A DA   9. Effective communication is an important requirement for managing change effectively.
A DA   10. Managers and training professionals need to work together for the transfer from "learning" to "behavior" to take place.

   1. Agree. Yes, everyone resists and/or resents change, but not all the time. It gets down to a pretty simple fact: "How will it affect me?" Probably the main reason people resist/resent a change is because it will affect them in a negative way. A good example is the move that Sears made in 1973. Management decided to build the tallest building in the world in the Chicago Loop and have all Sears's employees in the Chicago area move there. Not everyone was happy. Some of the reasons for resisting it were the additional cost of travel and parking and other expenses in Chicago; the additional time it would take; the crowded conditions on the elevator and other places in Chicago; the fear of heights; the lack of space—going from an office to a cubicle; and the separation from friends. On the other hand, many welcomed the change for a number of reasons, including being in the Loop for eating and shopping; prestige for being in the tallest building in the

world; being high up in a building where you could look out over the city; and having a place with better working conditions.

2. Disagree. It makes little difference whether or not "experts" made the decision or the boss made it. Many years ago, industrial engineering consultants (experts) were hired by manufacturing organizations to make decisions on reducing costs. In most cases, some people (usually 10 percent) lost their jobs. The attitudes and feelings of those who lost their jobs and of other employees were so strong that the promised effect of reducing costs did not occur in some organizations, because of the negative attitudes and lower productivity of their friends. Seldom will "experts" and or "facts" have the desired result when the feelings and attitudes of those affected are so strong.

3. Agree. George Odiorne wrote a number of management books before he passed away a number of years ago. I remember one of the concepts he stated: "If you want those affected by a change to accept it, give them a feeling of ownership." To illustrate this principle, when I taught my seminar on Decision Making, I used statements to describe the four choices a manager has when making a decision:

   a. Make a decision without any input from subordinates.
   b. Ask subordinates for suggestions and consider them before you decide.
   c. Facilitate a problem-solving meeting with subordinates to reach consensus.
   d. Empower your subordinates to make the decision.

In deciding on the best approach for making the decision, two factors are important to consider: quality and acceptance. Regarding quality, consider which approach will reach the best decision.

There is no assurance that one approach will let you come to a better decision than any of the others. But there is assurance that the more the involvement (ownership) by subordinates, the greater degree of acceptance. Therefore, if acceptance by subordinates is essential to getting the change implemented effectively, choice "a" should be avoided if possible and one of the other choices used to increase the chance of acceptance, which comes when you increase the degree of ownership.

4. Disagree. I say this because "it ain't necessarily so," as a songwriter put it. My pension benefits at the University of Wisconsin

were changed so I could retire at age sixty-two without losing any benefits. I don't know why the state of Wisconsin made the change, but I benefited from it and therefore did not resent it. Any change that will benefit employees will be welcome, whether or not they understand the reasons for it.

5. Agree. A practical definition of "empathy" is putting yourself in the shoes of other persons and seeing things from their point of view. This is one of the three principles I emphasize in my book *Managing Change Effectively*. It applies to training professionals and managers alike.

Training professionals must determine the needs of the learners so that the program will be practical. Whether using e-learning or classroom approaches, they must be able to communicate so that the learners will understand. And managers must know how to help them apply what they have learned. This means understanding their attitudes, desires, and what they have learned.

6. Disagree. A training professional once told me, "Don, I have no control over the learners when they leave the classroom, so it is up to their managers to see that change in behavior occurs." This person was right in saying "I have no control" but wrong in saying it is strictly up to the managers. My son, Jim, and I have just written a book called *Transferring Learning to Behavior*. (Chapter 10 describes its concepts in detail.) The key point is that training professionals will have to use "influence" instead of "control" to see that change in behavior occurs.

7. Agree. This is an obvious answer. What can they lose? And they might gain new practical ideas as well as build relationships with the person suggesting the change. In my "Management Inventory on Managing Change," I have the following "agree" or "disagree" item: "Most managers in my organization will welcome ideas and suggestions from other managers." Eighty-five percent of those who answered said "disagree." This is a terrible indictment on managers. But it is easy to understand why they don't accept suggestions. There is little if any difference between a "suggestion" and a "criticism," no matter how tactfully the suggestion is offered. To the receiver, a suggestion says one of two things: either "you are doing something you should quit doing" or "you should do something you aren't doing." Someone came up with an interesting and "practical" idea for improvement in performance. Instead of using the typical perfor-

mance appraisal approach where only the manager appraises the performance of subordinates and offers suggestions on how to improve, the "360-degree" approach was introduced to include appraisals and improvement suggestions from managers, peers, and subordinates. If managers don't even accept suggestions from peers, imagine how many managers will resent suggestions from subordinates. Organizations that have adopted the 360-degree approach are having trouble convincing managers that their subordinates are really trying to help instead of criticize.

8. Agree. This is a controversial answer. My answer is based on the principle that time can often change resistance to acceptance if the change is introduced gradually. An example is where an organization has decided to apply the principle called "job enrichment," which is based on research done by Frederick Herzberg. His research showed that the more challenge that could be put into a job, the more enthusiastic employees would be in doing it. An example is where a company decided to change from a line where six people each did one part in the process of assembling a radio to having each person assemble the entire radio. Needless to say, this was a drastic change. The need for empathy was obvious. When the employees were asked what they wanted to do, some were anxious to do it because they wanted to be able to be on their own and not be held back by the slowest person on the assembly line. Others were "scared to death" by the thought of working alone and doing all six jobs. The reasons for resisting the change were several, including the fear of failure. The organization could decide to proceed by training the ones who wanted the new opportunity and terminate or transfer those who did not want to change. Or the company could decide, We don't have to make the change immediately. For example, Jane, number 2 on the line, was asked, "If we give you the proper training, would you be willing to do job 1 and 3 as well as 2?" Because she was already somewhat familiar with the jobs before and after hers, she would say "yes." Likewise, number 5 would be willing to do jobs 4 and 6. Over a period of time, Jane would probably be willing to add 4 and so on. In other words, time, patience, and training could eventually move all or nearly all employees from the present process to the desired one.

The question is "What is the hurry?" A common example is where organizations changed the policy on smoking from one where it was allowed in certain places to one where no smoking was allowed on company property. In nearly every case, the change was introduced gradually to increase acceptance on the part of the smokers and those sympathetic to the smokers. In many cases, it took as many as six months before "no smoking" became a policy. During the six months, help was provided to smokers to encourage and help them to quit smoking or get adjusted to the change.

There are, of course, occasions where the change must be done immediately; organizations then do their best to sell the change and get acceptance using "ownership" concepts wherever possible.

9. Agree. This is one of the three key principles I stress in my book on Managing Change Effectively. It refers to upward as well as downward communication. Managers must be willing to listen even if they are being criticized (the "criticism" in many cases being meant as a helpful suggestion). It is obvious that instructors must be effective communicators by gaining and keeping the attention of the learner, using vocabulary that the learner understands, and listening to the questions and comments of the learners.

10. Agree. An important principle has to do with the "climate" that learners encounter when returning to the job after learning has taken place. If managers are "preventive" and operate on the attitude that "I am the boss and you will do it my way regardless of what you have learned," no change in behavior will take place. Not only will the learners be discouraged from changing, but they will also be upset by the fact that all the time spent in learning has been wasted. The ideal climate is where managers encourage learning and its application on the job. And this is where training professionals fit in. They must influence managers to have an encouraging attitude. This can be done by informing managers of the learning objectives, getting them involved in determining needs and offering suggestions on the curriculum, and possibly even involving them in the training process as members of an advisory committee or even as instructors. More details will be discussed in the next chapter, "Using the Balanced Scorecard to Transfer from Learning to Behavior."

The concepts, principles, and techniques illustrated by these ten items comprise the ingredients necessary for both training professionals and managers for managing change effectively. Managers must see the need and establish a climate to encourage subordinates to apply what they have learned. This is critical for the effective transfer of learning to behavior. Also, managers can help to determine needs by communicating the needs of their subordinates to the training department. Training professionals must be sure that the curriculum they establish will meet the needs of the learners. The training programs must have competent instructors so that learning takes place. The instructors must use empathy to understand the climate established by the managers. Then they must work with managers to help them establish an encouraging climate so that the learning will be transferred to behavior change and the results that will follow.

In summary, the three keys are empathy, communication, and participation.

References

Kirkpatrick, Donald L. *Managing Change Effectively.* Woburn, MA: Butterworth-Heinemann, 2001.

Note: The publisher has been bought out. Autographed copies can be ordered directly from Donald L. Kirkpatrick, *dleekirk1@aol.com* or 262/695-5851. Copies of the "Management Inventory on Managing Change" (MIMC) can also be ordered. Visit "Inventories" at *www.donald kirkpatrick.com.*

Chapter 10

Using Balanced Scorecards to Transfer Learning to Behavior

James D. Kirkpatrick, Ph.D.

I have asked my son, Jim, to write this chapter because of his knowledge and use of the Balanced Scorecard. In my description of moving from Learning to Behavior, I have concentrated on the motivation of the learners and the encouragement of their supervisors. I have described the various types of supervisors, including those who prevent or discourage the transfer. I have urged the trainers to work with the supervisors to help them become "encouraging" instead of "preventing" or "discouraging" bosses. I realize that this is not enough to be sure that the transfer takes place—hence this chapter on the Balanced Scorecard.

Don Kirkpatrick

I believe that transferring learning to behavior is one of training's biggest challenges. My father agrees—so much so that we recently wrote a book called *Transferring Learning to Behavior: Using the Four Levels to Improve Performance.* The University of Toyota (UOT), under the leadership of Russ Mundi and Chuck O'Keefe, also believes it to be true. *Transferring Learning to Behavior* contains "ten best" practice case studies, one of which is from Toyota and in which Russ outlines a corporate challenge to improve a critical element of customer satisfaction. Based on customer feedback, the UOT designed a ten-step program to do just that. The program is designed to ensure that training participants actually apply (level 3) what they learned (level 2) during training.

I believe that level 3 is the forgotten level. Lots of time, energy, and expense are put into levels 1 and 2 by training professionals because these are the levels that they have the most control over. Executives are interested in level 4, and that is as it should be. That leaves level 3 out there on its own with no one really owning it. I go so far as to say that it is the "missing link" in evaluation, since it is the level that contributes the most to the execution of strategy. Thus, it is the missing link not only between levels 2 and 4 but also between training and strategy execution.

There are several specific reasons why this transfer is important and difficult to achieve, and a few key things you can do to make it happen.

The Importance of Transferring Learning to Behavior

Let's say you have done a good job of collaborating with your internal partners and have identified several business objectives that you want to address through training. You then designed and delivered an excellent training program. It was not only well received by the participants (high level 1 reaction scores), but they learned what they were supposed to as evidenced by the high level 2 posttest knowledge and performance tests. Participants may even have received certificates to verify their (and your) good work. But the job is not done. Level 4 results—the business objectives—will not be achieved through high level 1 and 2 efforts. It will take participants going back to their jobs and *applying* what they learned in order for desired results to occur.

It is appalling to me how often I hear about the money that was spent and the training failures that occurred because of this lack of transfer. Here are the types of comments I have heard from senior leaders and department heads when the results are disappointing: "I guess we picked the wrong training program," or "My people need more training," or (worse) "I think we need to make some changes in our training department," or (the worst) "We need to make some cuts. How about training?" The sad part of this is that it typically happens with good programs, effective trainers, and determined effort. The reason for the failure is that the conditions were not in place to ensure the transfer of learning to behavior.

I recently left my job as Corporate University Director at First Indiana Bank in Indianapolis, Indiana. I learned much during my eight years there that relates to this exact situation. In 1997, I was directed to

questionnaire

implement "total quality management" (TQM) for the entire work-force. I did my best to do it but did not utilize the necessary methods to ensure the transfer of learning to behavior. As a result, TQM did not "stick"—not because it was a bad program, but because leaders and other employees never applied what they learned. On the flip side, in 2000 I was asked to design a program to move the bank to a "strategy-focused" way of conducting business. I applied (level 3) what I had learned (level 2) from the TQM fiasco and the effort was a success.

In summary, it is important to realize that level 3 drives the execution of strategy and achievement of organizational goals.

The Challenge of the Transfer of Learning to Behavior

The reasons that transfer exists as a great training challenge are numerous. I will touch on a few of the more significant ones. First, trainers lose their "control" when their training participants move from levels 1 and 2 to level 3. In other words, while participants are in the classroom or using e-learning methods, the instructor has total control over what is being taught and how it is being presented. Good trainers can therefore use their knowledge and skill to make sure that training is comfortable, relevant, and interesting (level 1) and that participants learn the objectives that have been set forth (level 2). Once the actual training is over and the participants go back to their jobs, all that is left for members of the training or learning team to use to achieve successful level 3 measures is *influence*. They become reliant on others—primarily the participants themselves and their supervisors—to see that application occurs.

This transfer is also a challenge because of the great amount of effort it takes to achieve successful level 3 measures. I personally don't think that the measures themselves are hard to determine. But it is difficult to get coaches and senior executives to apply the right amount of accountability and support to participants who have learned new behaviors. Another component of this reason is that many (most?) business leaders think it is the job of trainers to bring about new behaviors. They don't realize and accept the fact that they are the key people to make it happen. The other day I heard a well-meaning department manager say, "It is not my job to babysit my employees. It is my job to make sure that we make money!"

A final reason that this challenge is so difficult is human nature. Most of us tend to do things that we are familiar and comfortable with, even if there are better ways. As a result, it is very difficult to form new habits. Look at the concept of New Year's resolutions. A high percentage fall by the wayside because people simply don't find the accountability and support to hang in there until the new behaviors become part of "business as usual."

How to Ensure the Transfer of Learning to Behavior

I almost used the softer word *enhance* instead of *ensure*. But I am convinced that certain methods will work, so I am going to stay with "ensure." After all, the saying "What gets measured gets done" is very true when it comes to strategy execution and evaluation. If people know that level 3 behaviors are being tracked, they will be more likely to do them. And if trainers can get participants and leaders to apply the sales, customer service, coaching, and other mission-critical behaviors that they learned, then they are well on the way to positive results.

There are many methods that facilitate the transfer of learning to behavior, but you will have to read about all but one of them in our book, *Transferring Learning to Behavior*. The one my dad asked me to focus on in this chapter is the balanced scorecard. I will offer two versions of it. The first is my own modification of Robert Kaplan and David Norton's design, which they first presented in their book, *The Balanced Scorecard*. The other is a "dashboard" version, using methodology I learned from Megan Barrett, a friend and colleague of mine at Capital One University.

Balanced Scorecard Basics

Kaplan and Norton rightly point out that executing strategy is much more difficult than planning strategy. Strategy maps and their next of kin, balanced scorecards (BSC), are designed to display how a particular strategy is doing in regards to execution. The balanced scorecard is a visual and numeric representation of strategy in action. The measures are a balance of outcomes and drivers, sorted into four cate-

Table 10.1.

BSC Category	Category Description	Examples of Measures
Financial/ Production	These are bottom-line numbers—either financial or production—that represent what shareholders expect.	Return on investment, earnings per share, sales volume, budget
Customer	These measures represent what customers either say (in surveys) or do (buying patterns).	Loyalty, satisfaction, sales volume for a specified group, cross sales
Internal Systems	These measures show us what members of an organization need to excel at in order to please customers.	Profile scores, customer contacts, coaching sessions, quality measures
Learning and Growth	These measures are made up of steps that represent what an organization needs to have in place to set the foundation for success.	Competency scores, technology projects progress, employee satisfaction, market research

gories: financial/production, customer, internal systems, and learning/growth. Table 10.1 provides details.

Here is how this particular method works. Senior managers set financial/production goals and pass them along to department leaders. They, in turn, must decide what they need to put in place in order to set the table for success (learning and growth) that will then allow them and their employees to do what they need to do (internal systems) to please their customers (customer) to ultimately reach their goals (financial/production). The measures they choose to drive this process show up on the scorecard and are monitored (typically) every month to check to see that progress is being made. Remember that measures that are selected for a scorecard are the key ones that leverage or drive results.

Table 10.2 shows how a specific organizational goal can be broken down into objectives and subsequent measures and tracked using a balanced scorecard.

It is important to note that with Table 10.2, it is easy to see the progression or cause-and-effect relationships that tell the "cross-selling story." Training all customer service reps leads to effective use of the

Table 10.2.

Organizational Goals	Strategic Objective	BSC Measure
25% annual increase in no. of products per household	1. Get all customer service reps through training.	% Complete Training— Learning and Growth
40% annual $ volume increase from customers with 2+ accounts	2. Implement new customer profile methodology.	% of profile sheets that meet standard—Internal Systems
	3. Increase number of cross-departmental referrals made.	No. of referrals per individual and department—Internal Systems
	4. Increase % of customers with more than 2 accounts.	% of total customers with 2+ accounts— Customer
	5. Increase in $ volume from customers with 2+ accounts.	Total $ volume

new profile method, which then leads to an increase in the number of referrals, which leads to more customers with two or more accounts, which leads to an increase in volume (the ultimate goal). This is the type of presentation that usually impresses executives.

Table 10.3 displays the basics of a monthly balanced scorecard with the same organizational goal of increasing volume from customers with two or more accounts.

This simple example shows how the balanced scorecard can be used for three purposes. First, it can be used as an early warning system to uncover hitches that may detour financial and production goals. True "balanced" scorecards have a mix of lead measures, which make up this early warning system, and lag measures, which make up subsequent level 4 outcomes. Yellows and reds likely indicate problems that, if left unchecked, will lead to level 4 problems down the road. Interventions of cross-functional problem solving, coaching, training, staffing, process improvement, and the like can help get things back on track. Second, it can be used to communicate strategy, starting from the top and working down, and the execution of strategy, starting from the bottom and working up. The measures and colors lend themselves

Table 10.3.

No.	Strat	Financial/Production Measure	Actual	Target	Status	Change
F1	1a	Total loan volume from customers with 2+ accounts (000s)	15,000	15,000	Green	+
F2	1a	Total deposit volume from customers with 2+ accounts (000s)	8,520	10,000	Yellow	n.c.
		Customer Measure				
C1	2a	No. of products/household	2.3	2.5	Yellow	+
C2	2a	% increase in number of customers with 2+ accounts	12.5	15	Yellow	n.c.
C3	2b	Customer loyalty score for customers with 2+ accounts★	4.5	4.5	Green	+
		Internal System Measure				
IS1	2a	No. of customer contacts/banker/day	4.5	4.0	Green	+
IS2	2b	% of profile cards meeting standard	82	95	Red	+
IS3	2b	% of coaching logs meeting standard	92	95	Green	+
IS4	2c	No. Customer Impact errors	16	10	Yellow	−
		Learning and Growth Measure				
LG1	2a	% Managers through coaching course	85	100	Red	n.c.
LG2	2a	% Referral Tracking project completed	100	100	Green	+

★This score will be compared with the score of customers with two or fewer accounts.
Key: Green = Meeting Target
Yellow = Caution
Red = Needs Help
n.c. = No Change

well to explaining strategy and the story of evaluation to groups at every level. Third, this balanced scorecard system acts as a motivator to push the transfer of learning to behavior. I have seen many times where yellows and reds act as motivators toward improvement rather than discouragers. And that is primarily what this chapter is about.

As you can tell, the Internal Systems category is where level 3 behaviors and quality measures reside. The four measures in Table 10.4 represent key behaviors that three different groups of people need to perform successfully if the desired outcomes are to be achieved. Specifically, the customer contacts and profile cards are done by customer service reps; the coaching logs are filled out by supervisors; and the customer impact errors are monitored by service workers. Thus, there is behavioral accountability for each group.

Level 3 Balanced Scorecard Measures

Trainers constantly ask for examples, so here are some that either you can use or that may prompt you to come up with some of your own. Note in Table 10.4 that there are measures for both training participants and their managers. It is my strong belief that you need to have both in order for successful transfer to take place. Guess what I have found from my own experience? It generally takes more effort to get the supervisors to perform their new behaviors than it does the training participants. I suggest you plan the execution of your objectives with this in mind.

Science and Art of Scorecards

It is one thing to be able to design and develop scorecards and quite another to get managers to use them effectively. I learned this while working as the director of First Indiana Bank's Corporate University. The initial strategic directive that led to the scorecards was to "make us a bank that is strategy driven, not budget or tradition driven." I began this huge undertaking by gathering the senior leadership team and helping them (that is, us) to answer some very important questions, including: "What is our mission and vision?", "How will we differentiate ourselves from our competitors?", and "What will be our

Table 10.4.

Line-of-Business Objective	Training Programs	Participant Measures	Supervisor/ Coach Measures
Increase customer retention	Sales training for all sales associates. Coaching training.	No. customer contacts—phone No. customer contacts—face to face % use of new sales method % follow-up calls within 24 hrs.	% on time coaching sessions No. kudos to top sales associates No. joint sales calls No. reviewed call sheets
Decrease customer impact errors	Service training for all service associates	% service packets meeting standard % follow-up calls within 24 hrs. % resolved complaints	% on time coaching sessions No. service packets reviewed % weekly service meetings held
Increase employee retention	Engagement training for front line supervisors	% on time associate meetings % summary forms within standard No. recognition events per quarter	% on time coaching sessions No. kudos sent to top performers No. on-board interviews conducted

basic strategy?" Consensual answers came after much discussion, but they formed the foundation for us to move forward. Basically, we decided that we were to be a bank made up of employees who were to be *trusted advisers* to our internal and external customers, and that we were going to accomplish this through the general strategy of *discovery, delivery,* and *dialogue* (the 3 D's).

It was important at that point to work on getting the entire senior team on board with what lay ahead. This meant ownership and involvement, not just passive support. The next few months were spent by all of us learning about what it meant to be a strategy-focused organization. We used Kaplan and Norton's reference book *The Strategy-Focused Organization* to get many of our ideas. Once we had the table set for success, I went about the task of training leaders throughout the bank to develop strategy maps and subsequent balanced scorecards. This was the "science" of the whole initiative. From there, most of my time was spent developing methods to ensure that these knowledgeable (level 2) leaders actually put into practice (level 3) what they learned, in order to increase the banks' profitability and employee retention (level 4). Most of my Corporate University's team efforts centered around putting into practice two important concepts—*accountability* and *support*, the specifics of which are outlined in our book, *Transferring Learning to Behavior: Using the Four Levels to Improve Performance*.

Balanced Scorecards at Capital One University

The rest of this chapter is devoted to a "best practice" look at the work of a colleague of mine, Megan Barrett, a key member of Capital One University's Cross Functional Learning Team. Keep a lookout for the following basic scorecarding principles:

1. Purpose of scorecards
2. How to get started
3. The role of accountability

4. The role of benchmarking
5. How many metrics to use?

6. The evolutional process
7. Involving key stakeholders
8. Moving from operations to strategy
9. Continuing accountability
10. Measures from all four levels

———————

Capital One University Scorecard
by Megan Barrett

Purpose of Scorecards and why we decided to use one.   In late 2003, Capital One University formed from a series of disparate training functions across the organization. During this initiative, we combined and streamlined processes, including the metrics and evaluation strategy. Some teams had scorecards and explicit evaluation strategies, while others did not. Therefore, we had to determine what the optimal process would be for gathering and disseminating data and other information. In the new organization we had to be more accountable, justify costs, improve process, and show evaluation-based results. Because of this new accountability, a new structure under the Human Resources organization, Capital One University determined that a monthly scorecard to document our progress would be the most efficient way of demonstrating progress.

Main Audience.   University associates, University Leadership team, University Director, Vice President Career Development; Business Partners and other training partners

Implementation.   At the onset, the university began building a training scorecard by completing a series of internal and external benchmarking studies to gather a universe of metrics that we thought someone could possibly be interested in, about sixty altogether. We determined where the data would come from, how quickly we could implement the metric, and defined a possible owner. Through discussions with the leadership and internal teams we whittled the metrics universe down to about twenty metrics, some actionable, some just informational like "% of exempt population trained in 2nd quarter." Other metrics captured were "cost per student," "e-learning usage," and "class cancellation percentage." They were associated with the categories of Operational Excellence, Cost Effectiveness, Course Design/Delivery, and People/Service. The scorecard was assembled primarily of indicator and operational metrics, with low-level evaluation metrics built in. It was our intention to gradually include higher levels of evaluation as the University progressed. Due to the fact that many training groups combined to form the university, we had diverse ways of capturing level 1 information, including paper, online, and Scantron forms. With the large scale of training classes taught each day in the university, we determined that the most efficient way of capturing and reporting level 1 data was through our Learning Management system. After implementing our standard level 1, we included those satisfaction metrics and various level 2 and level 3 results on the monthly scorecard. Each month, metrics were gathered through the Learning Management system, analyzed, and presented with changes, issues, and recommendations for the senior leadership team to understand our growth. We defined benchmarks and goals over time from internal trends and external groups including the ASTD and the Corporate Executive Board (Learning and Development Roundtable).

The metrics on the scorecard remained consistent for all of 2004. However, the format and presentation of the metrics continued to evolve. We had trouble finding a format that was compelling for all parties. Instead of the standard categories like Operational Excellence, we decided that the best way to drive understanding of the evolution of the university was to align the metrics to our internal goals. Those goals had a natural progression from tactical to strategic, just as we wanted our metrics to illustrate (see Figure 10.1).

Six months after mapping the metrics to our internal goals, we revisited this scorecard with the leadership of Capital One University. We wanted to determine if these metrics were still meeting our need of showing the growth and impact of the training function. We realized that the time had come to move from an operations-based scorecard to a more strategic project–based structure. This is the natural progression of a new corporate university. We need to show impact, not just how many people came through a class and enjoyed it. Currently in 2005, we are building a new scorecard that will show greater value both to university associates and corporate leadership. It has not been fully defined but will be arranged in four broader, more strategic categories with sample metrics:

Customer Impact	*Delivery*
Client satisfaction	Operational indicators: cancellation, no-show
Requests fulfilled	Percent, e-learning usage
Behavior change	Course satisfaction
University Associates	*Financial Performance*
Team morale	Budget performance
Career fulfillment	Cost per associate

Figure 10.1.

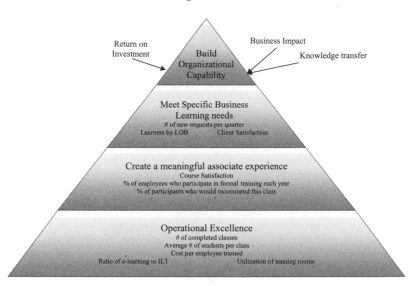

Lessons Learned.   A training scorecard can be an important tool for showing an organization's training progress and value. Since implemented, this scorecard has assisted the university in understanding its operational state and how it can be improved. The metrics that are gathered are used in every quarterly business review or presentation made by the University Leadership. It has helped us trend satisfaction data over time and provided a place to other evaluation results. However, one take-away from implementing a scorecard is to assign accountability and efficient process early in the building phase. Capital One University had a business management group that was responsible for the strategic formation of the scorecard and therefore ended up owning implementation and a large portion of the data. This created a disconnected metrics environment and associates had little understanding of how to impact the metrics in their own roles. By assigning owners to each of the metrics, you ensure that there is always a person responsible for raising awareness of metrics that are under or over the associate benchmarks. This creates action and buy-in of all associates in the university, who are also stakeholders in the business.

Chapter 11

So How Is E-Learning Different?

by William Horton

Many professional trainers are concerned with the evaluation of e-learning. No one is better able to provide answers than Bill Horton, who wrote the book *Evaluating E-Learning*, published by the American Society For Training and Development (ASTD). While details for evaluating e-learning at all four levels are described in the book, this chapter sets forth the principles and approaches for doing so.

Don Kirkpatrick

Evaluating E-Learning Is the Same, But . . .

How well can an evaluation framework conceived in the 1950s apply to twenty-first century e-learning and its blended-, mobile-, and ubiquitous-learning variants? Back then computers weighed tons and the term "network" referred to television stations. Yet, that four-level framework applies quite well.

Like all effective engineering models of evaluation it concerned itself solely with the results rather than the mechanisms used to accomplish those results. What we evaluate is not the artifacts or apparatus of learning but the outcome. The outcome of learning resides with the learners, not the pens, pencils, chalkboards, whiteboards, hardware, software, or other paraphernalia of learning.

Since we are measuring results rather than mechanisms, we can use this framework to evaluate e-learning as we do to evaluate other forms of learning. There are, however, some reasons why we might want to use different techniques and employ some different technologies to the evaluation process. And *that* is the subject of this chapter.

Here we will cover primarily electronic means of evaluating electronically delivered learning. Keep in mind, though, that conventional means can be used to evaluate e-learning and electronic means can be used to evaluate conventional learning.

Evaluating Level 1: Reaction

Reaction evaluations have gotten a bad reputation of late. Critics dismiss them as mere "bingo cards" or "smiley sheets." They rightly point out research showing no correlation between level 1 evaluations and actual learning. Just because someone liked training, they remind us, is no guarantee that they learned anything. So why bother evaluating e-learning at level 1?

In many situations, e-learning is a new experience for learners. For it to succeed, it must overcome natural skepticism and inertia. Level 1 evaluations help us monitor emotional acceptance of e-learning and can be essential in gathering the testimonials and statistics to generate a positive buzz around e-learning.

So how do you evaluate response electronically? Here are some suggestions.

Let Learners Vote on Course Design

Online polls and ballots give learners the opportunity to comment on aspects of e-learning design and delivery. Figure 11.1 shows a ballot that asks learners whether a particular lesson should be included in future versions of the course.

In live virtual-classroom sessions, you can use the built-in polling feature to ask for immediate feedback on the quality of presentation and delivery. Online testing and survey tools can also be used to post ballots like the one shown in Figure 11.1. Such ballots can then record scores over a period of time.

Figure 11.1. Question of the Day—Microsoft Internet Explorer

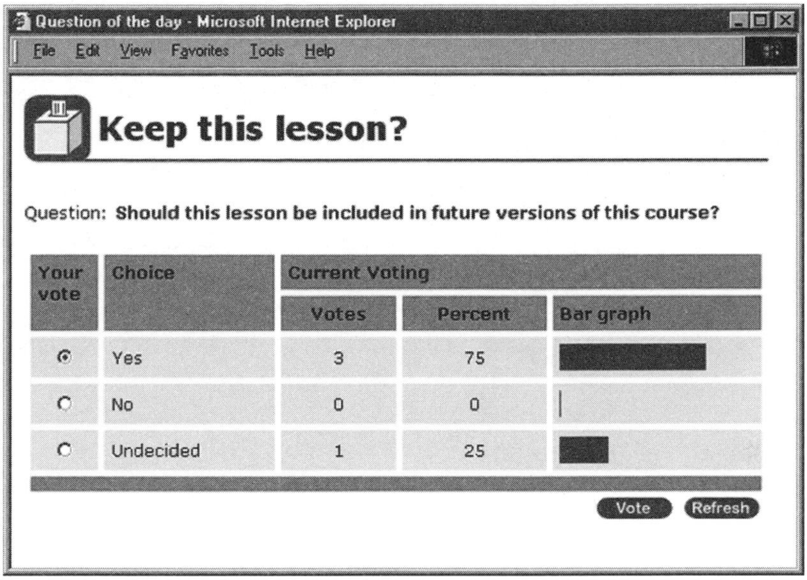

Set Up a Course Discussion Thread

Let learners talk about their experiences in taking e-learning. One way to do this is to set up a course discussion forum. Such a forum serves as a bulletin board where designers can post questions or issues for learners to respond to.

Figure 11.2 shows entries on one such forum that asks learners to evaluate one aspect of the design of the course.

In such discussions, learners can see other learners' comments and respond to them, creating an ongoing conversation that reveals more than a simple vote or numeric rating.

Discussion forums are a common feature within online-meeting tools and are also available as stand-alone online discussion tools. For a list of tools for discussion forums, check the list of tools and vendors at horton.com/tools.

Instead of a discussion forum, you may prefer to use a blog (Web log) that posts entries as an ongoing journal of comments. Blogs can be more spontaneous; discussion forums, more structured. Try both and see which harvests the kinds of comments you crave.

Figure 11.2.

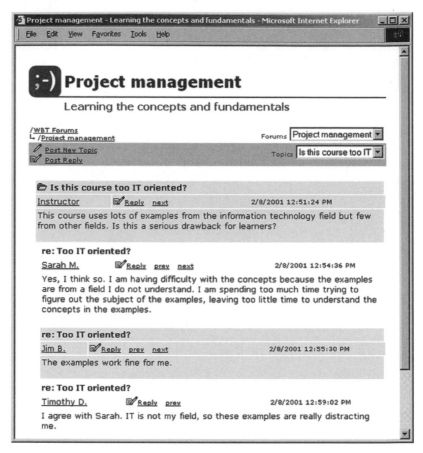

In either case, be sure to seed the discussion with questions that provoke meaningful discussion. Avoid questions that ask little more than "Did you like it?"

Use Chat or Instant Messaging for a Focus Group

Focus groups traditionally required a lot of travel and setup time. With chat and instant messaging, travel is no longer required. Participants just all join a chat session. Each person in chat sees the comments typed by the others.

Figure 11.3.

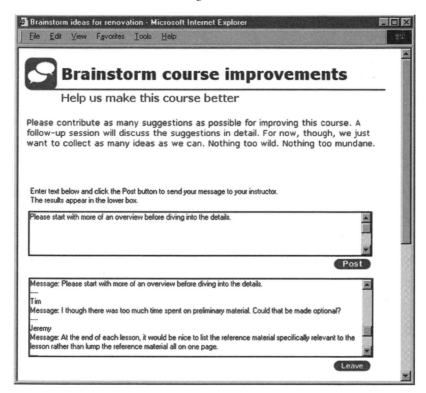

Figure 11.3 shows a brainstorming session to generate suggestions for improving a course. Brainstorming is especially suited for chat because it encourages a free flow of many ideas without criticism.

You could conduct focus groups with telephone conferencing, but chat has the advantage of leaving behind a written record, and there are no notes to transcribe.

If you have access to an online-meeting tool, such as WebEx, Centra, or LiveMeeting, you can conduct a conventional focus group with voice and shared display areas. If you do use such a tool, record the session so you can play it back for further analysis and for taking notes.

Figure 11.4.

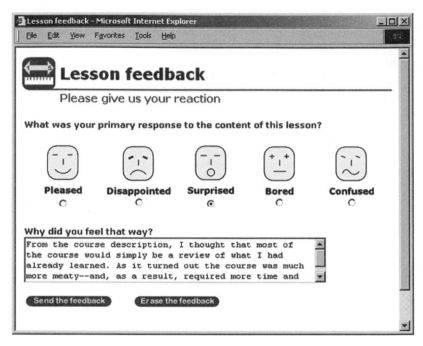

Gather Feedback Continually

With e-learning, you can embed evaluation events among the learning experiences. Figure 11.4 shows an end-of-lesson evaluation.

This example uses simple emoticons to let learners express emotions other than like and dislike. And it asks for their reasoning. This approach can reveal unanticipated reactions, such as a learner who did not like or dislike the lesson but was surprised at what it contained.

More frequent evaluations also solve the problem of e-learners who drop out before reaching the end of the course—and the end-of-course evaluation.

For such frequent mini-evaluations, keep the evaluation short and simple with only a question or two. Never subject the learners to a lengthy interrogation as their reward for completing a tough module.

Figure 11.5.

Gather Feedback Continuously

My personal choice is to enable feedback at any time throughout the learning experience. You can include a button on every screen that lets learners immediately comment on the e-learning or ask a question about it. Figure 11.5 is an example of how one system responds to such a button.

Providing the ability to send feedback at any time lets learners report problems, confusion, insights, and triumphs immediately. It prevents frustration from building to the point that the end-of-course or end-of-lesson evaluation becomes an emotional rant. It also provides an early warning to problems, so you can fix them. By the time the sixth learner encounters the problem area, you have fixed it.

Record Meaningful Statistics Automatically

Web servers, virtual-classroom systems, learning management systems (LMSs), and learning content management systems (LCMSs) all record detailed information about what the learner did while taking e-learning. By examining logs and reports from such systems, you can gather useful data such as:

- Frequency and pattern of accessing the course
- Number of pages or modules accessed
- Assignments submitted
- Participation in online chats and discussions
- Rate of progress through the course
- Answers to polling questions

When reviewing such data, look for trends and anomalies. You might notice that learners gradually pick up speed as they proceed through a course. Good. Or you might notice that 50 percent of your dropouts occur immediately after Lesson 6. Hmmm, either Lesson 6 needs improvement or maybe six lessons are enough for most learners.

Evaluating Level 2: Learning

E-learning greatly simplifies evaluating at level 2. In e-learning, tests can be automatically administered, scored, recorded, and reported. Automatic testing reduces the difficulty, effort, and costs of creating and administering tests. That means you can use tests more widely, such as:

- Pretests to see if learners are ready to begin a course or module.
- Diagnostic tests to identify the specific modules or learning objects learners should take.
- Posttests to confirm learning or shunt learners to remedial learning experiences.
- Within-course modules to help learners continually monitor accomplishment of learning objectives.

E-learning provides learners with inexpensive and easy-to-use tools to create tests and standards-based reporting mechanisms to record and report scores. Advanced e-learning applications use testing results to design custom learning programs for learners. Let's explore these differences.

Testing Tools

Many tools for authoring content include components to create test questions. In addition, separate tools can be used expressly to create and administer online tests. Here is a list of well-known tools:

Well-known authoring tools that can create tests	Well-known tools for creating and delivering tests
Captivate macromedia.com	CourseBuilder extensions for Dreamweaver (free) macromedia.com
ToolBook Instructor sumtotalsystems.com	QuestionMark Perception questionmark.com
Authorware macromedia.com	QuizRocket www.learningware.com
Trainersoft outstart.com	Hot Potatoes
Lectora Publisher lectora.com	web.uvic.ca/hrd/halfbaked/

In addition, many learning management systems and learning content management systems contain tools for creating and delivering tests. For more tools in these categories, go to horton.com/tools.

Standards-based Score Reporting

E-learning standards for communications between learning content and management systems promise that content developed in different authoring tools can deliver tests and report scores back to any management system—provided all the tools and content follow the same standard.

The advantage for evaluation is that the tedious and expensive process of distributing, conducting, gathering, grading, and recording tests is automated from start to finish. The effort and costs of tests are reduced, and the results of testing are available for immediate analysis.

A few years ago, getting results back from the learner's computer to a centralized database required either laboriously printing out results and then reentering them or doing some pretty sophisticated custom programming. Today, it can require as little as making a few clicks on dialogue boxes on the authoring tool and management system.

Figure 11.6 shows a dialog box used to set up reporting for a quiz developed in Macromedia Captivate. This example has chosen the SCORM standard (www.adlnet.org). Of the two standards, AICC and SCORM, SCORM is the newer.

The exact procedure varies considerably from tool to tool, but once the content is set up, each time the learner answers a test question, that score is recorded on the management system.

Manage Competence

Many large organizations are going beyond simply recording test scores. The immediate availability of test results provides these organizations a way to continuously guide learning in their organizations to ensure that targeted competencies are achieved.

Some LMSs and knowledge management tools are connecting testing and e-learning to more precisely target competencies needed by learners. Here, schematically is how it works.

The learner might be faced with a large, extensive course taking many hours to complete.

The learner, desiring a more efficient learning experience that takes into account what the learner already knows, clicks on the Customize button. (See Figure 11.7.)

Figure 11.6.

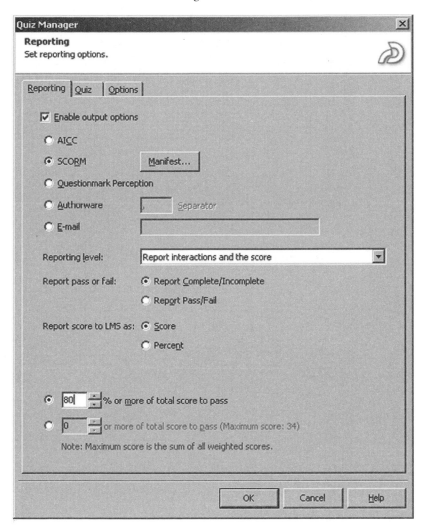

The learner engages in a test to identify gaps in knowledge and skills. (See Figure 11.8.)

The result of the test is a custom course consisting of just the modules the learner needs. The modules are fewer in number than the whole courses and are more specific. (See Figure 11.9.)

Figure 11.7.

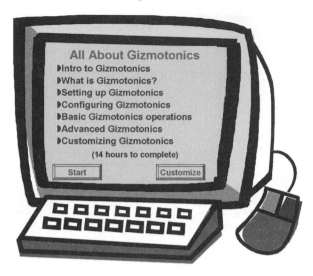

Figure 11.8.

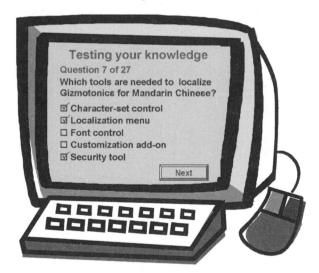

Figure 11.9.

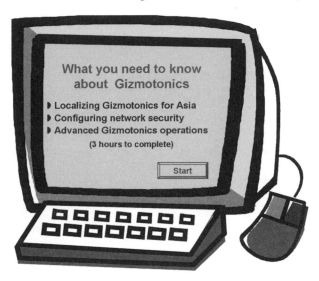

The learner can now begin a custom learning program that targets his or her competency gap.

Evaluating Level 3: Behavior

Since change in behavior occurs outside the e-learning proper, its evaluation is less coupled to the e-learning or to the technologies needed for e-learning. That means that you can use the same mechanisms to evaluate application for both the classroom and e-learning. This section, however, will consider electronic means of evaluation that rely on the same technologies as e-learning and are, hence, likely to be economical to implement.

Figures 11.10 and 11.11 rely on feedback from "those who should know," such as supervisors, colleagues, subordinates, customers, and the learner.

Figure 11.10.

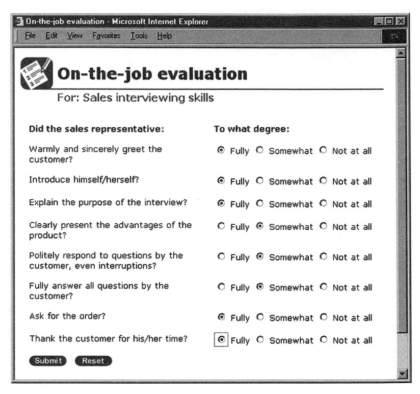

Measure On-Job Performance

We can use electronic questionnaires to compare trained and untrained individuals both before and after training to document improvements due to learning. Figure 11.10 shows a simple form that a supervisor might fill in to measure the performance of a sales representative.

Such appraisals of job performance might be gathered by human resources information systems (HRIS) or by some advanced learning management systems. Such data serves to evaluate not just the individual employee's job performance but the performance of the training designed to improve the job performance of many such employees.

Figure 11.11.

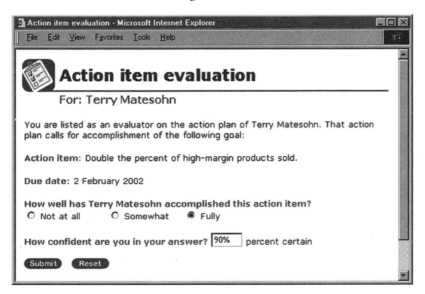

Evaluate Individual Action Items

E-mail, online forms, and discussion forums can also be used to measure whether distant learners have achieved specific performance goals. Figure 11.11 is an example that asks an evaluator to appraise one employee.

Notice that the evaluator can enter a "fudge factor," that is, a percentage that indicates how confident the evaluator is in the opinion.

Use Data Recorded by Other Corporate Systems

Many corporate information systems record data that directly measures human performance or from which human performance can be inferred. For example:

- Human resources information systems (HRIS), such as PeopleSoft, can reveal patterns of hiring, performance appraisals, promotion, turnover, and discipline.
- Enterprise resource planning (ERP), such as SAP, can reveal patterns of efficiency and effectiveness.

- Customers relationship management (CRM) tools, such as BAAN, and Contact management systems, such as ACT!, can reveal acquisition of new clients and customers.
- E-commerce systems, such as Oracle E-Business Suite, can reveal changes in sales levels and cost of sales for various product lines.
- Project management tools, such as Microsoft Project, can reveal timely accomplishment of project objectives.

Two caveats are in order. First, all this data can be a curse. Extracting meaningful trends and generalizations requires sophisticated analysis. The term for such efforts is *data mining*.

A second concern is that of the privacy of those whose performance is monitored. Be careful; some countries and other jurisdictions have regulations that limit what data can be collected and what data can be revealed.

Evaluating Level 4: Results

Evaluating results for e-learning is more difficult than it is for classroom training. The kinds of business and institutional changes you want to measure for level 4 seldom have only one cause. And they may take years to manifest. When evaluating at level 4, we may have to trade accuracy for credibility. Although you may not be able to state the effectiveness of e-learning to three decimal places, you can make statements that executives and managers will believe and trust.

First, Decide What Matters

Evaluating results works best if the people to whom you present your evaluation agree on what constitutes success. So, before you design your evaluation program or collect any data, answer this question:

> For the top management of my company, university, government, or institution, what is the single most important measure of success?

It does no good to report return on investment to executives who consider social responsibility or academic leadership the measure of success.

Estimate E-Learning's Value

One of the most straightforward methods for evaluating results is to ask those who can reasonably evaluate results. Good candidates include the learners themselves along with their supervisors, peers, subordinates, customers, and clients.

Figure 11.12 shows a Web form that just collects estimates of the value of an e-learning program. Although individual estimates may not be accurate, the average of many such measurements may have credibility with executives who trust the opinions of the groups you surveyed.

Notice that this form also gathers testimonials—useful for level 1 evaluations.

Figure 11.12.

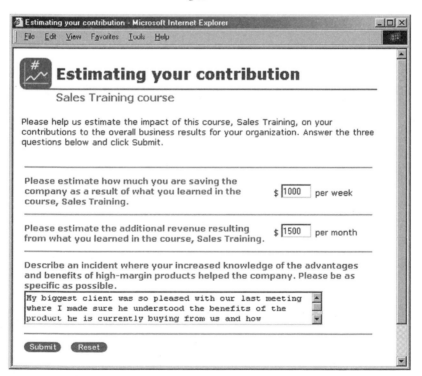

Estimate Confident Contribution

Earlier I said that credibility may be more important (and achievable) than accuracy in level 4 evaluations of e-learning. Figure 11.13 shows a double-conservative estimate of the value of e-learning.

The form asks the evaluator for an estimate of the monetary value of a change resulting *in part* from e-learning. It then asks for two factors to identify how much of the change is due to e-learning. The first factor asks what percentage of the change is due to e-learning and the second asks how confident the evaluator is in this estimate.

To derive a confident (conservative) estimate of e-learning's contribution, you just multiply the value of the change by the fraction attributed to e-learning and then further reduce this amount by the level of confidence in the figures.

Total value of change	$15,000	USD per month
× fraction due to training	55	percent
≈ Estimated value of training	$6,250	USD per month
× Confidence in the estimate	75	percent
≈ Confident estimate	$6,187	USD per month

Note: USD stands for U.S. dollars.

Figure 11.13.

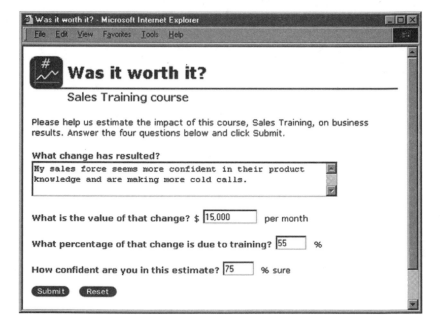

The result is a figure that you can confidently attribute to e-learning, especially if the executives receiving this estimate trust the evaluators.

Reference

Horton, William. *Evaluating E-Learning*. Alexandria, VA: American Society For Training and Development (ASTD), 2001.

PART TWO

CASE STUDIES OF IMPLEMENTATION

In order to make this book as practical and helpful as possible, I invited a number of training professionals to describe an evaluation that they had done in implementing one or more of the four levels. I looked for variety in terms of the type of program as well as the type of organization in which the evaluation had been done. I also wanted case studies of evaluations that ranged from the simple to the complex. All of the case studies were written especially for this book.

When you study these cases, it is important to understand that you can borrow forms, designs, and techniques and adapt them to your own organization. This may save you a lot of time and frustration when making decisions on what to evaluate and how to do it. If you want more details on the evaluations, I am sure that the authors will be happy to oblige.

Note: There are three case studies on Leadership training. I have purposely included all three because of the popularity of this program and the variations in program content and evaluation procedures.

Don Kirkpatrick

Chapter 12

Developing an Effective Level 1 Reaction Form

Reaction forms come in all sizes and shapes. And the information generated may or may not be used to improve training programs. This case study describes a thorough process of developing a form to evaluate the significant aspects of the program. Emphasis is on items that relate directly to job performance and desired results.

Duke Energy Corporation

W. Derrick Allman,
Plan, Manage, and Procure Training Services,
Duke Energy Corporation, Charlotte, North Carolina

Duke Energy is a world leader in the development, collection, distribution, and production of energy-related services. The company conducts business in the global marketplace through national and international offices, having two primary corporate locations: Charlotte, North Carolina, and Houston, Texas. The company employs 23,000 individuals worldwide.

Evaluation processes at Duke Energy Corporation have taken many turns through the years. As we enter the era of aggressive competition in the energy services market, we are increasing our interest in determining the value that learning and development contribute to the business. An essential element in the valuation of learning and development is the gathering and analysis of evaluation data associated with learning events. The following case tracks the history and development of an electronic level 1 evaluation process used by the company for a more rigorous evaluation at levels 1 and 3 of Kirkpatrick's model. Included is background information to assist in understanding the initial factors in implementing a more rigorous level 1 process. Methods applied in gathering levels 1 and 3 evaluation data are very important. Therefore, the case includes a discussion of how Duke Energy is working to refine the process through collaboration with an international benchmarking organization.

Duke Energy's roots are well established in serving the electrical needs of customers of central North and South Carolina for nearly ninety years. During that time, the company invested heavily in the development, construction, and operation of generating facilities. Three nuclear stations were constructed during the 1970s and 1980s. Experience gained in this highly regulated side of the business demonstrated the need for exhaustive training and education programs to ensure the safe operation of those nuclear units. In addition, particular focus on the training and education of nuclear industry employees developed during the late 1970s.

Eagerness to ensure competency in an employee's ability to perform resulted in extensive investment of resources in a systematic approach to training using job-task analysis, training program development, evaluation of lessons learned, and demonstration of competency. Through the experience gained in the years following this focused effort, the company gained insight into human performance through level 2 and level 3 evaluations. Many of the process lessons learned eventually spread from being used solely in the nuclear environment to other training areas of the corporation.

It was not until 1994 that Duke Energy sought to quantify the value of learning taking place and trend the experiences in order to monitor continuous improvement in programs. At that time, the initiating queue did not come from within the Training and Education function. In the early 1990s, Duke Energy had a strong focus on continuous improvement and quality performance measures. As a result, criteria for pursuing the Malcolm Baldrige Award (MBA) were adopted as a standard from which all corporate programs would be measured. It was thought that the use of the Baldrige criteria should be used for several reasons: (1) standardization—the award criteria were viewed as a standard by which we could directly compare our performance with other corporations across the country; (2) availability—a systematic process for evaluating programs was well established, including a network of examiners that would allow us to perform self-evaluations; and (3) success—it was viewed that compliance with Baldrige criteria would naturally result in excellence; it was later realized that excellence in all aspects of the business—and not the use of artificial criteria with which we were attempting to align practices—allows the corporation to succeed.

As a result of this effort, the Training and Education function was asked to produce reports in response to four areas of training. Later we learned that the four areas outlined in the MBA were actually the four levels of evaluation posed in Kirkpatrick's model for evaluating training and education. As proposed in the MBA, the four levels where a response and supporting data would be required were (1) reaction, (2) learning, (3) transfer to job, and (4) business results.

We immediately knew how to respond to the first of the four. Our "smile" sheets had been used for years to gauge end-of-class reaction to a course and instructor. However, as we began to learn more about the Kirkpatrick model of evaluation, we learned that our "smile" sheets were not capturing data adequate to demonstrate continuous improvement in the reaction to learning. The result of this awareness led to the development of a spreadsheet to begin capturing data from Corporate Training–sponsored events. Two weeks into the project, we discovered that an electronic spreadsheet would be incapable of providing the robust analysis necessary for continuous monitoring and improvement of programs, courses, instructors, and so on. Immediately, a project was chartered to construct a database system to perform these duties. At the center of this project were four criteria: (1) develop standard questions to apply across the enterprise, (2) develop a process for electronic gathering of data to reduce the human interface required, (3) secure the data in a manner so as to prevent any bias or tampering with results, and (4) be able to report the results of any event based on criteria important to the management of the Training and Education function. Within six weeks of the initial request, we had an operational database program capable of gathering data using an electronic scanner; analyzing data by course, instructor, location; and generating general and confidential reports for management.

When Duke Energy Training set about the development of standard level 1 reaction sheets, we knew that by their nature they would be very subjective. That is, they indicate the mood of participants as they leave training. The goal of level 1 evaluations is to "measure participant's perception (reaction) to learning experiences relative to a course, content, instructor, and relevancy to job immediately following the experience in order to initiate continuous improvement of training experiences." As a result, our project established three primary objectives:

1. Questions developed for the reaction level evaluation *must* measure the course, content, instructor, and relevancy to the job. These are four areas considered essential to successful training programs.

2. The form and delivery of the level 1 evaluation must communicate a link between quality, process improvement, and action. Participants *must* be made to feel as though their individual response is a factor in the continuous improvement process.

3. Action plans should be initiated to address identified weaknesses without regard to owner, political correctness, or other bias. If the results indicate poor quality, then appropriate corrective action should be taken. If excellence is indicated in an unlikely place, then reward and celebration should be offered commensurate with the accomplishment.

In addition to the primary objectives, several other objectives evolved. First was the need to identify the prerequisite processes that must be accomplished with each learning event. It became evident that the success of the level 1 process is directly linked to the proper completion of prerequisites for a course. Second, postmeasurement activities should be addressed by subsequent teams. During the initial database design, the team knew that certain reports would be required and others desired. Most reports were prepared during the first phase of development.

The initial computer project deliverables included the following:

- Proposed questions to be included on the level 1 evaluation
- Proposed measures from which management would determine actions to be taken when analyzing evaluation results
- Recommendations for deployment of the process within Corporate Training and Education, including roles and responsibilities

- Guideline for data collection, cycle times, reports, and analysis of data
- Schedule for developing, delivering, and measuring responsiveness of participants (generic level 1 assessment)
- Database and input program for manually gathering data
- Plans and scope document detailing a second (phase 2) project for automating the data acquisition process. (This document should include plans for using data collected in multiple ways—that is, requirements that header data be used to confirm enrollment/attendance, automated course completion, level 1 automated analysis and reporting, and so on.)

Along with the development of the computer program, a team worked on drafting an initial set of questions for the standard level 1 reaction sheets. These questions included the following:

1. Overall, my impression of this course was excellent.
2. The course objectives were clearly stated and used understandable terms.
3. This course met the defined objectives.
4. Both the facility and equipment used met *all* needs of the class/course. *Note:* Please describe any facility or equipment needs that did not meet your expectations.
5. The course materials were both useful and easy to follow. *Note:* Please describe any material that was not useful or easy to follow.
6. The instructor(s) demonstrated thorough knowledge and understanding of the topic. *Note:* The instructor(s) would be the facilitator(s) of any video, CBT, or audiotape.
7. The instructor(s) presented information in a clear, understandable, and professional manner. *Note:* The instructor(s) would include the facilitator(s) of any video, CBT, or audiotape.
8. The amount of time scheduled for this course was exactly what was needed to meet the objectives.
9. This course relates directly to my current job responsibilities.
10. I would recommend this course to other teammates.

These were measured using a five-point Likert scale with a value of 5 being assigned to "strongly agree" and a value of 1 being assigned to "strongly disagree."

A test period from November through December of 1995 was used to shake down the system and remove any "bugs" found. On January 1, 1996, the first electronic level 1 evaluation instruments were formally used. During the first month, less than 200 level 1 reaction sheets were returned for processing. In the ensuing months, acceptance and use of the questions as a basis for illustrating the effects of training grew. All of Corporate Training began using the level 1 reaction sheet to gather end-of-class data by March of 1996; volume grew to nearly 1,000 evaluation sheets per month. By the end of 1996, Corporate Training at Duke Energy had recorded over 12,000 evaluations on the reaction to training. By the end of 1997, the number using the standardized level 1 reaction sheet grew to over 25,000 participants. Analysis of the data began to reveal some very interesting trends. The growth also revealed the need to adjust the Corporate Training unit.

As we analyzed the data and produced reports, training management came to the realization that "the reaction to training and education is directly linked to the operation and business management aspects of the training unit." This led to the formation of a team to monitor business management and education quality. In theory, we concluded that the two are inseparable in (1) determining areas of continuous improvement, (2) measuring the success of programs and program participants, and (3) ensuring that corporate investments in training are providing an appropriate return on investment.

Along with full implementation of the level 1 process in March of 1996 came our joining of a national benchmarking organization composed of sixty member companies. In the fall of that year, the first subteam of this forum was commissioned to determine areas for which standardized performance metrics could be established. After two meetings, it was determined that standardized level 1 and level 3 evaluation questions should be developed. This team worked on the draft and completion of a standardized level 1 evaluation through the spring of 1997 and presented this to the larger body for use in April of 1997. We immediately set about the task of piloting the standard questions within our companies and continue to gather data for comparison at this time. In addition, the team is now completing work on the development of level 3 questions for use by the members. As a result of this effort, for the first time a standard set of data will be able to be analyzed in gauging the success of programs that literally span the globe. In doing so, the lessons learned from similar experiences will help in identifying successful practices and in avoiding the pitfalls others experience. Sometime in 1998 this information will be published and made available for other corporations to use.

Duke Energy Training stands at the threshold of a new era in evaluating the effectiveness of training. As we continue to analyze the reactions people have toward training, we are beginning to see indications that suggest a direct correlation between reaction (level 1) and transfer to the job (level 3). If this correlation is correct, the use of sophisticated techniques for analyzing participant reaction will be warranted. On the other hand, if all we are able to glean from the data are indications of areas needing improvement, then we will still be able to implement corrective actions in programs. When used effectively, analysis of level 1 evaluation data can help in the early detection of areas that need improvement or support the conclusion that a good result was achieved.

Chapter 13

Evaluating a Training Program for Nonexempt Employees

This case study is an example of a relatively simple approach for evaluating at all four levels. It includes a reaction sheet and a survey form that can be tabulated on a computer. The evaluation of results compared turnover figures for those trained with figures on those who were not trained. These figures were then converted into dollar savings. The design of the evaluation is readily adaptable to other organizations.

First Union National Bank

Patrick O'Hara, Assistant Vice President
Human Resources Division, Training and Development,
First Union National Bank, Charlotte, North Carolina

CARE

A major goal of First Union is to let employees know how much they and their contribution to the success and growth of First Union are valued. Personal development is one strategy.

CARE I is a program that was developed to provide a developmental opportunity for the nonexempt employees who historically have not been the focus of personal development training. As the corporation has expanded over the last several years, there has been tremendous change and upheaval. During mergers and consolidations, employees have the pressures that all this change has brought to bear. CARE is a one-day program devoted to the bank's largest population, the nonexempt employees who have shouldered major responsibilities throughout this growth cycle at First Union.

CARE is an acronym for Communication, Awareness, Renewal, and Empowerment. The learning objectives are:

- Increase self-awareness by use of self-assessment tools and group feedback.
- Increase understanding of communication styles and develop flexibility in one's own communication style.
- Increase communication effectiveness by exposure to and practice in assertiveness concepts and skills.
- Understand and implement the steps of goal setting as a tool in career renewal.

Input from employee focus groups was instrumental in developing the course design.

The program is offered on an ongoing basis for new employees. The majority of CARE I training occurred in 1991. More than 10,000 employees have attended CARE I.

Here is a brief description of the CARE program, with an indication of the activities and materials used:

Morning:
- Johari Window
- Self-awareness: DESA instrument explained and processed
- Assertiveness in communication, lecturette, role playing, discussion on using a journal to help increase assertive behavior
Lunch: As a group
Afternoon:
- Assertiveness continued
- Creating your future: goal-setting process as a tool for personal renewal (process explained and exercises processed)
- Personal empowerment: where and how it begins (discussion to tie the day's activities to the overriding theme of empowerment)
Closing ceremony: three gifts

- Gift from corporation: a mustard seed in a lucite cube with the CARE logo
- Gift from each other: positive quotes for other participants sealed in an envelope to be opened in one month
- Gift to self: have participants write down what they want to give themselves in the coming year (could be a healthier body, etc.), put in sealed envelope, and open in two months

Evaluation Plan

Because this was such a massive effort on the part of the corporation, it was decided that the results should be evaluated. It was decided to start with the four-level Kirkpatrick evaluation model and create several measurement instruments.

1. Participant reactions

Our standard end-of-course evaluation form was modified to fit the CARE program. Because it was a personal development course, the intent was to ask participants how it related to their personal development. The questionnaires were administered at the end of the day by the trainer and collected and returned to the Corporate Training and Development Department for processing. Exhibit 13.1 shows the evaluation form.

2. and 3. Learning gains and behavior changes

Again, because CARE was a personal development course, it was felt that both the learning and any resulting changes in behavior were of a very subjective and personal nature. To evaluate on the second and third levels (learning gain and behavior change), the company sent a questionnaire to a random sample of the participants asking them about their learning and changes in their behavior. This instrument was mailed to participants at the end of each quarter, so that the longest period of time between the class and the questionnaire was about ninety days. The completed forms were returned to the Corporate Training and Development Department for processing. Exhibit 13.2 shows the questionnaire.

4. Organizational impact

Exhibit 13.1. CARE Evaluation Form, National Computer Systems

---

Name of Instructor _____

Location _____

Date _____

National Computer Systems

Instructions: When marking each answer:

- Use a No. 2 pencil only.
- Circle appropriate number.
- Cleanly erase any marks you wish to change.

Please use the following scale to record your thoughts about the course content:

1 = *Disagree strongly*
2 = *Disagree*
3 = *Neither agree nor disagree*
4 = *Agree*
5 = *Agree strongly*

Content

1. The skills taught in this class are relevant to my personal development.   1   2   3   4   5

2. This class helped me develop those skills.   1   2   3   4   5

3. The material was clearly organized.   1   2   3   4   5

4. The course content met my needs.   1   2   3   4   5

5. Comments:

Instruction

The course instructor

6. Facilitated class discussions effectively.   1   2   3   4   5

7. Listened carefully to participants.   1   2   3   4   5

8. Assisted in linking concepts to actual interpersonal situations.   1   2   3   4   5

9. Had excellent presentation skills.   1   2   3   4   5

10. Comments:

Overall

11. Rank your overall satisfaction with the program.   1   2   3   4   5

Thank you for taking the time to give constructive feedback on this course. Your responses will be used to improve future courses.

Exhibit 13.2. Insti-Survey, National Computer Systems

Directions: Thank you for taking the time to complete this short survey.

Please use a No. 2 pencil. Cleanly erase any responses you want to change.

Please use the following scale:

A = *Agree strongly*
B = *Agree somewhat*
C = *Neutral*
D = *Disagree somewhat*
E = *Disagree strongly*

Because of my CARE Class, I

1. Am more self-aware.	A	B	C	D	E
2. Am better able to communicate with others.	A	B	C	D	E
3. Am seeking more feedback on strengths and areas to improve.	A	B	C	D	E
4. Feel more personally empowered.	A	B	C	D	E
5. Can better respond to aggressive behavior.	A	B	C	D	E
6. Can better respond to nonassertive behavior.	A	B	C	D	E
7. Am more likely to assert myself now.	A	B	C	D	E
8. Am better able to set goals for myself now.	A	B	C	D	E
9. See how goal setting helps me make some positive changes.	A	B	C	D	E
10. Feel more valued as a First Union Employee now.	A	B	C	D	E

It was determined that the best way to evaluate the impact on the organization was to look at turnover. The rationale was that, if employees did indeed feel valued by the company, they would be less likely to leave. Turnover is also one of the most reliable bits of information tracked at First Union.

Numbers on turnover were kept not only for employees who had participated in the program but also for those who had not. The employees selected to participate in the CARE program were determined in a fairly random manner, since the intent of the program was that eventually all nonexempt employees would participate. An extra step was taken, and statistics were run on other information kept in our Human Resource database to determine whether we had other information about participants that might be related to turnover. Last, some simple calculations were made to determine what a reduction in turnover might have saved the corporation in real dollars.

Evaluation Results

The results of the evaluations were surprising, to say the least.

1. Participants' reactions

Our course evaluation was separated into three categories: content, instruction, and an overall evaluation of the program. We used a five-point scale to scale responses, with 5 being the highest response possible and 1 the lowest. For the CARE program, we consistently received the following scores:

Content	4.45
Instruction	4.76
Overall	4.69

While it is felt that these scores can always be improved, they are high.

2. and 3. Learning gains and behavior changes

The responses to the various questions are combined to determine a score for the achievement of the course objectives overall. Once again, a five-point scale was used in which 5 was the best and 1 signaled cause for concern. On this measure, an average of 3.9 was received. Given the fact that time had passed and that learning and behavior changes normally drop off over time, this, too, is a very good score.

4. Organizational impact

The results of the level 4 evaluation were probably the most exciting from an organizational perspective. We found that the difference in turnover was 14 percent. Turnover rates for the CARE group were running at about 4.2 percent for the year, while for the non-CARE group they were 18.2 percent. This finding was extremely exciting.

In addition, we pulled several pieces of data from the corporate Human Resources database on all participants. We checked things like gender, age, and time with the company to see whether some other variable might affect the results. We brought in a consultant to help determine what information might be looked at, and the consultant ran a discriminant analysis on the resulting data for us. Nothing else could be found that seemed to be contributing to the reduction in turnover among the CARE group. This was pretty good evidence that the program was influencing the reduction in turnover.

As the last step in the process, we calculated real dollar savings for the program. To do this, we determined our cost for hiring and training tellers. First Union has a lot of tellers, and we know a lot about their hiring and training costs. Tellers also made up about 33 percent of the CARE participants.

It costs $2,700 to hire and train a teller. It costs $110 to put a teller through CARE. If CARE training saves the company from having to hire and train a teller, we save $2,590. Given the number of tellers put through the CARE program, the estimated savings to the company were over $1,000,000 in 1991, and that was for only one-third of the CARE group. It is expected that the costs of hiring and training for the other two-thirds are the same or higher on average. This means that the corporation saved a lot of money by offering the program to employees. This saving would have more than funded the entire CARE program.

After conducting what is felt to be a fairly rigorous evaluation of the CARE program in a business environment, we know that

- Participants reacted very favorably to the program.
- Participants feel that they learned and are using new skills.
- More participants than nonparticipants are staying at First Union.
- First Union not only helped employees grow and develop personally but also benefited in a real, quantifiable way.

Chapter 14

Evaluating a Training Program on Developing Supervisory Skills

This case study is based on a research project that was designed to measure changes in behavior and results. The program covered six topics and lasted for three days. Patterned interviews were conducted three months after the program with the participants and their immediate supervisors.

Management Institute, University of Wisconsin

Donald L. Kirkpatrick,
Professor Emeritus
University of Wisconsin, Milwaukee

Developing Supervisory Skills, a three-day institute conducted by the University of Wisconsin Management Institute, included six three-hour sessions on the following topics: giving orders, training, appraising employee performance, preventing and handling grievances, making decisions, and initiating change. All the leaders were staff members of the University of Wisconsin Management Institute. Teaching methods included lecture, guided discussion, "buzz" groups, role playing, case studies, supervisory inventories, and films and other visual aids.

Research Design

Each participant completed a questionnaire at the start of the program. Interviews of each participant were conducted at his or her workplace between two and three months after the conclusion of the program. On the same visit, the participant's immediate supervisor was also interviewed. Out of a total enrollment of fifty-seven participants, data were obtained from forty-three and from their bosses, and those data are included in this study. Exhibit 14.1 shows the findings on demographics and general issues.

Exhibit 14.1. Questionnaire Responses: Demographics

1. Describe your organization:
   a. Size
       (4)   Less than 100 employees
       (10)   100–500 employees
       (3)   500–1,000 employees
       (26)   More than 1,000 employees
   b. Products
       (15)   Consumer
       (11)   Industrial
       (12)   Both
       (5)   Other

2. Describe yourself:
   a. Title
       (33)   Foreman or supervisor
       (10)   General foreman or superintendent
   b. How many people do you supervise?
       (1)   0–5
       (9)   6–10
       (6)   11–15
       (8)   6–20
       (19)   More than 20
   c. Whom do you supervise?
       (26)   All men
       (11)   Mostly men
       (6)   Mostly women
   d. What kind of workers do you supervise?
       (14)   Production, unskilled
       (23)   Production, semiskilled
       (12)   Production, skilled
       (2)   Maintenance
       (9)   Office

Exhibit 14.1. Questionnaire Responses: Demographics
(*continued*)

---

    e. Before attending the program, how much were you told about it?
       (3)   Complete information
       (8)   Quite a lot
     (20) A little
     (12) Practically nothing
    f. To what extent do you feel that you will be able to improve your supervisory performance by attending this program?
     (21) To a large extent
     (22) To some extent
      (0)   Very little

3. How would you describe your top management?
     (31) Liberal (encourages change and suggestions)
      (9)   Middle-of-the-road
      (3)   Conservative (discourages change and suggestions)

4. How would you describe your immediate supervisor?
     (35) Liberal
      (8)   Middle-of-the-road
      (0)   Conservative

5. How often does your supervisor ask you for ideas to solve departmental problems?
     (19) Frequently
     (19) Sometimes
      (5)   Hardly ever

6. To what extent will your supervisor encourage you to apply the ideas and techniques you learned in this program?
     (14) To a large extent
     (14) To some extent
      (1)   Very little
     (14) Not sure

Research Results

In this situation, it was not possible to measure on a before-and-after basis. Instead, interviews were used to determine how behavior and results after the program compared with behavior before the program. Both the participant and his or her immediate supervisor were interviewed, and their responses were compared.

The first part of each interview determined overall changes in behavior and results. Exhibit 14.2 shows the responses. The second part of the interview determined changes related to each of the six topics discussed in the program. The reader should note that all

Exhibit 14.2. Questionnaire Responses: Behavior Changes

---

1. To what extent has the program improved the working relationship between the participant and his or her immediate supervisor?
   (23, 12)   To a large extent
   (51, 32)   To some extent
   (26, 56)   No change
     (0, 0)   Made it worse

2. Since the program, how much two-way communication has taken place between the participant and his or her immediate supervisor?
   (12, 5)   Much more
   (63, 46)   Some more
   (25, 49)   No change
     (0, 0)   Some less
     (0, 0)   Much less

3. Since the program, how much interest has the participant taken in his or her subordinates?
   (26, 5)   Much more
   (67, 49)   Some more
   (7, 46)   No change
     (0, 0)   Some less
     (0, 0)   Much less

---

responses in Exhibit 14.2 and Tables 14.1 through 14.8 are given in percentages. When two figures are given, the first is the percentage response from participants, and the second is the percentage response from their immediate supervisors.

One question that was asked was: On an overall basis, to what extent has the participant's job behavior changed since the program? Table 14.1 shows the responses in regard to changes in performance and attitude. Positive changes were indicated in all nine areas, with the greatest improvement occurring in attitudes.

In regard to the question, What results have occurred since the program?, Table 14.2 shows the responses from participants and immediate supervisors. Positive results were observed in all eight categories. In four areas, one or two supervisors observed negative results. And one participant (2 percent) indicated that employee attitudes and morale were somewhat worse.

It is interesting to note that, in nearly all cases, participants were more likely than supervisors to indicate that positive changes had taken place. There is no way of telling who is right. The important fact

Table 14.1. Change in Behavior

Supervisory areas	Much better	Somewhat better	No change	Somewhat worse	Much worse	Don't know
Giving orders	25, 12	70, 65	5, 14	0, 0	0, 0	0, 9
Training	22, 17	56, 39	22, 39	0, 0	0, 0	0, 5
Making decisions	35, 14	58, 58	7, 23	0, 0	0, 0	0, 5
Initiating change	21, 9	53, 53	26, 30	0, 0	0, 0	0, 7
Appraising employee performance	21, 7	50, 42	28, 36	0, 0	0, 0	0, 12
Preventing and handling grievances	12, 7	42, 40	46, 46	0, 0	0, 0	0, 7
Attitude toward job	37, 23	37, 53	26, 23	0, 0	0, 0	0, 0
Attitude toward subordinates	40, 7	42, 60	19, 30	0, 0	0, 0	0, 2
Attitude toward management	42, 26	26, 35	32, 37	0, 0	0, 0	0, 2

Table 14.2. Results

Performance benchmarks	Much better	Somewhat better	No change	Somewhat worse	Much worse	Don't know
Quantity of production	5, 5	43, 38	50, 50	0, 2	0, 0	0, 5
Quality of production	10, 7	60, 38	28, 52	0, 0	0, 0	0, 2
Safety	21, 7	28, 37	49, 56	0, 0	0, 0	0, 0
Housekeeping	23, 14	32, 35	42, 46	0, 5	0, 0	0, 0
Employee attitudes and morale	12, 7	56, 53	28, 32	2, 5	0, 0	0, 2
Employee attendance	7, 2	23, 19	67, 77	0, 0	0, 0	0, 0
Employee promptness	7, 2	32, 16	58, 81	0, 0	0, 0	0, 0
Employee turnover	5, 0	14, 16	79, 79	0, 5	0, 0	0, 0

Table 14.3. Giving Orders

	Much more	Somewhat more	No change	Somewhat less	Much less	Don't know
Since the program, is the participant taking more time to plan his orders?	17, 23	58, 60	16, 12	9, 0	0, 0	0, 5
Since the program, is the participant taking more time to prepare the order receiver?	24, 17	71, 57	5, 19	0, 0	0, 0	0, 7
Since the program, is the participant getting more voluntary cooperation from his employees?	26, 0	37, 56	37, 23	0, 0	0, 0	0, 21
Since the program, is the participant doing more in the way of making sure the order receiver understands the order?	51, 21	44, 44	5, 7	0, 0	0, 0	0, 28
Since the program, is the participant taking more time to make sure the order receiver is following instructions?	21, 16	60, 58	19, 12	0, 0	0, 0	0, 14
Since the program, is the participant making more of an effort to praise his employees for a job well done?	24, 30	50, 22	8, 7	0, 0	0, 0	0, 41
Since the program, is the participant doing more follow-up to see that his orders were properly carried out?	37, 21	39, 42	24, 26	0, 0	0, 0	0, 11

is that both participants and supervisors saw positive changes in both behavior and results.

Tables 14.3 to 14.8 show the responses to the questions asked on each of the six topics that the program covered. The responses are uniformly positive.

Table 14.4. Training Employees

Questions	Yes Participant always Does not apply	No Participant usually Much more	Not sure Participant sometimes Somewhat more	No change	Somewhat less	Much less	No new or transferred employees Participant never Don't know
Since the participant attended the program, are his or her new or transferred employees better trained?	63, 46	9, 0	23, 43				6, 11
Before the program, who trained the workers?	16, 13	42, 45	34, 31				8, 11
Since the program, who trained the workers?	15, 18	45, 42	32, 29				8, 11
Since the program, if someone else trains the employees, has the participant become more observant and taken a more active interest in the training process?	14, 11	22, 16	40, 27	24, 30	0, 0	0, 0	0, 16
Since the program, if the participant trains the employees, is he or she making more of an effort in seeing that the employees are well trained?	8, 5	42, 24	42, 42	8, 18	0, 0	0, 0	0, 11
Since the program, is the participant more inclined to be patient while training?	8, 11	24, 5	47, 50	21, 20	0, 3	0, 0	0, 11
Since the program, while teaching an operation, is the participant asking for more questions to ensure understanding?	8, 21	27, 14	46, 46	9, 8	0, 0	0, 0	0, 11
Since the program, is the participant better prepared to teach?	8, 11	29, 18	47, 52	16, 8	0, 0	0, 0	0, 11
Since the program, is the participant doing more follow-up to check the trainees' progress?	0, 0	41, 21	38, 49	21, 14	0, 0	0, 0	0, 16

Table 14.5. Appraising Employees' Performance

Is the participant required to complete appraisal forms on his or her subordinates?

		Yes 62, 69		No 38, 31	
	Does not apply	Large extent	Some extent	Little	Don't know
Before the program, if the participant conducted appraisal interviews, to what extent did he or she emphasize past performance?	48, 40	10, 5	40, 12	2, 14	0, 29
Before the program, to what extent did the participant try to determine the goals and objectives of his or her employees?	—	5, 15	65, 52	30, 30	0, 3
Before the program, to what extent did the participant praise the work of his or her employees?	—	8, 12	77, 52	15, 18	0, 18

	Does not apply	Much more	Somewhat more	No change	Somewhat less	Much less	Don't know
Since the program, is the participant doing more follow-up to see that the objectives of the appraisal interview are being carried out?	48, 40	10, 5	24, 21	14, 19	2, 0	0, 0	0, 14
Since the program, during an appraisal interview, is the participant placing more emphasis on future performance?	48, 40	24, 7	17, 10	10, 14	0, 2	0, 0	0, 26
Since the program, is the participant making more of an effort to determine the goals and objectives of his or her employees?	—	22, 15	60, 50	18, 18	0, 0	0, 0	0, 18
Since the program, how much does the participant praise his or her employees?	—	22, 10	40, 38	38, 38	0, 2	0, 0	0, 12

Table 14.6. Preventing and Handling Grievances

Do participant's employees belong to a union?

Yes	No
69, 69	31, 31

	Participant always	Participant usually	Participant sometimes	Participant never
Before the program, if an employee had a grievance, who usually settled it?	10, 12	64, 38	24, 43	2, 5
Since the program, who usually settles employee grievances?	10, 12	69, 48	21, 38	0, 2

	Always defended management	Usually defended management	Acted objectively	Usually defended employees	Always defended employees	Don't know
Before the program, to what extent did the participant defend management versus the employees in regard to grievance problems?	34, 17	22, 39	44, 20	0, 10	0, 0	0, 15

	Much more	Somewhat more	No change	Somewhat less	Much less	No union	Don't know
Since the program, is the participant more inclined to the management viewpoint regarding grievances and complaints?	19, 14	31, 29	48, 48	2, 0	0, 0	0, 0	0, 9
Since the program, has there been a change in the number of grievances in the participant's department?	2, 5	7, 14	81, 71	10, 5	0, 0	0, 0	0, 5
Since the program, has the degree of seriousness of grievances changed?	0, 0	2, 2	74, 74	24, 12	0, 7	0, 0	0, 5
Since the program, has the participant been better able to satisfy employee complaints before they reach the grievance stage?	17, 7	31, 52	26, 24	0, 0	0, 2	26, 14	0, 5

Table 14.7. Making Decisions

	Yes		No		Don't know
Participants only: Since the program, is the participant making better decisions?	88		2		10
	Much better	Somewhat better	No change	Somewhat worse	Much worse	Don't know
	12	68	10	0	0	10
Supervisors only: Since the program, is the participant making better decisions?					
	Frequently	Sometimes		Hardly ever	Don't know
Before the program, how often did the participant's boss involve or consult him or her in the decision-making process in the participant's department?	40, 65	45, 30	15, 5	
Before the program, to what extent did the participant involve or consult employees in the decision-making process?	24, 26	57, 38	19, 24	0, 10

Table 14.7. Making Decisions *(continued)*

	Much more	Somewhat more	No change	Somewhat less	Much less	Don't know
Since the program, how often does the participant's boss involve him or her in the departmental decision-making process?	13, 23	25, 17	60, 55	3, 3	0, 3	0, 0
Since the program, how often does the participant involve employees in the decision-making process?	26, 0	38, 43	33, 33	3, 7	0, 3	0, 14
Since the program, does the participant have less tendency to put off making decisions?	0, 0	0, 0	36, 33	36, 40	28, 22	0, 5
Since the program, is the participant holding more group meetings with employees?	12, 5	26, 17	62, 55	0, 0	0, 0	0, 24
Since the program, does the participant have more confidence in the decisions he or she makes?	29, 19	60, 60	12, 21	0, 0	0, 0	0, 0
Since the program, is the participant using a more planned approach to decision making (taking more time to define the problem and develop an answer)?	40, 14	50, 71	10, 7	0, 0	0, 0	0, 7
Since the program, does the participant take more time to evaluate the results of a decision?	24, 3	60, 62	14, 12	3, 0	0, 0	0, 24

Table 14.8. Initiating Change

	Frequently	Sometimes	Hardly ever
Before the program, when the need for change arose, how often did the participant ask his or her subordinate for suggestions or ideas regarding the change or need for change?	21, 21	64, 52	14, 21
Before the program, how often did the participant inform his or her employees of the change and the reason for it?	50, 26	36, 55	14, 14

	Much more	Somewhat more	No change	Somewhat less	Much less	Don't know
Since the program, is the participant doing more follow-up to the change process to make sure it is going in the right direction?	38, 17	50, 60	12, 12	0, 0	0, 0	0, 12
Since the program, how often has the participant involved his or her subordinates by asking them for suggestions or ideas?	17, 2	43, 40	40, 38	0, 7	0, 0	0, 12
Since the program, is the participant doing more in the way of informing employees of impending change and the reasons for it?	33, 10	38, 45	29, 26	0, 2	0, 0	0, 17

Summary and Conclusions

Because this program is repeated a number of times a year, it was worthwhile to spend the time and money that it takes to do a detailed evaluation. It was rewarding to find such positive responses from both the participants and their immediate supervisors. Because it was not possible to measure behavior and results on a before-and-after basis, the evaluation design took the alternative approach: to determine how behavior and results after the program differed from what they had been before the program.

The important thing for the reader of this case study is not what the researchers found out as a result of the research but what they did. You can borrow the design and approach and use them as is or modify them to meet your own situation. For example, you may want to add another set of interviews with subordinates of the participant and/or others who are in a position to observe the behavior of participants. You may even want to use a control group to eliminate other factors that could have caused changes in either behavior or results. In any case, consider evaluating in terms of behavior and even results, especially if the program is going to be repeated a number of times in the future.

Chapter 15

Evaluating a Leadership Training Program

This case illustrates an organized approach to evaluating a leadership training program at all four levels. Forms and procedures are included as well as the results of the evaluation. The approach can be adapted to any type of organization.

Gap Inc.

Don Kraft, Manager, Corporate Training
Gap Inc., San Bruno, California

Introduction: Why Leadership Training?

In 1994 the need for leadership training was identified for the store-manager level for the Gap, GapKids, Banana Republic, and International divisions of Gap Inc. The focus was on supervisory and leadership skills—how to influence and interact with store employees.

The program selected to meet this need was Leadership Training for Supervisors (LTS). By providing store managers the opportunity to attend LTS, managers would not only improve their performance with supervisory and leadership skills, but job satisfaction would also increase.

As one manager shared after attending LTS, "This was the most rewarding experience I've had with the company in my four years as a manager." Equally important, LTS would also provide managers with the necessary tools for developing people, so the business could remain competitive and continue to grow.

Getting to Level 4 Evaluation

Program

The LTS program was developed through a partnership between Blanchard Training and Development (BTD) and Gap Inc. Corporate Training Department. The content and delivery were customized to be applicable to the needs of the company. The three-day program focuses on the Situational Leadership® II model, as well as communication skills, goal setting, action planning, monitoring performance, giving feedback, and providing recognition.

The program continues, and training occurs throughout all divisions of the organization. The widespread use of one program connects employees at Gap Inc. by providing a shared philosophy and common language.

Audience

In 1994, the program rollout began and included general managers, area managers, district managers, and regional managers for Gap, Gap-Kids, Banana Republic, and International divisions. In 1995 and 1996, LTS was rolled out to store managers. The program continues today, focusing on new store managers and the additional participation of general managers from Gap Inc.'s division, Old Navy.

Evaluation Strategy

From the onset of planning the 1995 rollout to store managers, Gap Inc. Corporate Training Department was committed to evaluating the effectiveness of the LTS program. The evaluation strategy included measuring the program's effectiveness on four levels:

1. *Level 1: Evaluating Reaction.* Determining participants' initial *reactions* to the LTS program: Were they satisfied with the program?
2. *Level 2: Evaluating Learning.* Determining if participants *learned* the fundamental concepts of Situational Leadership® II during the program: What new knowledge was acquired as a result of attending the program?
3. *Level 3: Evaluating Behavior.* Determining participants' *change in behavior* since attending the LTS program: How has the program affected on-the-job performance?
4. *Level 4: Evaluating Organizational Results.* Determining the *impact* of the LTS program on the company: How has the program contributed to accomplishing company goals?

Evaluation Methods

Level 1: Evaluating Reaction

Participant reaction was evaluated both qualitatively and quantitatively using the LTS Program Evaluation form. Each participant completed an LTS program evaluation at the end of the program. See Exhibit 15.1 for the LTS Program Evaluation questionnaire, grouped with the other exhibits at the end of the chapter.

Level 2: Evaluating Learning

Participant learning was evaluated using the LTS Questionnaire. The LTS Questionnaire is a "fill-in-the-blank" test with fifty-five possible answers (see Exhibit 15.2). A sample of 17 percent of total participants completed the questionnaire at the end of the LTS program. The questionnaire was completed anonymously. While completing the questionnaire, participants were not permitted to use any notes or program materials. Results were then aggregated by division.

The facilitators who delivered the program received detailed written and verbal instructions on how to administer the questionnaire. Participants were told on the first day of the training that a questionnaire would be administered to determine the effectiveness of the LTS program.

Exhibit 15.1. LTS Program Evaluation

Please help us evaluate the Leadership Training for Supervisors Program by answering the following questions. Give the completed evaluation to your facilitator(s), who will then forward your comments to the Training Department. Your candid feedback will be key in creating a strategy for future roll-out of the program and in improving its facilitation.

	Entirely ineffective			*Very effective*	
1. Rate how well this program met your expectations. Comments:	1	2	3	4	5
2. Rate the relevance of the program to your job. Comments:	1	2	3	4	5
3. Rate how helpful the *Participant's Workbook* was as an in-class tool. Comments:	1	2	3	4	5
4. Do you think you will refer to the *Participant's Workbook* at a later time? If Yes, how?	Yes		No		

5. What three key skills will you apply immediately?

   a.

   b.

   c.

6. What is the most significant thing(s) you learned about:

   • Leadership
   • Coaching and developing employees
   • Communication
   • Goal setting and action planning
   • Monitoring performance
   • Problem solving and decision making
   • Recognizing accomplishments

(continued)

Exhibit 15.1. LTS Program Evaluation (*continued*)

---

7. Overall, was the material appropriate for your skill level? Select the best response.

    _____ Entirely too elementary

    _____ Somewhat elementary

    _____ Just right

    _____ Somewhat advanced

    _____ Entirely too advanced

    Please comment:

8. Overall, how was the pace of the program? Select the best response.

    _____ Entirely too quick

    _____ Some sections were covered too quickly

    _____ Just right

    _____ Certain sections were covered too slowly

    _____ Entirely too slow

    Please comment:

	Entirely ineffective			*Very effective*	
9. How effectively did the activities (i.e., role-plays, games, and practices) reinforce the concepts discussed? Which activities did you find interesting? Dull? Challenging? Overly simple? Please comment:	1	2	3	4	5

10. How would you improve this program?

	Poor		*Good*		*Excellent*
11. Overall, how do you rate this program?	1	2	3	4	5
12. Overall, how do you rate the facilitator's presentations?	1	2	3	4	5

13. Additional comments:

Exhibit 15.2. LTS Questionnaire

Check your division: Gap _____   GapKids _____   Banana Republic _____
                                UK _____   Canada _____

Check your manager level: District manager _____   Store manager _____
                                      General manager _____   Area manager _____

Complete the following questions by filling in the blanks.

1. What are the three skills that situational leaders use when working to develop people to eventually manage themselves?

    1. _____
    2. _____
    3. _____

2. A person at D2 (Disillusioned Learner) has _____ competence and _____ commitment.

3. Diagnose the development level of the individual in this situation.

    Eric has begun working on a merchandising project that is important to his store. He has successfully completed previous merchandising projects in the past but feels there is some pressure on him. He is already involved in other projects and is beginning to feel discouraged because of the time crunch.

    Eric's development level on this project is _____ .

4. Competence is a measure of a person's _____ and _____ related to the task or goal at hand.

5. Describe what a style 4 leader (Delegating) does. List three behaviors/actions you would see a style 4 leader take.

    1. _____
    2. _____
    3. _____

6. A person at D4 (Peak Performer) has _____ competence and _____ commitment.

7. In order to listen well, a supervisor must concentrate. What are two examples of concentration techniques?

    1. _____
    2. _____

8. Commitment is a measure of a person's _____ and _____ with regard to the task or goal at hand.

9. Describe what a style 2 leader (Coaching) does. List three behaviors/actions you would see a style 2 leader take.

    1. _____
    2. _____
    3. _____   *(continued)*

Exhibit 15.2. LTS Questionnaire (*continued*)

---

10. Define "leadership."

11. Who takes the lead in goal setting, feedback, decision making, and problem solving in leadership styles 1 and 2?

12. A person at D1 (Enthusiastic Beginner) has _____ competence and _____ commitment.

13. Define the acronym for a SMART goal.

    S _____

    M _____

    A _____

    R _____

    T _____

14. When contracting, whose perception should prevail if a supervisor and employee do not agree on the same development level?

15. Describe what a style 3 leader (Supporting) does. List three behaviors/actions you would see a style 3 leader take.

    1. _____

    2. _____

    3. _____

16. To create a positive interaction with an employee, a supervisor's attention must be focused on _____ and _____ .

17. List four examples of what you see someone doing or hear someone saying to be a good listener.

    1. _____

    2. _____

    3. _____

    4. _____

18. When monitoring performance, supervisors reinforce performance standards by using three methods of giving feedback. They are _____ , _____ , and _____ .

19. Suppose you have a sales associate, Becky, who needs to improve her listening skills. Create a goal for improving Becky's listening skills using the formula for a clear goal.

20. Encouraging dialogue means using attentive body language. What are two examples of body language?

    1. _____

    2. _____

Exhibit 15.2. LTS Questionnaire (*continued*)

---

21. Interactions a supervisor has with an employee that have a positive or negative impact on that person's performance and satisfaction are called _____ .

22. A person at D3 (Emerging Contributor) has _____ and _____ commitment.

23. Describe what a style 1 leader (Directing) does. List three behaviors/actions you would see a style 1 leader take.
    1. _____
    2. _____
    3. _____

24. When communicating, a sender sends a message three ways:
    1. _____
    2. _____
    3. _____

25. Who takes the lead in goal setting, feedback, decision making, and problem solving in leadership styles 3 and 4?

The LTS Questionnaire was scored on a percentage basis by the number of correct answers. Each blank was equal to one point. All questionnaires were scored by Gap Inc. Corporate Training Department.

Level 3: Evaluating Behavior

Short–Term Behavior Change. Behavior change was measured quantitatively by interviewing participants and their direct reports using the LTS Post-Program Survey. A random sample of 17 percent of total participants from each division was selected for this evaluation method. See Exhibits 15.3 and 15.4 for LTS Post-Program Surveys.

The LTS Post-Program Survey is an absolute rating scale survey of twelve questions. There are two versions of the survey. A store manager version was completed by interviewing the managers who attended the program no less than three months prior to the interview. A second version, with the same question content, was completed by interviewing two to three of the store managers' direct

Exhibit 15.3. LTS Post-Program Survey: Store Manager Version

Store Manager _____ Division _____

This survey is designed to describe your experiences with your employees since completing the LTS program. Please answer the questions by identifying the number that corresponds to your response.

	Much better	Somewhat better	No change	Somewhat worse	Much worse	Don't know

Since attending the LTS program,

1. How would you describe your ability to look at a situation and assess the development level of your employees? (e.g., skills, knowledge, past experience, interest, confidence level, etc.)

	6	5	4	3	2	1

Comments:

2. How effective are you with choosing the most appropriate leadership style to use to develop your employees' skills and motivation?

	6	5	4	3	2	1

Comments:

3. How would you describe your ability to use a variety of the four leadership styles comfortably?

	6	5	4	3	2	1

Comments:

4. How is your ability to provide direction? (e.g., setting clear goals, training, setting priorities, defining standards, etc.)

	6	5	4	3	2	1

Comments:

5. How is your ability to provide support? (e.g., praising, trusting employees, explaining why, listening, allowing mistakes, encouraging, etc.)

	6	5	4	3	2	1

Comments:

6. How is your ability to reach agreement with your employees about the leadership style they need from you in order to complete a task or goal?

	6	5	4	3	2	1

Comments:

Exhibit 15.3. LTS Post-Program Survey: Store Manager Version (*continued*)

	Much better	Somewhat better	No change	Somewhat worse	Much worse	Don't know
7. To what extent have your listening skills changed? (e.g., encouraging dialogue, concentrating, clarifying, and confirming) Comments:	6	5	4	3	2	1
8. How would you describe your ability to communicate information in a clear and specific manner? Comments:	6	5	4	3	2	1
9. How are your skills with creating clear goals with your employees? Comments:	6	5	4	3	2	1
10. How would you describe your ability to provide timely, significant, and specific *positive* feedback? Comments:	6	5	4	3	2	1
11. How would your describe your ability to provide timely, significant, and specific *constructive* feedback? Comments:	6	5	4	3	2	1
12. To what extent have you changed with providing recognition for employee accomplishments? Comments:	6	5	4	3	2	1

reports. The results of the survey determined managers' perception of changes in behavior since attending LTS as well as perceptions of their direct reports.

Division facilitators completed the survey by conducting telephone interviews without recording participants' or direct reports' names. Results were aggregated by division, not by individual. No names or

Exhibit 15.4. LTS Post-Program Survey: Associate/Assistant Manager Version

Associate/Assistant Manager_____ Division _____

This survey is designed to describe your experiences with your store manager since their completing the LTS program. Please answer the questions by identifying the number that corresponds to your response.

	Much better	Somewhat better	No change	Somewhat worse	Much worse	Don't know
Since your store manager attended the LTS program,						
1. How would you describe their ability to look at a situation and assess your skills, knowledge, past experience, interest, confidence level, etc.?	6	5	4	3	2	1
Comments:						
2. How effective have they been with helping you develop your skills and motivating you?	6	5	4	3	2	1
Comments:						
3. How would you describe their ability to use a "different strokes for different folks" approach when helping you accomplish a task or goal?	6	5	4	3	2	1
Comments:						
4. How would you describe their ability to provide you direction when needed? (e.g., setting clear goals, training, setting priorities, defining standards, etc.)	6	5	4	3	2	1
Comments:						
5. How would you describe their ability to provide you support when needed? (e.g., praising, trusting, explaining why, listening, allowing mistakes, encouraging, etc.)	6	5	4	3	2	1
Comments:						
6. How is their ability to reach agreement with you about what you need in order to complete a task or goal?	6	5	4	3	2	1
Comments:						

Exhibit 15.4. LTS Post-Program Survey: Associate/Assistant
Manager Version (*continued*)

	Much better	Somewhat better	No change	Somewhat worse	Much worse	Don't know
7. To what extent do they listen to what you say?	6	5	4	3	2	1
Comments:						
8. How would you describe their ability to communicate information that is clear and specific?	6	5	4	3	2	1
Comments:						
9. How have their skills changed with creating clear goals with you?	6	5	4	3	2	1
Comments:						
10. How would you describe their ability to provide timely, significant, and specific *positive* feedback?	6	5	4	3	2	1
Comments:						
11. How would you describe their ability to provide timely, significant, and specific *constructive* feedback?	6	5	4	3	2	1
Comments:						
12. To what extent have they changed with recognizing your accomplishments?	6	5	4	3	2	1
Comments:						

store numbers were used in the results. All completed interview surveys were mailed to Gap Inc. Corporate Training Department.

Long-Term Behavior Change. Leadership skills assessments were administered to store managers' direct reports prior to the training as well as six to nine months after attendance. Quantitative results were determined by comparing the preleadership skills assessment score with the postleadership skills assessment score. See Exhibit 15.5 for the Leadership Skills Assessment questionnaire.

This evaluation method measured the percent of change between

Exhibit 15.5. Situational Leadership® II Leadership Skills Assessment

---

Directions: The purpose of the Situational Leadership® II Leadership Skills Assessment is to provide feedback to your immediate supervisor or manager on his/her use of Situational Leadership® II. Because your responses will be used by your supervisor or manager in his/her professional development, your honest and accurate evaluations are crucial.

The information you and others provide will be analyzed by computer, and the results will be provided to your manager in summary form so that no individual responses are identified. To ensure confidentiality, *do not put your name* on the questionnaire, but make sure that your *manager's name* is on the LSA questionnaire.

Assume that the person who gave you this questionnaire is the supervisor/manager described in each of the thirty situations. For each situation, mark the point on the scale that you think best describes your supervisor's/manager's recent behavior. Mark *only one* choice. *Please answer all questions. Do not leave any blank.* Choose the answer that is closest to how you believe your manager would respond. Be sure to read each question carefully.

At most, this questionnaire should take twenty-five minutes to complete. Once you have completed the questionnaire, put it in the envelope and mail it back to Blanchard Training and Development, Inc., today.

Manager's or supervisor's name: _____ Date: _____

Mail by: _____

	Never	Rarely	Sometimes	Frequently	Almost always	Always
1. When I am able to perform a task and am confident in my ability to do so, I am given the flexibility to determine the best way to accomplish it.	1	2	3	4	5	6
2. When I am new to a particular task and learning how to do it, my manager provides me with enough direction.	1	2	3	4	5	6
3. If I am making progress but become discouraged in learning a new task, my manager tends to encourage me.	1	2	3	4	5	6
4. When I know I have the skills to complete a task but feel apprehensive about an assignment, my manager listens to my concerns and supports my ideas.	1	2	3	4	5	6
5. When I begin to learn how to complete a task and develop some skill with it, my manager listens to my input on how to better accomplish the task.	1	2	3	4	5	6

Exhibit 15.5. Situational Leadership® II Leadership Skills Assessment (*continued*)

	Never	Rarely	Sometimes	Frequently	Almost always	Always
6. If I have shown I can do a job, but lack confidence, my manager encourages me to take the lead in setting my own goals.	1	2	3	4	5	6
8. When I have demonstrated expertise in my job but am not confident about making a particular decision, my manager helps me problem-solve and supports my ideas.	1	2	3	4	5	6
9. If I have not performed at an acceptable level while learning a new task, my manager shows and tells me once again how to do the job.	1	2	3	4	5	6
10. When I get frustrated while learning a new task, my manager listens to my concerns and provides additional help.	1	2	3	4	5	6
11. My manager delegates more responsibility to me when I have demonstrated the ability to perform at a high level.	1	2	3	4	5	6
12. When I begin to learn new skills and become discouraged, my manager spends time with me to know what I am thinking.	1	2	3	4	5	6
13. When I am new to a task, my manager sets goals that tell me exactly what is expected of me and what a good job looks like.	1	2	3	4	5	6
14. To encourage me, my manager praises my work in areas where I have skills and experience but am not totally confident.	1	2	3	4	5	6
15. When I have shown I can do my job well, my manager spends less time observing and monitoring my performance.	1	2	3	4	5	6
16. When I am new to a task, my manager tells me specifically how to do it.	1	2	3	4	5	6
17. When I have developed some skill with a task, my manager asks for input on how he/she wants me to accomplish it.	1	2	3	4	5	6
18. Once I have learned a task and am working more independently, my manager encourages me to use my own ideas.	1	2	3	4	5	6

(*continued*)

Exhibit 15.5. Situational Leadership® II Leadership Skills Assessment *(continued)*

	Never	Rarely	Sometimes	Frequently	Almost always	Always
19. When I am confident, motivated, and have the skills, my manager only meets with me once in a while to tell me how well I am doing.	1	2	3	4	5	6
20. When I am learning a new task, my manager frequently observes me doing my job.	1	2	3	4	5	6
21. When I am performing a task well, my manager lets me set my own goals.	1	2	3	4	5	6
22. When I am learning how to do a new task, my manager provides me with timely feedback on how well I am doing.	1	2	3	4	5	6
23. When I feel overwhelmed and confused with completing a new task, my manager is supportive and provides me with enough direction to proceed.	1	2	3	4	5	6
24. My manager observes my performance closely enough in areas where I have skills so if I lose confidence or interest, he/she is there to help me.	1	2	3	4	5	6
25. When communicating information or feedback to me, my manager is clear and specific.	1	2	3	4	5	6
26. When talking to me, my manager's tone is positive and respectful.	1	2	3	4	5	6
27. If my manager is unsure of what I am saying, he/she asks questions to clarify my message.	1	2	3	4	5	6
28. When I talk to my manager, he/she listens to me and does not get distracted.	1	2	3	4	5	6
29. During conversations, my manager restates and asks questions about what I said to avoid miscommunication.	1	2	3	4	5	6
30. My manager is able to communicate with me in a way that gets his/her message across while keeping my self-esteem intact.	1	2	3	4	5	6

Source: Reprinted with permission by Blanchard Training and Development, Inc., Escondido, CA.

pre- and postassessment, specifically for eight skill areas—directing, coaching, supporting, delegating, goal setting, observing performance, providing feedback, and communication.

Level 4: Evaluating Organizational Results

To investigate the impact LTS had on organizational results, Gap Inc. Corporate Training Department, in partnership with Blanchard Training and Development, conducted an impact study to determine if improvement in leadership and supervisory skills had a positive impact on areas such as store sales, employee turnover rates, and shrinkage.

Sales. It was assumed that if the leadership skills of store managers improved, employee performance would improve, customers would be served better, and sales would increase.

Employee Turnover Rates. Studies indicate that recruitment, hiring, and on-the-job training costs are about 1.5 times the first-year salary for a job. Therefore, any training intervention that reduces turnover contributes directly to the bottom line.

Shrinkage. It was also assumed that by improving store managers' effectiveness, shrinkage as a percent of sales should go down.

Interpreting LTS Results

Interpreting Level 1: Reaction

When reviewing the averages from the LTS program evaluation (Exhibit 15.1), use the following ranges as guidelines for responses to *expectations, relevance, facilitator's presentation,* and *overall program*.

Range	Interpretation
1–2	Participants had serious concerns about the training.
Low–mid 3	Training provided some value, but could have been better.
High 3–4	Participants found real value in the training and indicated a positive reaction.
High 4–5	Outstanding! Participants indicated strong positive reaction.

Use the following ranges as guidelines for responses to *appropriate for skill level.*

Range	Interpretation
1–2	Participants' reactions indicated the material of the program was entirely too elementary.
2–3	Participants' reactions indicated the material of the program was somewhat elementary.
3	Participants found the material "just right" for their skill level.
3–4	Participants' reactions indicated the material was somewhat advanced.
4–5	Participants' reactions indicated the material was entirely too advanced.

Use the following ranges as guidelines for responses to *pace of program.*

Range	Interpretation
1–2	Participants' reactions indicated the pace of the program was entirely too quick.
2–3	Participants' reactions indicated some sections were covered too quickly.
3	Participants' reactions indicated the pace was "just right."
3–4	Participants' reactions indicated certain sections were covered too slowly.
4–5	Participants' reactions indicated the pace of the program was entirely too slow.

Figure 15.1 shows the results of LTS Program Evaluation. Table 15.1 shows a breakdown of these results. Store managers attending the LTS program responded to the training with incredible enthusiasm. They reacted favorably; their expectations were met and the training was relevant to the job. Reaction was also extremely positive to the overall program and the facilitators' presentation of the material.

As regards appropriateness of material for store manager skill level and the overall pace of the program, store managers responded overwhelmingly positively, with "just right" to both questions.

Figure 15.1. LTS Program Evaluation Results (all sessions)

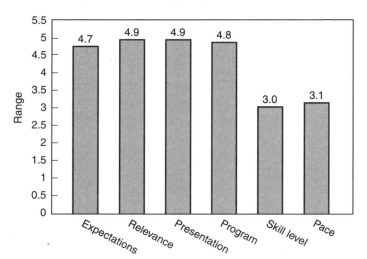

Table 15.1. LTS Program Evaluation Results, by Division

Category	All divisions	Gap	GapKids	Banana Republic	Canada	UK
Average of expectations	4.7	4.7	4.7	4.7	4.7	4.6
Average of relevance	4.9	4.9	4.9	4.9	4.9	4.8
Average of presentation	4.9	4.9	4.8	4.9	4.8	4.7
Average of program	4.8	4.8	4.7	4.7	4.8	4.6
Average of skill level	3.0	3.0	2.9	3.0	3.0	3.0
Average of pace	3.1	3.1	3.2	3.2	3.2	3.2

Interpreting Level 2: Learning

Although store manager reaction was extremely positive, the question to ask was, Did they *learn* while attending the session? The following guidelines were used to interpret learning scores from the LTS sessions:

Range	Interpretation
Less than 50%	More than half of the participants did not increase their knowledge.
50–60%	Little over half the participants improved their knowledge.
60–80%	The majority of participants gained new knowledge as a result of the training.
80–100%	Outstanding! Almost all participants gained new knowledge.

The results from the LTS Questionnaire shown in Figure 15.2 indicate that significant learning did occur during the program. *The average score for all divisions from the LTS Questionnaire was 87 percent.* Store managers were unfamiliar with LTS concepts before attending the session. The score of 87 percent indicates that new learnings were used to successfully complete the LTS Questionnaire.

Interpreting Level 3: Change in Behavior (Short Term)

Store managers' reactions were positive, and significant learning occurred during the training. Now the question to ask was, Did the managers *change* their behavior on the job as a result of the training?

Figure 15.2. LTS Questionnaire Results

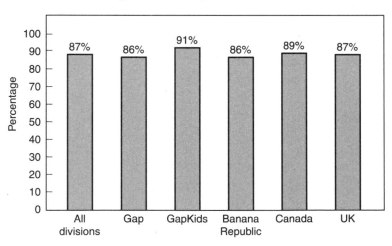

The LTS Post-Program Survey measured the degree to which managers' behaviors changed in twelve skill areas, according to their own perceptions as well as their direct reports' perceptions. Each of the survey questions focuses on a skill from the LTS program. Following are the skills surveyed:

Skill	*Interpretation*
1. Diagnosing	The ability to look at a situation and assess the developmental needs of the employee involved.
2. Leadership styles	The patterns of behavior a leader uses as perceived by others.
3. Flexibility	The ability to use a variety of leadership styles comfortably.
4. Direction	What supervisors use to build an employee's knowledge and skills with accomplishing a task.
5. Support	What supervisors use to build an employee's commitment, both confidence and motivation.
6. Contracting	The ability to communicate with employees and reach agreement about which leadership style to use to help them develop competence and commitment to achieve a goal or complete a task.
7. Receiver skills	Supervisors in this role can make communication effective by encouraging dialogue, concentrating, clarifying, and confirming a sender's message.
8. Sender skills	Supervisors in this role can make communication effective by analyzing their audience, being specific, and using appropriate body language and tone.
9. Goal setting	A function of leadership for ensuring standards are clarified. A clear goal creates a picture of what good performance looks like.
10. Positive feedback	Positive feedback focuses on the employee's positive behavior.
11. Constructive feedback	Constructive feedback focuses on the employee's behavior that needs improvement.

Table 15.2. LTS Post-Program Survey Results (all interviews)

Skill	Store managers	Assistant/associate managers
1. Diagnosing	5.3	5.0
2. Leadership style	5.1	5.0
3. Flexibility	4.9	4.9
4. Direction	5.1	4.9
5. Support	5.2	5.0
6. Contracting	4.8	4.9
7. Receiver skills	5.1	5.0
8. Sender skills	4.9	4.8
9. Goal setting	5.0	4.9
10. Positive feedback	4.9	4.9
11. Constructive feedback	5.0	4.9
12. Providing recognition	5.0	5.0

12. Providing recognition	Reinforcing desired performance by acknowledging progress and celebrating accomplishments.

When looking over the results of the Post-Program Survey shown in Tables 15.2 and 15.3, the following ranges can be used as guidelines:

Range	Interpretation
Less than 4	No improvement. In fact, since attending LTS the participant's leadership behavior has changed for the worse.
4–5	Some measurable improvement did take place back in the stores. Store managers are somewhat better with using the skill since attending LTS. This is a positive change in behavior.

Table 15.3. LTS Post–Program Survey
Results (all interviews), by Division

| | Store Managers | | | | | | Associate/Assistant Managers | | | | | |
Skill	All	Gap	GapKids	Banana Republic	Canada	UK	All	Gap	GapKids	Banana Republic	Canada	UK
Diagnosing	5.3	5.5	5.1	5.1	5.0	5.7	5.0	5.1	5.0	5.0	4.6	4.9
Leadership styles	5.1	5.3	5.0	4.9	5.0	5.3	5.0	5.1	5.0	5.0	4.8	5.1
Flexibility	4.9	4.9	4.9	4.9	4.3	5.0	4.9	5.0	4.8	4.9	4.3	4.7
Direction	5.1	5.2	4.9	4.9	5.0	5.2	4.9	5.0	4.8	4.9	4.3	5.0
Support	5.2	5.3	4.9	5.0	5.3	5.2	5.0	5.1	5.0	5.0	4.6	5.0
Contracting	4.8	4.9	4.6	4.7	4.5	4.9	4.9	4.9	4.9	4.8	4.4	4.9
Receiver skills	5.1	5.1	5.1	5.1	5.0	5.2	5.0	5.1	5.2	4.8	4.9	4.9
Sender skills	4.9	5.0	4.9	4.9	4.5	5.2	4.8	4.8	4.9	4.7	4.9	4.9
Goal setting	5.0	5.0	4.7	5.1	4.5	5.3	4.9	4.9	4.8	4.8	4.6	4.7
Positive feedback	4.9	5.0	4.8	5.0	4.0	5.0	4.9	4.9	4.8	4.7	4.6	5.1
Constructive feedback	5.0	5.1	4.9	4.9	5.0	5.1	4.9	5.0	4.7	5.0	5.0	4.7
Providing recognition	5.0	4.9	5.2	4.9	4.8	4.9	5.0	5.1	5.1	4.8	4.9	4.7

Greater than 5   Any rating in this range is very positive and indicates the store managers improved dramatically in using the skill they learned since attending LTS.

As seen in Table 15.3, store managers believe they have become "somewhat better" to "much better" in using all of the leadership skills included in the program. Specifically, store managers believe they have significantly improved their leadership skills in four areas:

1. *Diagnosing* the development level of their employees
2. Using the correct *leadership style* with each development level
3. Providing *direction* to employees when needed
4. Providing *support* to employees when needed

Table 15.3 also illustrates associate and assistant managers' perceptions of their store manager. All responses indicate a dramatic improvement in leadership skills since the managers attended LTS. In fact, five out of the twelve questions asked have an average score of five.

Interpreting Level 3: Change in Behavior (Long Term)

As store managers continued to focus on developing their supervisory and leadership skills, measurement of their ongoing success continued. In 1996, store managers participated in the post-leadership skills assessment.

A comparison of all pre- and posttraining leadership skills assessment (LSA) results indicated that according to store employees, store managers had improved in all skill areas measured by the LSA—namely, directing, coaching, supporting, delegating, goal setting, observing and monitoring performance, feedback, and communication. In fact, seven of the eight skill areas included in the assessment showed improvement at a statistically significant level. In other words, the odds of the increased effectiveness occurring by chance were highly improbable, or less than 50 in 1,000. In summary, this important information indicated that store managers had actually changed their behavior as a result of the training.

Interpreting Level 4: Evaluating Organizational Results

Store managers' reactions were positive, new learnings occurred during the training, and behaviors changed on the job since attending LTS. The next question was, How has the training contributed to organizational results?

Recent statistical analyses have revealed positive correlation between improved LSA scores and increased sales, decreased turnover, and increased loss prevention in stores from which managers attended the training. The study examined stores with increased sales, reduced turnover, and reduced shrinkage that had the same managers in place one year prior to the training and one to one and a half years after attending LTS.

For each month, quarter, or year of store performance data examined, the number of managers with increased sales, reduced turnover, and reduced shrinkage was compared with the number of managers with increased LSA scores and increased performance on these three measures. Of the stores with increased sales, reduced turnover, and reduced shrinkage, 50 to 80 percent of the time managers had also increased their LSA scores. In other words, store managers increased their leadership effectiveness and had a positive impact on store performance.

Over time (one to two years after training), the trend in the data is also very positive; the percentage of store managers with improved LSA scores and positive business results steadily increases.

Summary

On four levels of evaluation, LTS was a success. Store managers

1. Had a positive reaction to the LTS program
2. Learned new skills and knowledge while attending the program
3. Used those learnings to improve their performance as leaders on the job
4. Impacted their stores' business

Chapter 16

Evaluating a Leadership Development Program

Introduction

Recognizing a shortcoming of future leaders, an anticipated large-scale retirement cohort in the decades to come, and spurred by the passage of the Government Performance and Results Act of 1996, the U.S. Geological Survey in 1999 established a Leadership Program to provide direct opportunities for its employees to learn about, and foster, leadership development. Starting in 2001, Walden Consulting was contracted to evaluate the efficacy of the program in a long-term study. The research project was premised on Kirkpatrick's four levels of evaluation and infused with concepts from the literature on adoption of new ideas, primarily drawn from Everett Rogers' seminal work, *Diffusion of Innovations*. Through a conceptual framework of the learning process, this research offers a new way for evaluators and designers to imagine greater impacts training programs can have on participants and their coworkers.

U.S. Geological Survey, Walden Consulting, Granville, Ohio

Dr. Abram W. Kaplan, Principal Investigator
Jordan Mora, Gillian Poe, Jennifer Altzner, and Laura Rech
Reston, Virginia

Through previous research in other contexts, the principal investigator (Kaplan and Kishel 2000; Kaplan 1999) has developed a learning model that hypothesizes a series of phases that leads a participant from ignorance to action, and that then can be extended to observe changes in co-workers as their exposure to the new material increases (see Figure 16.1).

Figure 16.1. Learning Model, USGS Leadership Program Evaluation

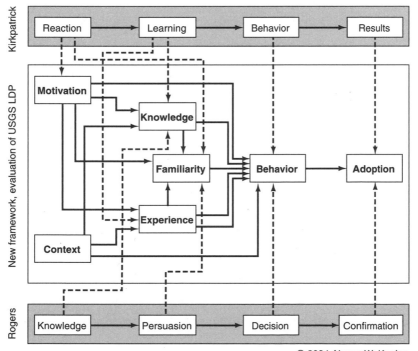

© 2004 Abram W. Kaplan

This case study provides an overview of the process and the findings of the first four years of investigation.

The USGS Leadership Program, directed by Nancy Driver as Program Manager, is a remarkable effort to enhance the organizational culture of the survey. A series of classroom experiences are offered for groups of about twenty-four participants at a time. The Leadership 101 course is a week-long, intensive workshop taught at the National Conservation Training Center in Shepherdstown, WV, by a team of ten instructors in a series of modules designed specifically for the program. All but three of the instructors are USGS managers; the others are experts brought in to contribute particular segments. Participants are selected through an extensive nomination process, and there is a waiting list for admission to the course. Prior to the 101 class, all participants undergo a full 360-degree evaluation, completing a lengthy survey assessing their own behavior and requesting that a similar survey be completed by eight to ten of their co-workers. During the first days of the course, the relevant 360-degree feedback is compiled and distributed to each participant, and a buddy system is established to formulate action plans based on the comments provided from the surveys. Follow-up meetings by buddy pairs are required, and other modes of follow-up reinforce the classroom learning. The rest of the 101 week is devoted to a wide variety of leadership issues, including negotiation, supervision, team building, communication, and mentoring.

Some eighteen to twenty-four months later, the same cohort of participants returns to Shepherdstown for the 201 class, another full week follow-up course with a subset of instructors and a new set of issues to address, with a heavy emphasis on the importance of story-telling as part of the leadership learning process. Another 360-degree evaluation is done prior to the 201 course, and new action plans are developed during the week. Then, about a year after that course, a third tier has been added, offered on one occasion at this writing: a "train the trainer" (T-3) course where participants are provided the tools necessary to become leadership instructors themselves. After a series of trial runs, pairs of T-3 graduates become co-facilitators for two-day "Leadership Intensive" (LI) workshops, offered ten times per year at USGS facilities all around the country. The LIs are intended to provide a subset of 101/201 content for USGS employees who have not been nominated for the full-blown Leadership Program, and to expand the impact of the program across the bureau. Given that the 101/201 sequence is only offered twice per year (thus reaching about forty-eight people), the LIs offer a diffusion opportunity for 250 people each year.

The Leadership Program does not content itself with offering these various course offerings. It has facilitated monthly lunch gatherings at the two largest USGS offices—in Reston, VA, and Denver, CO. It has established a bureauwide annual leadership award, conferred by the director of the agency and given much publicity. It has created the "leadership coin" program, with a small number of special coins minted with the inscription "The most important quality of a leader is that of being acknowledged as such" (Andre Maurois). The coins are given to employees in recognition of special acts of leadership, and their stories are published on the agency's Web site. A Web-based "chat room" and various e-mail Listservs have been created to foster interaction among participants, and the Leadership Program's Web site itself (via *http://training.usgs.gov/*) maintains an active presence in helping to promote leadership development around the survey.

Conceptual Development

Our evaluation project focuses upon the measurement of five primary variables: Motivation, Knowledge, Experience, Familiarity, and Behavior. The ultimate goal in the measurement of all of these variables is to better understand the processes of leadership diffusion and adoption throughout the survey. Refer to Figure 16.1 for the causal links among these variables.

Motivation accounts for the reasons people are inclined to be involved in leadership activities. If someone has as his or her sole aspiration to become director of USGS, we might worry a little bit about the kinds of responses such a person offers, as compared to someone who wants to improve his or her negotiation skills. A typical Motivation question is "How interested are you in interacting with your co-workers in a teamwork setting?"

The *Knowledge* variable evaluates individuals' knowledge of specific topics addressed during the leadership class. Therefore Knowledge measures the technical, formal aspects of the educational process. As Kaplan has previous shown, an individual's knowledge of a subject is just one variable related to behavior and is insufficient on its own for predicting behavior. However, when knowledge is combined with experience, the ability to predict behavior is dramatically increased. Therefore, it is critical to measure individuals' experience. *Experience*, in the current project, refers to the application of techniques acquired through exposure.

Experience can be either direct, through experimentation and utilization of skills, or vicarious, as in hearing leadership success stories from colleagues. The Experience variable examines individuals' leadership experiences both within and beyond the classroom. "Have you watched true leaders at work?" is an example of a possible measure of Experience. Experience is considered a necessary building block in the development of leadership behavior.

The *Familiarity* variable examines how comfortable people are with the suggested ideas (in this case, leadership ideas promoted during the class), and how confident they are in their own abilities to try them out. Familiarity can be thought of as the intermediate in which we can look at the direct result of learning facets that develop before we can observe leadership behavior. Our model suggests that the ingredients of knowledge and experience mix together in varying amounts to produce familiarity, and only when familiarity reaches a critical level can we expect the behavior "bulb" to go on. As leadership behavior continues to expand, we then can measure adoption—the immersion of tendencies into the culture of an agency. "How comfortable would you be in a leadership position?" is one example of a question on familiarity.

Behavior measures individuals' engagement in specific leadership activities and how they utilize leadership knowledge and skills—what people actually do. And our ability to determine whether these ideas are getting adopted more broadly in the agency requires us to measure behavior repeatedly, both of class participants and of other people where the leadership ideas might rub off through their own vicarious experiences. One of the behavior questions from our surveys inquires whether the respondent prefers to let other people lead or to be in a leadership position.

Evaluation Methodology

Walden Consulting's evaluation has been an evolutionary process; first it examined just the 101 course and now it incorporates nearly all aspects of the program. From the inception of the research effort, the idea of diffusion has been of paramount interest, due primarily to the Leadership Program's vision of creating a "leadership-centered culture" throughout the USGS. Because of this focus, it has been critical to incorporate feedback from participants' colleagues as well as the participants themselves, in order to measure and observe the "osmosis" effects of the program beyond its direct target group.

In order to acquire this potentially difficult layer of data, our evaluation team came up with an innovative idea: to piggy back on the 360-degree evaluation already administered before each course. (Note that this only works for the full-week classes; there is no current effort to measure the diffusion of the LI workshops, which, admittedly, will be a more difficult undertaking.) The program manager e-mails all participants about two months before each course, asking them to fill out their own copy of the 360-degree evaluation, and to forward the e-mail to eight to ten co-workers, who are directed to fill out a parallel form. That form includes questions that are necessary for the participant feedback process just described, as well as a series of questions that assess the evaluator's own behavior and learning process.

Because the feedback and action planning processes are so fundamental to the leadership curriculum, the program manager insists that all participants complete the survey and that they secure responses from their co-workers. As a result, our evaluation team obtains 100 percent response rates from participants (24 per 101/201 group), and more than 200 evaluator responses (which would equate to eight evaluators per participant) for each course. We ask all respondents to provide a unique identifier (based on their birth month, state/country of birth, and partial digits from Social Security number) so that we can track anonymous responses over time and ensure the confidentiality of their sensitive and personal information. We also request information from all evaluators regarding their own familiarity with the Leadership Program, to ascertain the exposure they have received prior to their evaluation response. With this information, we can begin to assess the diffusion of the concepts introduced in the courses.

Furthermore, our research design includes a biennial control survey of USGS employees having no exposure to the Leadership Program, a three-year follow-up survey of Leadership Program participants who have either completed the course sequence or who terminated their involvement before graduating, as well as a pre-post survey sequence for the LI participants. In all, we gather between 1,500 and 2,000 survey responses per year for this study, and these give us an outstanding opportunity to assess the growth and development of this 10,000-employee federal agency.

Measurement: Levels of Evaluation

As indicated in the learning model above, this evaluation does not rely explicitly on the Kirkpatrick levels, nor on the Phillips levels that have been offered as an extension therefrom. But our conceptual layers are similar in many ways, and we offer the following measurement rubric:

Reaction and Planned Action

Each Leadership course includes extensive course evaluation materials by participants, both at the module level and for the entire course. In the 101 course, for instance, each of fourteen modules is assessed with these questions, asked in a daily "green sheet" form:

1. How would you rate the session overall (1 = disappointing; 5 = outstanding)
2. How much of the session's content could you relate back to your duties at work (1 = not much; 5 = very much)
3. On a scale from 1 to 5, with 5 being outstanding, how would you rate the session's instructor(s)? Preparation? Presentation? Inspiration? Overall?
4. What suggestions would you offer for future improvements of this session?
5. What parts of this session did you find most useful for the future?

These are contained in a half-sheet section. Then, at the end of the week, our level 1 forms ask:

1. How would you rate the course overall (1 = disappointing; 5 = outstanding)

2. How valuable was this course to your development as a leader within the USGS (1 = not valuable; 5 = very valuable)
3. What suggestions would you offer for future improvements of this course?
4. What element(s) of this course did you find most useful?
5. Additional comments or suggestions? Thank you!

We complement in-class course evaluations with questionnaire items in our pre-201 surveys asking participants for longer-range recollections of the 101 class, and these measures provide a valuable check on the immediate reactions during the workshop.

Motivation

One facet of our model that does not match up easily with the Kirkpatrick levels is what we call "motivation": the reasons an employee might choose to be involved in the Leadership Program. We measure this variable by asking respondents about the specific interests that led them to the course. For instance:

How interested are you in the following?	*Not Very–Very*				
a. Taking a leadership role within the bureau	1	2	3	4	5
b. Interacting with co-workers in a team setting	1	2	3	4	5
c. Learning about leadership skills	1	2	3	4	5
d. Personal advancement or enhanced personal opportunities	1	2	3	4	5
e. Learning about negotiation and conflict resolution	1	2	3	4	5

Learning

In our case, "learning" is a construct that cannot be measured in one variable. Rather, it is a combination of measurements about the formalized knowledge acquired in the classroom, the opportunities to experience the material—either in hands-on fashion or through vicarious stories of other people's experience—and the outcome of these activities in terms of familiarity: the degree of comfort and confidence a person might achieve through effective learning opportunities.

Knowledge measures include items such as these:

Indicate how different you think the following
pairs of terms are: *Not Very–Very*

  a. Leader and manager   1 2 3 4 5
  b. Collaboration and compromise   1 2 3 4 5
  c. USGS Vision Statement and Mission
      Statement   1 2 3 4 5

Experience items include:

How much influence do these items have on your
leadership development?   *Not Very–Very*

  a. Observing others in leadership positions   1 2 3 4 5
  b. Practicing particular leadership skills yourself 1 2 3 4 5
  c. Hearing leadership success stories   1 2 3 4 5
  d. Taking a leadership class to learn in a formal
      setting   1 2 3 4 5

Familiarity questions might look like this:

How comfortable do you feel about: *Not Very–Very*

  a. Taking a leadership role in a small group?   1 2 3 4 5
  b. Asking input from others?   1 2 3 4 5
  c. Delegating responsibilities?   1 2 3 4 5
  d. Negotiating with your colleagues?   1 2 3 4 5
  e. Expressing the goals and vision of the USGS?   1 2 3 4 5
  f. Communicating concerns to a supervisor?   1 2 3 4 5

Behavior

Our questionnaires seek a wide variety of behavioral self-reports from participants, and these are complemented by identical questions asked of evaluators, who have been asked to comment on the participants. The survey incorporates a large group of behavioral measures, and these are repeated in multiple surveys to provide pre-post and treatment–control comparisons. Here are examples:

When working with other people, how likely
are you to: Not Very–Very

a. Retreat from a (potentially conflictual)
   situation?   1   2   3   4   5
b. Hold team members accountable?   1   2   3   4   5
c. Communicate effectively with colleagues?   1   2   3   4   5
d. Volunteer for a leadership role?   1   2   3   4   5
e. Maintain focus/intensity when you're
   confronted with adversity?   1   2   3   4   5

How effectively do you think you: Not Very–Very

a. Coach and mentor?   1   2   3   4   5
b. Listen to ideas and concerns?   1   2   3   4   5
c. Think and plan strategically?   1   2   3   4   5
d. Keep everyone focused on the purpose
   of the team?   1   2   3   4   5

In your estimation, how much do you: Little–Lots

a. Open yourself up for feedback?   1   2   3   4   5
b. Commit to improving areas of weakness?   1   2   3   4   5
c. Work to maintain the goals and objectives
   of the USGS?   1   2   3   4   5
d. Actively support others?   1   2   3   4   5

Results

There are innumerable ways to derive conclusions about the impact
of a program beyond the improved behavior of its direct participants.
In our case, the most immediate gauge are the conversions—in
behavior as well as in other parts of the learning model—for co-
workers. This requires very careful study of the term "culture," and
requisite attention to the criteria by which cultural change can be
assessed. If, by some agreed-upon measures, we can demonstrate that
USGS employees, on the average, reveal higher leadership capacity
due to the availability of the Leadership Program courses, then that
would draw a conclusion that the culture is altered. If we cannot show
behavioral change but we observe increases in knowledge and famil-

iarity, is that sufficient? This is not the place to argue—or answer—these questions, but suffice it to say that our objective is to maximize changes on all facets of the learning model, and to create reliable measures whose data can reveal valid conclusions about cultural change in the organization.

What We're Finding

Our evaluation results to date suggest that this innovative program has a significant impact on the federal agency within which it resides. The U.S. Geological Survey is a bastion of hard science, home to a larger percentage of PhDs than perhaps any other federal organization. Its reputation is built on careful, systematic, and objective research about the earth's geology, water, biological resources, and geographical facets. That set of lenses is not lost on the designers of this program, as they clearly see the need to infuse the scientifically minded bureau with a greater sense of leadership and purpose. Changing that culture is no small task—far more challenging than reforming a government agency like the Office of Personnel Management (OPM), populated by many employees with a Human Resources background, for instance. We knew, in evaluating this effort, that the prospects for dramatic change were small, and that the skepticism about our social science approach to measurement would be vast. Indeed, in our first presentation to the USGS director after the first year of study, we felt the need to establish ourselves as legitimate scientists in our own right, to equate the rigor of our work with that of the hydrologists and geomorphologists in the audience.

Reaction-level results for this program have been outstanding from its inception: participants are energized by the weeklong workshops and return to their offices enthusiastic and satisfyingly fatigued. This in itself is no small feat, since many participants come to the classes with a rather grumpy fortitude: they have lots of work to do back home, they don't understand why leadership is something they have to deal with, and they certainly don't want to do anything touchy-feely. (The class is relatively touchy-feely and has a kind of in-your-face quality at points.) Typical course evaluation results look like these (averages for 2004 classes on a 1–5 scale):

Course evaluation item	101	201
How would you rate the course overall?	4.6	4.9
How valuable was this course to your development as a leader within USGS?	4.9	5.0

Across the four years of our research, we rarely have any respondents answer with less than a "4" on the five-point scale for any of our quantitative items, and typically in the range of 60–70 percent of participants rate the course and its value at level "5."

But reaction is a dead-end in the views of this research unit. Without any greater assessment of anticipated results, it is only a gauge of relative happiness. Participants may be entertained, or may secretly be glad to have escaped their home offices, and that has little bearing on the results we may or may not see emanating from the classes. This extends to queries about course value as well, where the euphoria (and fatigue) at the week's end inevitably produces distorted responses about an intervention. It is our view that a "life-training" experience like leadership development is especially sensitive to this sort of bias, as it is very easy for a participant to conflate the salience of leadership skills as applied at work with that which may be useful at home. The USGS course covers negotiation skills, team building, supervision, communication, vision, action planning, mentoring, and many other facets that any parent would likely find useful irrespective of his or her employment. This is why none of the reaction facets are included in the learning model of Figure 16.1, for they offer no causal insights.

More critical is our effort to understand the learning process of the skills transmitted through the two main leadership classes and the diffusion of those skills both in the Leadership Intensive workshops and the "osmosis" of home office interactions with colleagues. Figure 16.2 provides a set of bar charts summarizing the big picture of this assessment, but it is only a broad-brush way of looking at some very complex and intriguing patterns. For starters, here are the results as they pertain to the participants in the leadership courses (see Figure 16.2). Following that, we will explore the diffusion patterns.

Motivation.   There is a very clear self-selection bias among participants in the Leadership Program, which comes about in one of two

Figure 16.2. Summary Charts of Results, Years 1–4,
USGS Leadership Program Evaluation

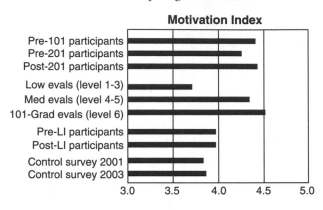

Motivation Index

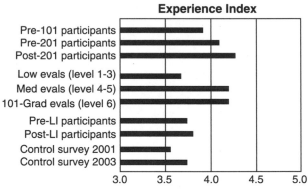

Experience Index

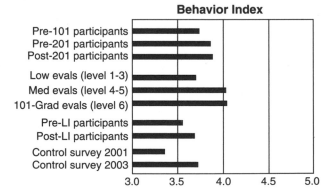

Behavior Index

Figure 16.2 Summary Charts of Results, Years 1–4 (*continued*)

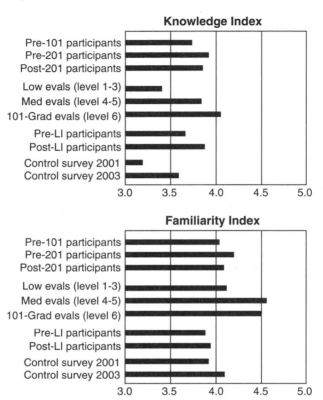

ways: either the nomination process effectively identifies highly motivated employees or the nomination process causes employees to become highly motivated. In either case, we see motivation among participants start high and stay there. The control group and the LI population both show far lower interest, and show little change over time.

Knowledge. Here we see mild increases from pre-101 to pre-201, and no gain at all from pre-201 to post-201. This might be horrific to some evaluation experts, but we see this as relatively minor: the courses tend to devalue straightforward knowledge transmission, and the timing of our surveys (as much as a two-year gap between pre-101 and pre-201) is likely to produce mediocre recall of facts. What is fascinating is that the LI participants do show a significant knowledge gain in their two-day class, suggesting that the instructors in that setting endeavor to provide a lot of factual information that is more likely to be prioritized in a shorter class. We also see a big increase in the control group results which we can—at this point—only attribute to an "osmosis" effect, thanks to Leadership Program marketing and interactions with participants.

Experience.   This is where we would hope to see some marked gains in our 101/201 participants, and indeed we do. The more exposure these employees have to leadership opportunities, the stronger their responses are to questions on those subjects. LI participants have fewer chances to experiment with leadership and are exposed to fewer stories from other people who have attempted those same tasks. Interestingly, the control group shows gains on this front, and again, we can only speculate that there is some impact resulting from the Leadership Program such that employees across the bureau are hearing more success stories, witnessing colleagues changing their behavior, and/or gaining opportunities to try out relevant skills themselves.

Familiarity.   According to our learning model, familiarity is the linchpin in behavioral change: if someone secures enough knowledge and experience to produce an affective change—an increase in one's own comfort and confidence with the material at hand—then there is a foundation for converting that material into habit. To use Rogers' terminology, we might see someone persuaded to adopt the innovation. So it is fundamentally important to observe the familiarity patterns in this setting. What we find most intriguing is that the 101 course does seem to promote greater confidence in trying out leadership skills, but the 201 course serves as a reality check; in fact, a lot of what leadership is about really is quite complex and challenging, and the 201 curriculum pushes its participants hard to get beyond the superficialities of valuing each other and listening well. The LI workshops do not provide sufficient exposure to have much effect, and the control group gains are marginal at best.

Behavior.   Finally, we look to see whether behavioral change takes place. At the outset of our study, we acknowledged the challenge inherent in this. Actually demonstrating long-range alterations in individual behavior over large groups of people without built-in incentives for change is a high threshold for any organizational intervention. People just do not change readily, nor do they (we) typically hang on to major changes without constant reminders about the necessity of those new practices. So we are thrilled to see even slight gains in behavior, and are struck that the control group has gained, in a two-year period, to the point where the pre-101 participants start. While there is a long way to go in ascertaining major behavioral improvements in leadership, we do observe incremental gains in the right direction.

Diffusion of Leadership

So this underscores the successes of a program for its participants, and the comparative impacts on the general population of USGS employees, where there undoubtedly are some clear gains in awareness about the importance of leadership. But the middle of the Figure 16.2 charts are perhaps the most interesting of all, for they represent our findings from the "piggyback 360-degree"—the self-reported values by evaluators of 101 and 201 participants. On the premise that the creation of a leadership-centered culture will start through the interactions of participants with the people they work with on a day-to-day basis, we would want to measure the learning process of those colleagues to know whether those interactions make a difference.

We ask evaluators, "How familiar are you with the USGS Leadership 101 course?" with a scale from "1" signifying "not familiar" to "5" meaning "very familiar" and "6" for those respondents who themselves had completed the 101 course. We also know, for each evaluator, what his or her structural relationship is to the participant (supervisor, peer, or employee); this is our "relation" variable. And we ask the evaluators how well they feel they know the participant, so that we can assess the quality of their responses; we refer to this as "acquaintance." In our multiyear analyses, neither relation nor acquaintance has a major effect on evaluator variability on any of our five indices. But their connection to the Leadership Program turns out to be huge.

Without expanding on each of the five charts in Figure 16.2, the patterns are very similar. Evaluators with little connection (values of 1–3 on the "how familiar are you . . ." item) have relatively low values on all five indices, and their responses are significantly depressed in comparison to the other two groups. More astonishing still, the medium-level (4–5 on the "how familiar" scale) and high-level (101 graduates) evaluators showed significantly higher scores on both familiarity and behavior than Leadership Program participants them-selves. In other words, not only are the ideas about leadership diffus-ing to co-workers, but the participants are functioning as such outstanding opinion leaders—and even as informal change agents—that they are propelling their colleagues to levels *beyond* their own performance. This may, in fact, be the most important leadership suc-cess story of all: the program clearly promotes change on all fronts, and it hits hardest where it counts the most.

Implications and Concluding Thoughts

Many organizations look on leadership as a valuable enhancement of their ongoing activities, and they devote considerable budgets to training. Rarely do they take the opportunity to observe the impacts of those expenditures long-term, or to establish a rigorous model for assessing the real, on-the-ground results that arise from the training investment. In the U.S. Geological Survey, we have had the unique opportunity to evaluate an innovative program for an extended period, and to measure the critical facets of learning and diffusion. While we are not yet at a point where anyone can claim success or a clearly changed culture, we do have solid data to support the original vision of this program. After six years of course offerings for a highly selective pool of employees, more than 300 graduates have been pro-duced. In an agency of 10,000 people, that is an insignificant dent. But a few of those graduates have become LI instructors, and they have invigorated another 500 participants in those workshops. And far more important than any of their personal improvements are the clear effects they have transferred to the USGS employees around them: the colleagues in their own offices and the broader realm of employ-ees having no connection to the program at all. As the Leadership Program steering team looks for more opportunities to enhance the experiences of its participants and to increase the confidence of that crowd in making a difference, it will leverage a cascading effect on the broader population. It takes patience and courage to administer a pro-gram with those kinds of far-reaching impacts in mind, but truly, is that not what leadership is all about?

References

Kaplan, Abram W. "From Passive to Active about Solar Electricity: Innovation Decision Process and Photovoltaic Interest Generation." *Technovation* 19:8 (Aug. 1999): 467–81.

Kaplan, Abram W., and Shannon M. Kishel. "Adaptive Farming Decisions: Lessons from the Amish." Presented at the "Role of Culture in the Agriculture of the Twenty-First Century" Conference, San Antonio, Texas, 2000.

Rogers, Everett M. *Diffusion of Innovations*. 5th ed. New York: The Free Press, 2003.

Chapter 17

Evaluating a Leadership Development Program

Caterpillar won the overall Corporate University Best In Class (CUBIC) award in 2004. In addition, it received the CUBIC awards for Evaluation Technique and the CUX Xchange Best Measurement. This case study describes the program that was one of the reasons for the awards. It evaluated this program at levels 1 (Reaction), 3 (Behavior), and 4 (Results). It will be of interest to the readers for both the subject content and the forms and procedures that can be adapted to organizations of all sizes and types.

Caterpillar, Inc.

Caterpillar University
Merrill C. Anderson, Ph.D. CEO, MetrixGlobal, LLC
Chris Arvin, Dean, Leadership Development
Peoria, Illinois

Introduction

The announcement of Caterpillar's business growth goals thrust its leaders into a world of paradoxes: operate with autonomy to run a business unit but in a way that collaborates with other business unit leaders; be accountable to drive higher business unit profits but in a way that does not suboptimize profits in other business units; maximize the near-term value of current assets but be prepared to make investments that take advantage of global opportunities.

This leadership challenge was not just to develop more leaders, it was to develop *different* leaders: leaders who epitomize collaboration, business acumen, and a global mind-set. Meeting this challenge to develop a new kind of leader also required new ways of *thinking* about leadership development.

Caterpillar has a rich history of growing its own leaders. In the 1970s and 1980s the annual management course at the Starved Rock State Park in Illinois exposed leaders to the latest thinking about leading people and organizations. This course evolved into the Caterpillar Advanced Management Program that prepared leaders to effectively expand Caterpillar's business base. With the establishment of Caterpillar University and the College of Leadership in 2001, Caterpillar had an exciting new capability to develop leaders. Building a unified approach to leadership development across Caterpillar became the focus.

The Leadership Development Pilot

This new leadership initiative, launched in 2002, represented a bold departure for Caterpillar with the intention of creating a new kind of leadership. The initiative featured multisource feedback, a two-day workshop and a follow-up session to further drive application and business impact. Participants in this initiative received multisource feedback that was structured around the new leadership framework. They reflected upon this feedback to chart their own unique course of development. The workshops deepened their understanding about how they needed to change and how to make this change happen.

The centerpiece of the Leadership Development initiative was a two-day experiential workshop for department heads and their intact leadership teams. These workshops featured feedback on individual and organization climate surveys to develop self-awareness, and action planning to apply key insights to improve performance. Each participant completed an action plan. Over the course of three months the participant (and others) took actions to remedy this issue and document their actions in the form of a case study.

A second, one-day session was then conducted with the leader and his or her intact team three months after their initial two-day workshop. The intention of this session was to reinforce and accelerate how participants applied what they learned to their work environment. Case studies were reviewed, obstacles were identified, potential solutions were brainstormed, and successes were highlighted. Participants also explored the potential impact of their case studies on the performance of people and the organization.

The Caterpillar CEO and his senior leaders decided to first conduct a pilot of this new approach to leadership development. Evaluating the results of this pilot was critical to learning how best to deploy leadership development throughout Caterpillar.

Evaluation Approach

The evaluation plan consisted of three elements that were organized according to the four Kirkpatrick (1998) levels (Table 17.1):

Table 17.1. The Evaluation Plan for the Leadership Development Pilot

Level	Activity	Description
1	Leadership Development Feedback (Exhibit 17.1)	The evaluation was conducted at the conclusion of the two-day workshop and addressed the quality of facilitation, workshop content, relevance of the workshop and additional items.
3	Quick Wins Score Sheet (Exhibit 17.2)	The evaluation was conducted about two months after the workshop had been completed and just prior to participation in a one-day follow-up session. This evaluation addressed how well leaders applied what they learned in the workshop, their assessment of improved effectiveness, and areas of business impact.
3, 4	Value Narratives	This evaluation was conducted about four months after the one-day follow-up session and probed specific examples of application and business impact. Business impact was captured in terms of monetary as well as intangible benefits.

Level 1.   Reaction data were gathered via a questionnaire completed by each pilot participant at the conclusion of the workshop (Exhibit 17.1). Areas addressed included the quality of facilitation, workshop content, relevance of the workshop, and additional items.

Level 2.   Learning data was not formally collected as part of the evaluation plan. Given the senior levels of the leaders in the organization, it was felt that a learning comprehension test would not be appropriate. Learning data were collected as part of the value narratives, in addition to application examples and business impact as part of the storytelling process.

Level 3.   Change in behavior data were collected via the Quick Wins Score Sheet about two months after the completion of the workshop and about one week prior to participation in a one-day follow-up meeting (Exhibit 17.2). The score sheet began by asking for an example of how the participants applied what they learned in the workshop. Then, based on this example, participants offered their assessment of improved effectiveness on their performance, the performance of their teams and the performance of the organization. If respondents indicated that performance had improved as a result of their participation in the LD initiative, then they checked off one or more of the particular areas of the business they thought were impacted. Examples of these areas included productivity, employee engagement, product quality, and other areas.

Level 4. Business results data were collected about four months after the one-day follow-up session. Specific examples of behavior change and business results were probed in one-on-one interviews according to an innovative values narrative process. A value narrative is defined as the written representation of events and people producing value in an organization. It is, in essence, a short story. There are three main elements to these stories:

1. The first element is to capture background information about the leaders and the particular situation that they faced.
2. The second element describes what leaders did as a result of their participation in the Leadership Development Initiative. Actions must be specific enough to support further probing into business impact.
3. The third element probes the impact that the leaders' actions

Exhibit 17.1. Leadership Development Workshop: Feedback

Instructions: We appreciate your participation in the pilot workshop. Please complete this questionnaire so that we may learn from you about how to improve the content and delivery of the Leadership Development Workshop. Space is provided to give feedback on each facilitator. Thank you!

Please select a response category for each item that best reflects your views:

  1 **Strongly Disagree**

  2 **Disagree**

  3 **Somewhat Disagree**

  4 **Somewhat Agree**

  5 **Agree**

  6 **Strongly Agree**

Items	1	2	3	4	5	6
Facilitator Name:						
1. The facilitator was prepared and organized for the workshop.						
2. The facilitator was responsive to participants' needs and questions.						
3. The facilitator kept all participants actively engaged.						
Facilitator Name:						
1. The facilitator was prepared and organized for the workshop.						
2. The facilitator was responsive to participants' needs and questions.						
3. The facilitator kept all participants actively engaged.						
Workshop Content						
4. The objectives for the workshop were clearly explained.						

(continued)

Exhibit 17.1. Leadership Development Workshop: Feedback (*continued*)

5. The workshop content/materials were sufficient to achieve the workshop objectives.						
6. The length of the workshop was appropriate for the workshop objectives.						
Relevance of the Workshop						
7. This workshop was relevant to my work.						
8. I have gained new skills and knowledge that will improve my effectiveness.						
9. I will apply what I have learned to my job.						
Additional Items						
10. I would recommend this workshop to my colleagues and co-workers.						
11. What was the most valuable piece of new learning you received in this program?						
12. How could this workshop be improved?						

have had on the business. Results were captured in terms of monetary as well as intangible benefits.

Results of the Evaluations

Level 1: Reaction of Leaders to the Workshop

Overall, the leaders rated the workshop highly, averaging 87 percent favorable (defined as either a 6 or a 5 favorable response on the six-point scale.) Lowest rated was the workshop content (79 percent aver-

Exhibit 17.2. Quick Wins Score Sheet

Name: _____

Please respond to the following questions in preparation for the one-day Leadership Development follow-up session. In addition to helping you prepare for this session, your responses will help us to better understand how you have applied what you have learned. This information will help us to learn from the pilot experience and ultimately improve the full deployment of the Leadership Development initiative.

1. What are you doing differently as a result of what you have learned from Leadership Development?

   _____

   _____

   _____

   _____

   _____

   _____

2. Have these actions improved:

   a. Your effectiveness as a leader?   Yes_____ No_____ Not Sure_____

   b. Your team's effectiveness?   Yes_____ No_____ Not Sure_____

   c. Your organization's performance?   Yes_____ No_____ Not Sure_____

3. If you feel that your actions have improved effectiveness, please indicate in what areas:

   i. Productivity   _____

   ii. Employee engagement   _____

   iii. Quality of work   _____

   iv. Decision making   _____

   v. Clarity about priorities   _____

   vi. Communications   _____

   vii. Collaboration   _____

   viii. Time to complete projects   _____

   ix. Other: _____   _____

4. What other benefits have you, your team and/or the organization realized so far from Leadership Development?

   _____

   _____

Exhibit 17.2. Quick Wins Score Sheet (*continued*)

_____

_____

_____

_____

Thank you!

age for the three items), in particular, leaders felt that the workshop objectives could have been better explained (73 percent favorable). Workshop relevance was rated high (93 percent) and almost all leaders (96 percent) would recommend the workshop to colleagues. The level 1 data suggested several enhancements to the workshop. These enhancements were made and reaction scores soared to over 95 percent favorable in all three areas.

Level 3: Change in Behavior

Leadership participants from two Leadership Development pilots indicated that they were able to readily apply what they learned from the leadership sessions to create meaningful impact on the organization. Heightened employee engagement and increased clarity of leadership team members on strategic priorities topped the list of eight impact areas. All but two leaders cited examples of how they were able to apply what they learned from LD to their workplace. These actions were credited with improving their effectiveness as leaders by 81 percent of the respondents, improving team effectiveness by 56 percent, and improving organization performance by 44 percent of the respondents.

Respondents identified specific ways in which their LD experiences increased effectiveness. Figure 17.1 presents the percent of respondents who identified one or more of eight effectiveness categories. Topping the list of eight was engagement with 81 percent. One team leader reported taking actions to improve organization climate and provide employees with greater recognition for their efforts. Greater engagement seemed to be extended to leadership teams as well. Respondents reported encouraging more open dialogue in leadership team meetings, allowing more input by team members, and providing greater latitude for the teams to be engaged in problem solving.

Three additional impact areas were selected by over 50 percent of

Figure 17.1. The Percent of Leadership Development Participants Whose Actions Impacted the Eight Business-Impact Categories

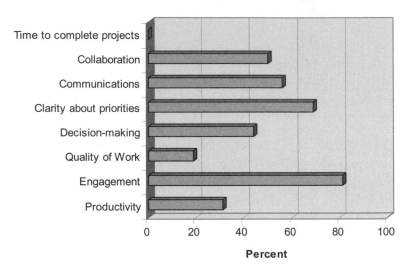

the respondents: clarity about priorities, communications, and collaboration. Written comments by the participants indicated that leaders had increased alignment of their leadership teams to strategy and business direction. Some leadership teams were reorganized to accomplish this alignment. Improved communication effectiveness also facilitated strategic alignment. Better delegation, improved listening, and increasing the quality of leadership team meetings were cited as examples of improved communication. Many respondents indicated that they were spending less time in meetings and yet getting more accomplished. Coaching skills had improved. Leaders reported that they were not necessarily acting in a more collaborative way. Rather, they were using collaboration more effectively and perhaps even more sparingly. For example, one respondent wrote that there was in his leadership team less collaboration on areas requiring his direct decision.

Other intangible benefits were cited by the respondents. These included having one common language to talk about leadership and a shared understanding of the required competencies, having their leadership group being seen by stakeholders as more cohesive and more capable of leading the growth strategy, team members gaining a better understanding of each other, and an increased energy and focus on developing leaders.

Level 4: Business Results

Given the very senior levels of the participants and the need for high-quality data, it was decided to conduct value narratives with a 25 percent sample of leaders from the two pilot groups. Four leaders who participated in one of two pilots were interviewed to further explore how they applied what they learned to impact their respective businesses. These interviews were written up as brief narratives or stories. Intangible benefits and, when appropriate, monetary benefits were documented as part of the narrative-building process. Monetary benefits were expressed in dollars or hours and directly attributed to actions taken as a result of participation in the leadership development initiative. Of course, there were many other potential influencing factors on producing these benefits, so when monetary benefits were identified, the leaders were also asked two additional questions (Anderson 2003; Phillips 1997). The first question required leaders to attribute a percentage of the monetary benefit directly to their LD experience. The leaders were then asked to express as a percentage their confidence in this attribution. The monetary benefit was discounted by these two factors (attribution and confidence). This resulted in monetary benefits that were qualified and conservative in nature.

Two value narratives are excerpted and offered as examples of how these data were collected (see Exhibits 17.3 and 17.4). The leaders identified many important intangible benefits that were produced by their actions. These included:

1. Improved strategic focus in decision making, enabling leaders to focus on the most strategically critical decisions, and not just those decisions that were the most urgent and not necessarily the most strategic.
2. Improved performance management of subordinate leaders, as clearer expectations for performance were set and more effective leadership styles were adopted.
3. Increased accountability for results, as leaders became more involved in setting performance targets and their personal roles in achieving these targets were given greater visibility.
4. Increased insights into personal development needs, as leaders better grasped how their actions impacted the climate of

Exhibit 17.3. Value Narrative No. 1

Background

Diane's (a fictitious name) predecessor ran the marketing group with a strong team concept that emphasized consultation and involvement in all aspects of decision making. The group's high employee engagement scores were in large part attributed to the highly consultative team environment created by the group's leaders. Diane continued this style when she took over the group about a year ago, although it was at times frustrating. She felt that her group could be more responsive to changes in the external environment. Her participation in the LD initiative helped her explore the downside of this highly consultative style. Diane's key learning was that consultation, while important, needed to be better focused on only those decisions that required a broader base of information, and not just reflexively applied to all decisions.

Change in Behavior

Encouraged by her LD experience, Diane implemented better screening of issues that required decisions. Specific accountabilities for making the decisions were clarified. Ground rules for bringing certain kinds of decisions to the attention of decision-making bodies were specified. Decision-making bodies such as Diane's leadership team gained added focus as their time was better spent on more strategic issues. Leaders were consulted when their specific expertise and knowledge were required. Decisions that Diane needed to make that did not require other leaders' input did not go through the gauntlet of consensus building. Meetings and the topics covered were streamlined. The team concept continued to flourish and engagement levels remained high.

Business Results

Diane estimated that at least a 10 percent to 15 percent improvement in team productivity was realized for herself and her team of ten direct reports. She attributed 100 percent of this productivity gain to LD and was 70 percent confident in this estimate.
The monetary benefits of the productivity gain were:

11 people × $85 hour × 40 hours per week = $37,400 total per team per week

$37,400 × 10% productivity gain = $3,740 productivity gain per week

$3,740 × 48 weeks = $179,520 of annualized benefit

$179,520 × 100% (attribution) × 70% (confidence) = $125,664

A total monetary benefit of $125,664 was gained from LD through increased productivity.

Intangible benefits included:

- Improved strategic focus in decision making
- Improved and more efficient communications
- Clearer expectations
- Better risk management
- Increased insights into personal development needs
- Stronger teams
- Facilitated culture change

Exhibit 17.4. Value Narrative No. 2

Background

The timing of Frank's (a fictitious name) leadership development experience was excellent, given that Frank's team had gone through a process of great change. Frank recently replaced someone who was in the role for twenty years. While the group was considered to be successful, it had, in the last few years, become rather set in its ways. The employee opinion survey results were trending down for the group, and the group did not seem strongly connected with the broader business enterprise.

Frank assumed his new role and immediately led a change in the group's approach to working with business partners. Frank's approach was to roll up his sleeves and manage every aspect of the group's business. His strong orientation to detail enabled him to set the pace in working with his people so that they understood what Frank expected from them. Frank's hands-on management style was successful. During this transition phase, the group went from being perceived to be on the fringe of the core business to becoming a more vibrant and central partner to the other business units. Frank's business grew as dealers were reengaged and stronger partnerships with dealers were forged.

Frank's style of personally setting the pace was effective during the transition phase. However, with the transition completed, a different approach to leadership was required. While relationships with other business units and the dealers were improved, Frank's own team was becoming dispirited. They often felt that they needed to wait for Frank in order to make the right decision. Teamwork was low and employee engagement was trending downward.

Change in Behavior

Frank participated in the LD initiative and learned that his strong pacesetting style was no longer the appropriate style for his group. In lieu of any overarching strategy, people did not feel empowered to make decisions. His weekly staff meetings, which had become quite lengthy, were nothing more than data dumps so that Frank could make the appropriate decisions. Encouraged by LD, Frank decided to take a more strategic approach. He stopped his weekly staff meetings and instead facilitated monthly off-sites. The purpose of these off-sites was to delve more deeply into strategic issues. Frank began engaging his people in creating the group's strategy so that they could make decisions independently and still know that these decisions were in line with the strategy. Decision making improved. Employee engagement jumped to 72 percent from 37 percent, and Frank attributed a significant chunk of this increase to his leadership development experience. The team went from running hard to running smart.

Business Results

According to Frank, these actions freed up at least two to three hours of Frank's time per week. He attributed 50 percent of this gain to LD and was 90 percent confident in this estimate. Monetary benefits were determined as follows:

2 hours per week $\times$ 48 weeks $\times$ \$85 per hour = \$8,160 in annualized benefits

\$8,160 $\times$ 50% (attribution) $\times$ 90% (confidence) = \$3,672 in qualified benefits

(continued)

Exhibit 17.4. Value Narrative No. 2 (*continued*)

Intangible benefits included:

- Improved decision making
- Higher employee engagement
- Increased teamwork and enthusiasm
- Increased empowerment
- Increased strategic focus
- Improved communications

the organization and the performance of their teams and managers.

5. Higher employee engagement, as the organizational climate improved and people were able to make a stronger link from their behavior to achieving the organizational goals. People felt more empowered to act without necessarily having to go through a series of approval steps. Teamwork improved and communications became more effective and focused.

In addition to these benefits, a total of $141,576 in qualified, annualized, monetary benefits were identified by a 25 percent sample of the leaders included in the value narrative process. These benefits compare favorably with the out-of-pocket cost of $134,000 for conducting the sessions with both of the pilot teams. It is fair to say, based on the sample data collected, that the two Leadership Development pilots more than paid for themselves while delivering substantial, strategic, and sustainable value.

Conclusion

The value narratives completed the successful story of the Leadership Development pilot at Caterpillar. The story began with the leaders' initial workshop experience being rated very favorably. The story continued with the Quick Wins Score Sheet, which documented significant examples of application to the work environment. The value narratives enabled leaders to tell their stories in a way that really resonated with others. While monetary benefits were only one element of these stories, the monetary benefits that accrued from the leadership development initiative more than paid for the investment in the initiative.

References

Anderson, Merrill C. *Bottom-Line Organization Development*. Boston: Butterworth-Heinemann, 2003.

Kirkpatrick, Donald L. *Evaluating Training Programs: The Four Levels*. 2nd ed. San Francisco: Berrett-Koehler, 1998.

Phillips, Jack J. *Handbook of Training Evaluation and Measurement Methods*. 3rd ed. Houston: Gulf Publishing, 1997.

Chapter 18

Evaluating Desktop
Application Courses

This case study from Australia concentrates on the evaluation of desktop application courses, including Word, Excel, and Power Point. The training company also teaches and evaluates soft skill courses. It evaluated at all four Kirkpatrick levels. Particular emphasis is placed on communicating with the participants before, during, and after the courses. Of special interest will be the many contacts between the trainers and the learners and their bosses.

Pollak Learning Alliance

Heather Bolster, General Manager, Professional Services
Antoinette Chan, General Manager, Marketing
Sydney, Australia

Description of Our Organization

Pollak Learning Alliance is a large and long-standing Australian training company that has been providing learning solutions to both corporate and government for over twenty years. We train in excess of 35,000 participants a year in learning centers located throughout the country, with a head office in Sydney. We have a staff of around sixty.

We provide learning solutions in both desktop and soft skills, supplemented with e-learning tools. Our focus is on learning transfer to improve performance in the workplace. We support the training with a range of consulting services, including training-needs analysis, applications development, and tailored training.

Description of the Evaluation Program

Evaluating the effectiveness of training has long been a key focus for us, and we have many stories to tell in the measurement area. But for the purpose of this exercise we would like to describe the evaluation program we have put in place across the board for our desktop application courses—Word, Excel, PowerPoint, and so on, which are mostly one- or two-day courses. (We train soft skills as well but have a different methodology for evaluating in that domain.) We feel we have broken some ground here and are pleased to take this opportunity to describe it.

Background

It began with a marketing event we hosted for key clients at the Sydney Opera House. We decided to have an open discussion with them about return on investment—to hear from our clients what they had done, their case studies, war stories, key challenges, things still unresolved. We wanted a chance to hear them, really, and to let them hear each other about this alone-in-the-wilderness topic.

If you are reading this book, you are someone who can imagine the themes that emerged—primarily of course the extreme difficulty of providing evidence that the training they do actually produces results for the business. Their budgets, they said, go elsewhere, where evidence *can* be provided. And they have no real way of measuring the effectiveness of their training providers. We found that although these were large corporations and government agencies, there actually were very few ROI case studies, and not even a lot of war stories. It's just too hard.

So we decided to take it on. Our Managing Director, Steve Lemlin, had been at the seminar and was piqued by the topic. As an ex-accountant, he had been involved always in eliciting proof of return on investment. And he knew there had to be a way to measure return on training investment.

Thus began our journey.

Our Objectives

We based our thinking from the beginning around Kirkpatrick's four levels of assessment. And we decided (controversially?) that when it comes right down to it what any business is interested in is not fundamentally the first three levels; it's great if people have enjoyed the training, it's great if they learn and if they change behaviors, given spending all that time on the course, but it's not central to the objectives of the business. What is important to the CEO is whether the training has actually impacted the business objectives and driven the organization closer in some way to reaching its desired outcomes.

So we decided to focus on level 4: has the training impacted the business objectives and how can that be measured? And equally important, if we're going to do all this measuring and evaluation, how can we make it actually add to the process, increasing the effectiveness of the training rather than just driving everyone mad?

When we looked at the financial drivers of a business (simply put, to earn more or spend less), we saw that what we could actually measure is time saved. This would be our primary ROI measure, and we would enrich it with a variety of other "softer" measures also known by a business to be important.

Specifics of the Evaluation

The process we have developed is called Prepare—Learn—Apply—Measure (known affectionately as PLAM internally.) It works like this:

Before the Course

1. When participants register for any of our courses (e.g., Word, Excel, Access, at intro, intermediate, or advanced levels), they are asked to appoint a "sponsor." This is a *learning* sponsor, someone who will support their learning back in the workplace. Often it is their manager.
2. They are also e-mailed a link to a Web site. They go online to an attractive screen that asks them to specify their learning outcomes for the course. They are also asked whether their

outcomes have been discussed with their sponsor, and if the outcomes are aligned to their job role.

3. Our trainers review these outcomes in advance of the course.

During the Course

1. Participants go online after each and every module of the course and are asked to speculate briefly about how they will use the software's feature after the program, and how much time they may save by using the feature after the course.
2. They are also asked at the end of the day to rate any changes in their confidence, the potential quality of their work, their ability to problem-solve, and their attitude to their job.
3. They go online and create an action plan.
4. They complete a traditional evaluation of the program (level 1).

After the Course

1. They are reminded to work with their sponsor toward accomplishing their action plan.
2. Four weeks after, they are asked to go online again and complete a survey about time saved and changes in the way they are approaching their work.

Summary of the Levels Being Evaluated

Level 1.   The process evaluates level 1 in the usual way, with a comprehensive questioning about their reaction to the trainer, the course, the service, and the like.

Level 2.   Level 2 evaluation is done during the training itself, indirectly, with exercises built in to the program. We also have online testing software and occasionally clients will take advantage of the offer to test participants before and/or after their training.

Level 3.   Participants define outcomes before the course and create an action plan during the course. Afterward, we find out if they have achieved their outcomes and accomplished their action plan.

Level 4.   Level 4 is at the heart of what we're up to with this program. The data we collect is about time saved, and how that translates into dollars, as well as about what participants and their sponsors see in regard to how the training has impacted their roles and results and the business overall.

Results of the Evaluation

Because this is a new process for us, results are only beginning to flow in. Some of our observations at this stage:

- *Reporting:* We can of course turn this data into a wide spectrum of reports for our clients. The most popular reports are:
  1. Participation Reports (e.g., who has done what stages of the process, who the popular sponsors are)
  2. Perceived Value Reports (summarizing the "soft data" from the process—increase in confidence, increase in quality of work, and so on)
  3. Dollars Saved Reports (summarizing clients' speculation about how much time they will save and actually have saved in using the features, and translating that into dollars)
- *Client reaction:* Our client contacts at senior levels in the organization love it. Response to the reports, in particular the Dollars Saved Reports, has been very positive, with strong feedback by both HR managers and CEOs.
- *Participant reaction:* Both trainers and participants report favorably about the process. The extra discipline of thinking through how the software is going to be used back at work, and how their jobs will be impacted by it, is generally seen as a valuable investment. As one of our trainers put it, the biggest impact is probably people's buying into the fact that they've actually got an impact on the business.
- *Participation:* Currently about half the participants are engaging in the precourse stage (remembering that ours is a large, across-the-board client base, this is not too bad a result— which we're working to improve). Virtually all participants do the on-the-day stage. And, finally, it's too early to have good statistics on the postcourse stage. This will be the tough one and will demand our attention in making it happen.

Our Communication

During the pilot process, several client focus groups were formed to gather feedback. This group consisted of senior HR professionals from some of our top corporate clients, who were very keen to participate.

Upon completion of the pilot, e-mail marketing was executed to our top-tier corporate clients, advising them of the initiative. Information has also been posted on our Web site and collateral (brochures) to incorporate the new training methodologies. We also communicated the new tools and measures internally, reinforcing our objective of strengthening long-term relationships with our clients by undertaking this initiative.

The results have been very positive, with clients responding favorably. We will be convening another focus group sometime in the next two months to review the reports and the response to the program generally.

We are enormously excited by the possibilities opening up for us and for our clients from this initiative.

Chapter 19

Evaluating an Orientation Program for New Managers

This program, referred to as "jump start," was evaluated at all four Kirkpatrick levels. The content of the program will be of interest to all readers who are eager to get their new managers off to a good start. Also, the evaluation approaches and forms will be of special interest and adaptable to organizations of all sizes and types.

Canada Revenue Agency, Pacific Region

David Barron, Regional Learning and Development Advisor
Vancouver, British Columbia

Introduction

Canada Revenue Agency (CRA) forms part of the Federal Public Service of Canada. Nationwide the agency has approximately 40,000 employees. The agency's Pacific Region, covering the province of British Columbia and the Yukon Territory, has roughly 4,600 employees.

CRA Pacific Region's Jump Start to Management Program was developed to provide new managers throughout Pacific Region with the opportunity to learn what they need to perform effectively in their new roles. The design and development of the program was undertaken in collaboration with all prospective stakeholders in response to clearly defined urgent regional needs.

In order to most effectively meet the learning needs of new managers a four-phase model was developed:

Phase I: A Local Orientation Checklist was developed
Phase II: A three-day Regional Orientation Session was designed and delivered
Phase III: A Compendium of Core Learning Events was developed
Phase IV: An inventory of Advanced Learning Events was projected and initial development work was undertaken.

This case study focuses on the evaluation process used to assess the effectiveness of Phase II: the Regional Orientation Session. The theme of the Regional Orientation Session was "Balancing management with leadership," and great stress was laid on effective people management as the key to effective program management. The session contained modules on values and ethics, inspirational leadership, self-assessment, achieving corporate goals, coaching as a management practice, priority management and meeting management, as well as a full-day hands-on exercise on managing performance and the opportunity to learn from a senior manager in an informal armchair session. An overview of a typical Regional Orientation Session can be found in Appendix 19.1.

Four three-day sessions were held between September 2003 and February 2004.

Evaluation Approach

An in-depth formal evaluation strategy was developed for the Regional Orientation Session to assess its effectiveness at all of Kirkpatrick's four levels: reaction, learning, behavior, and results. Instruments used included Learner Reaction Questionnaires, Content Analysis Questionnaires, random follow-up contacts, and postsession focus groups.

Level 1 Reaction: Relevance and Satisfaction

Participants were asked to evaluate how relevant they found the content of the Regional Orientation Session to their jobs and to rate

Appendix 19.1. Overview of Jump Start Regional Orientation Session

DAY 1		DAY 2		DAY 3	
8:30–9:00	Introductions Facilitated by Learning and Development Team	8:30–9:00	Networking and recap of and links to day 1 Facilitated by Learning and Development Team.	8:30–9:00	Networking and recap of and links to days 1 and 2 Facilitated by Learning and Development Team
9:00–10:30	Opening Remarks Frankly Speaking: Exploring the Leadership Mindset Guest: Senior Manager	9:00–12:00	Performance Management Presented by Learning and Development Team supported by various HR Subject Matter Experts Performance Management . . . continued Participants examine the leader/manager's role in the Performance Management process through work-related scenarios.	9:00–11:15	Coaching Practices for Managers Workshop Presented by National Manager's Community representatives or . alternate manager Coaching continued
10:30–10:45	Health Break	10:30–10:45	Health Break	10:30–10:45	Health Break (Included in Coaching Session)

Appendix 19.1. Overview of Jump Start Regional Orientation Session (*continued*)

Time	Track 1	Time	Track 2	Time	Track 3
10:45–12:00	The Corporate World of the CCRA: An overview		Performance Management . . . continued	11:15–12:00	Meetings Bloody Meetings: Meeting Management and the use of Bob Chartier's Tools for getting the most out of meetings
	Facilitated by Intergovernmental and Corporate Affairs				Presented by Learning and Development Team
12:00–1:00	Lunch: a networking opportunity	12:00–1:00	Lunch: a networking opportunity	12:00–1:00	Lunch: a networking opportunity
1:00–2:00	Inspirational Leadership Facilitated by George Matthews	1:00–2:45	Performance Management . . . continued	1:00–2:15	Managing Priorities: the Key to Time Management
2:00–2:45	Balancing the Role of Leader and Manager				Presented by Learning and Development Team
	Facilitated by Learning and Development Team				
2:45–3:00	Health Break	2:45–3:00	Health Break	2:15–2:30	Health Break
3:00–4:30	Self-Assessment: A Time to Reflect	3:00–4:30	Performance Management . . . continued	2:30–3:50	Ethics and Values
	Facilitated by Learning and Development Team				Facilitated by a Senior Manager
				3:50–4:30	Concluding Remarks: Summary and Transfer of Learning Plan
					By Learning and Development Team

their overall satisfaction with the session in terms of a five-point scale where 5 is the highest and 1 is the lowest. A copy of the form used to evaluate level 1 can be found in Appendix 19.2.

Level 2 Learning

For the content sessions on Day 1 and Day 3 participants were asked to complete content evaluation questionnaires designed to capture what they thought they had learned. The hands-on performance management simulation on Day 2 was evaluated separately by narrative report. Copies of the forms used to evaluate level 2 can be found in Appendix 19.3a and Appendix 19.3b.

Level 3 Behavior

In order to assess transfer of learning, two focus groups were held with participants in April/May 2004—that is, some considerable time after they had attended Jump Start Phase II. At these focus group events participants were asked what they had been able to apply on the job from that which they had learned in Jump Start. A question schedule for these focus groups can be found in Appendix 19.4.

Level 4 Results

In an attempt to gain insight into how participation in Jump Start Phase II could positively impact business results, focus group participants were asked to gauge the effect of implementing what they had learned from Jump Start Phase II in terms of:

- Morale
- Teamwork
- Turnover
- Production

Results

Level 1

Over 80 percent of the participants found the topics covered in the session either relevant or very relevant to their jobs and were satisfied

Appendix 19.2. Example of Learner Reaction Questionnaire (Level 1 Evaluation)

Jump Start to Management Regional Orientation Session
February 10–12, 2004
Learner Reaction Questionnaire

Your feedback will be used to help us continually improve our products and services.

1. Position Title: Level: Work Location:

2. How much total experience have
   you had in a management role
   (including acting)?   _____years _____months

3. Did you complete Jump Start
   Phase I (Local orientation)
   before attending this session?   YES   NO

4. Why did you attend this session?

5. How would you rate the importance
   level of the topics covered in this
   session to your job?   Low _____High

                                                1   2   3   4   5

6. To what extent was your learning
   enhanced by the opportunities to engage
   in activities with senior managers
   and HR representatives?   Low _____High

                                                1   2   3   4   5

7. Overall, what was your level of
   satisfaction with this session?   Low _____High

                                                1   2   3   4   5

8. What is your confidence level in applying
   to your job what you learned through
   your participation in this learning event? Low _____High

                                                1   2   3   4   5

(continued)

Appendix 19.2. Example of Learner Reaction Questionnaire
(Level 1 Evaluation) (*continued*)

9. Please describe aspects of this learning
   event you found particularly meaningful.

10. What specific elements of the three-day
    session had the most positive impact
    on you and why?

11. Is there anything else that would have
    facilitated your learning? If so, please
    describe.

12. Are there any changes you feel we
    need to make to this workshop? If so, please describe.

Name: (optional) _____

Thank You!

Appendix 19.3a. Example of Content Evaluation Form Day 1
(Level 2 Evaluation)

November 18, 2003   Name:_____

Session: The Corporate World of the CCRA

Objective

• To give new managers an understanding of how and what they contribute to
  the organization as a whole

After participating in this session do you feel you now have a better understanding of
how your work as a manager contributes to the achievement of corporate goals?
Please explain.

Session: Balancing Management and Leadership

Objectives

• To examine the leadership expectations of a CCRA manager
• To illustrate why a CCRA manager must balance management and leadership
  roles in order to be successful.

After participating in this session do you now better understand why you need to balance management and leadership? Please explain.

November 18, 2003   Name:_____

Session: Understanding the Possibilities for Leadership

Objectives

• To energize
• To inspire
• To motivate
• To reflect

(continued)

Appendix 19.3a. Example of Content Evaluation Form Day 1
(Level 2 Evaluation) (*continued*)

After participating in this session, how energized, inspired, and/or motivated do you feel about your new role? Please explain.

Did you have an opportunity to reflect on your new role? What was the outcome of your reflection?

Session: Ethics and Values

Objectives

- To raise awareness of the roles values and ethics play in effective leadership
- To raise awareness of the Public Service Values
- To profit from the experience of senior managers

After participating in this session, do you now better understand the role that ethics and values play in effective leadership? Please explain.

How useful did you find the case studies?

Appendix 19.3a. Example of Content Evaluation Form Day 1
(Level 2 Evaluation) (*continued*)

November 18, 2003   Name:_____

Session: Self-Assessment and Reflection

Objectives

- To introduce participants to the Managing for Success instrument
- To develop self-awareness and self-understanding prerequisites to effective management
- To introduce the concept of reflective practice

After participating in this session, what have you learned about yourself as a manager?

How useful did you find the Managing for Success instrument?

---

or very satisfied with the workshop. On their own, these are very high average figures. They might well have been even higher had not a number of more experienced managers been sent to a workshop designed for new managers.

Level 2

The results received from the content evaluation questionnaires illustrate that the overwhelming majority of Jump Start to Management participants reported that due to having taken part in a Phase II session they now felt better equipped to do their jobs. Specifically: 83 percent of participants reported that they now felt they could manage meetings more effectively, 82 percent reported a better understanding

Appendix 19.3b. Example of Content Evaluation Form Day 3
(Level 2 Evaluation)

November 20, 2003   Name:_____

Session: Coaching Practices for Managers

Objectives

- To familiarize participants with Paul Lefebvre/National Managers Network coaching tool kit
- To provide practice on how to use the tool

After participating in this session, do you feel you now have a better understanding of coaching as a management practice? Please explain.

To what extent do you feel that you can apply what you have learned in this session?

Session: Meeting Management

Objective

- To rethink the role and use of meetings so the time is used more effectively

After participating in this session, do you feel you can now manage meetings more effectively? Please explain.

Appendix 19.3b. Example of Content Evaluation Form Day 3
(Level 2 Evaluation) (*continued*)

Session: Priority Management—the Key to Time Management

Objective

- To familiarize participants with the Covey model of priority setting

After participating in this session do you now feel that you are better equipped to manage your time more effectively? Please explain.

Session: Armchair Session (Innovation)

Objective

- To allow participants to profit from the experience of an experienced senior manager (knowledge transfer)

What was the most valuable learning you gained from this session?

---

of ethics and values' role in leadership, 79 percent felt they were now better equipped to manage time, 77 percent found the self-assessment exercise useful, 73 percent found the inspirational leadership session energizing and inspirational, 72 percent felt they better understood how their work linked to the achievement of corporate goals, and 64 percent reported that they now better understood the need to balance management and leadership. In addition, many participants commented on the value of the armchair session, and indeed on the positive effects of senior management's demonstrated support of the program.

The hands-on one-day practical performance management workshop, which formed Day 2 of Phase II, was evaluated by narrative

Appendix 19.4. Focus Group Question Schedule (Levels 3 and 4)

Jump Start to Management Regional Orientation Session Focus group questions

1. What did you learn in Jump Start that you found relevant to your work?
2. From what you learned in Jump Start, what have you been able to apply?
3. What has been the effect of applying what you learned in terms of:
   - morale
   - teamwork
   - turnover
   - production
4. What, if anything, has made it difficult for you to apply what you learned in Jump Start?
5. Since participating in Jump Start, have you identified further learning needs?
6. What help do you need to meet your ongoing learning needs?

---

response. Participants reported learning from the personal experiences of others: they commented on the way that colleagues' issues and suggestions were very useful in putting things into perspective. Participants also reported learning from the various Human Resources subject matter experts from Staff Relations, Alternative Dispute Resolution, Employee Assistance Program and Competencies who were on hand to help them work through the scenarios. Participants found these resource persons very beneficial in discussing issues that had, or could potentially, come up in the workplace, while their presence also reinforced the fact that managers can turn to Human Resource advisers when in need of help. Various tools such as the 5Ps, Appreciative Inquiry, and SMART Goals were found to be very useful and of great potential in the workplace since these tools were important in understanding people's values, interests, and passions. Additionally, the exercise on Vision, Goals, and Objectives was regarded as a potentially powerful way to help differentiate corporate goals from smaller team goals.

Level 3

As can be expected, the answers differed from individual to individual. In general, however, the participants found that Jump Start to Management Phase II helped them realize the importance of taking the time to get to know their employees as individuals. Their work was put into perspective, affecting a decrease in stress level when deciding the urgency of demands from HQ versus those that existed in their work areas. They also reported that attending the session resulted in great improvements in team communication. With the tools that they have learned from Jump Start, they had been able to involve their team members in coming up with different and better solutions to problems that their teams might be facing.

Specifically, as illustration of how they had transferred what they had learned in Phase II into practice, participants made reference to:

Appreciative Inquiry

- Discovering new ways of doing things
- Reflecting more

Managing Priorities

- Learning how to say no
- Beating the terror of e-mails
- Learning to distinguish between urgent and important
- Being better organized
- Being more available for team members

Managing Meetings

- Encouraging participation
- Rotating meeting functions
- Doing joint minutes with a related team
- Being better organized

Performance Management

- Being more effective at career management
- Using 5 Ps as a good tool to create more interesting and effective feedback sessions
- Helping to get buy-in to performance management process

Armchair Session

- Being yourself
- Treating others the way you want to be treated

Coaching

- Investigating the commitment behind the complaint

Level 4

Most comments recorded focused on the increase in team morale through better people management. In one focus group almost everyone reported a noticeable increase in morale, which they attributed to their changed behavior (e.g., modeling values, more "hands-off" management) as a result of having participated in Jump Start. Several participants commented on the close link between an increase in morale and improved teamwork, which itself was reflected in improved production. In one case an example was cited where two closely related teams, divided by a wall, had now learned to work around this wall. Turnover was not found to be an issue.

Communication of Results

A full evaluative report was compiled on the entire Jump Start program. This report was presented to CRA Pacific Region's senior management, distributed among the stakeholders who had collaborated in the design of the program, and submitted to Training and Learning Directorate of Canada Revenue Agency in Ottawa. Jump Start has since been recognized by the National Managers Council of the Public Service of Canada as a best practice.

Chapter 20

Evaluating Training for an Outage Management System

This comprehensive case study describes in detail the strategy, planning, implementation, and evaluation of the training program at levels 1 (Reaction), 2 (Learning) and 3 (Behavior). In addition to using Kirkpatrick's "four levels" as the basis for evaluation, it used the work of three other authors in developing an effective training program.

PacifiCorp

Dan Schuch, Power Learning Training Developer
Portland, Oregon

PacifiCorp is a large, internationally owned utility, based in Portland, Oregon, that generates more than 8,400 megawatts (mw) and delivers power to 1.5 million customers in six western states. The company has 15,000 miles of transmission line, 44,000 miles of overhead distribution line, and 13,000 miles of underground distribution line. PacifiCorp operates as Pacific Power in Oregon, Washington, California, and Wyoming and as Utah Power in Utah and Idaho. There are approximately 6,140 employees within the company whose duties range from those involving the maintenance and operation of electrical power lines to those normally found in a large business.

PacifiCorp is committed to the professional and personal development of its employees and community members. We firmly believe that, in a constantly changing environment, continuous learning and the acquisition of new skills and knowledge are essential for personal development and the overall success of the company. To this aim, PacifiCorp has built an extensive and varied training program, including an extensive distance education program, a number of separate training facilities, computer-based training opportunities, and relationships with universities and colleges located in our service territory. Power-Learning is one of the training branches of PacifiCorp. This past year PowerLearning conducted over 750 courses equating to over 15,000 training days to its employees.

Early in 2004, PowerLearning reexamined its training program with the intent to improve it and to better match training with on-the-job performance. This strategy was in line with the leading work in effective training programs. A comprehensive training and evaluation strategy was developed. It was based on the leading research and best practices in the design and development of effective training and includes Kirkpatrick's work, Shrock and Coscarelli's book on criterion-referenced test development, Dick and Carey's instruction design model, Robinson and Robinson's work in performance, and learning theories from Gagné.

Kirkpatrick's four levels of evaluation for training programs was the standard selected for the evaluation component. Specifically, Kirk-patrick's levels 1 to 3 (Reaction, Learning, and Behavior) were integrated into our training strategy. Business results and return on investment issues were separated from our basic training strategy. In this chapter, a specific training class will be described in detail complete with level 2 and 3 evaluation outcomes highlighted. Discussion will follow how Kirkpatrick's evaluation levels were integrated into our training strategy, outcomes from this training, and benefits received—especially in reference to the integration of level 3 activities early in the training development process.

New Outage Management System Training—Case Study

In March 2004, PowerLearning developed and conducted training on a new system. This event has turned out to be an ideal case study when determining the effects of training on job performance.

Early in 2004, PacifiCorp facilities in California were upgraded to a new outage management system. This new computer software provided an important link between the centralized dispatch centers and the various offices scattered across our service territory. Company offices in the other states had already been using this system for some time. Upgrading the California offices to the new system would enable the entire company to be using the same outage management system.

However, once the new system was implemented the outdated one would be turned off. It was not possible to run the old and the new systems simultaneously. The company's California employees using this new system were required to master the new system before the previous one was permanently shut down. None of the employees had any previous experience with this new system prior to the training. Needless to say, training was critical. Mistakes made using the new system could result in delays in service during outages to the company's California customers or could place our employees working in the field at risk of injury. This training took place from March 8 to March 10. The new system was activated on March 15, 2004.

The training team included the company subject matter expert on the new system, a representative from the central dispatch group, and the trainer. This team was assembled to address any questions or problems pertaining to the new system, interactions between the field and the central dispatch office, or the training itself. These resources were provided so that the right people were available to handle any possible problem or question that might arise with the system or groups affected by the new system. In addition, all supervisors of the employees participating in the training were present during the training and participated as well.

Training consisted of demonstration of the system, discussion of the impacts and risks, followed by the students practicing and demonstrating proficiency of the specific tasks to the instructors. Each participant was provided with documentation on the system as well as a job aid describing the process step by step. This training lasted a day and a half.

It was important to accurately assess the performance of the employees taking this training in order to identify any gaps in competence and close them. All employees participating in this training completed level 1 and level 2 assessments upon completion of the training. The level 2 assessment was developed such that each question simulated actual performance on the system or checked critical verbal information material required to operate the new system. Immediately after the class completed the level 2 assessment, the training team reviewed the questions and answers and used this time as a learning opportunity. Though the performance on the assessment was outstanding, all found this immediate feedback to be invaluable and helpful in clearing up all outstanding issues. Both learners and supervisors strongly felt that the training more than adequately prepared them to use the new system—which was scheduled to be implemented the very next week.

Here's the rest of the story. During the first day that the new system had gone live, a transmission line went down in Crescent City, causing a large power outage in the area that affected numerous customers. As a result of some unforeseen factors, this outage quickly became a complex one. However, as a result of the thorough training, the employees handled the situation smoothly and efficiently. They were confident in their abilities and performed them with the new system flawlessly. In this instance, there was no time gap between the training and the major outage in which the participants had time to practice their new skills. The transfer between training and performance of the job was clearly evident. In this specific instance, the effectiveness of the training and comprehensive assessment strategy without any confounding variables can be clearly demonstrated.

Structured level 3 (Behavior) evaluations were conducted via interviews over the phone with these supervisors of the employees of the California offices who participated in the training. All expressed favorable performance results from their employees. The manager from the office experiencing the large outage stated that their employees were well able to handle the outages with the new system. He was very satisfied with their training and confident that they would be able to use the system. He also mentioned that a couple of his employees had expressed appreciation to him for the training.

Why the Training Was Successful

The success of this training was a result of a number of factors. While it is difficult to identify the specific contribution of any one of these factors, it can be confidently stated that the outcomes from the training were very successful and the attitude about the training from the participants and management was great.

When developing the training, the entire system involving and surrounding the new outage management system was considered. Training included more than just learning the specifics of the new application; it also included content about other computer systems interacting with the new one and interactions with other groups in the organization affected by the new system.

The training involved true simulation training. Each participant worked in a training environment identical to production, with one person per computer. The learners worked through realistic scenarios. The training tasks provided matched the actual ones performed in the field.

The training team received complete management buy-in and involvement. Supervisors participated in all phases of training development, including the development of specific job tasks, identification of performance objectives, approving training materials, signing off on level 2 and 3 assessments, and even participating in the actual training along with their employees.

The right resources were made available for training. Training activities matched actual job performance. The computer training environment mirrored the production environment. Subject matter experts in all areas of the new system were present during the actual training. A comprehensive training development strategy was implemented to develop the training, including a thorough job task analysis, sound behavioral objectives, and well-written assessment items.

Evaluation Strategy as a Component of a Broader Training Strategy

Our training development model was designed using the leading evaluation, instructional design, and performance improvement models. Dick and Carey's instruction design model, *The Systematic Design of Instruction*, provides the overall training development strategy and foundation from which the model was built. Kirkpatrick's book, *Evaluating Training Programs: The Four Levels*, tells us what type of evaluation questions to ask and who should answer them. Shrock and Coscarelli's book, *Criterion-Referenced Test Development*, provides sound advice on the specifics of how to develop the evaluations. Our model also integrated learning theories from Gagné's book, *The Conditions of Learning*, as well as Robinson and Robinson's work on performance, *Performance Consulting: Moving Beyond Training*.

The evaluation strategy used at PacifiCorp is a subset of a broader training strategy. PacifiCorp PowerLearning has developed a Training

Development Model that outlines the training development strategy in a ten-step process, and the evaluation component is an integral part of this model. The steps of the training strategy are provided here as well as details of their evaluation component.

Ten-Step Model of Training Development

1. Identify Business Goals
2. Assess Needs
3. Conduct Instructional Analysis
4. Conduct Learner Analysis
5. Write Performance Objectives
6. Develop Assessment Instruments
7. Develop Instructional Strategy
8. Develop and Select Instructional Materials
9. Implement Instruction
10. Evaluate Program

Step 1: Identify Business Goals. When first meeting with the manager or supervisor, it is important to provide an overview of the training development process. A part of this debriefing will include a description of the evaluation components. Evaluation is important to the manager/supervisor/client because it will tie the training to the performance on the job. In short, the evaluation strategy will determine if the participants were satisfied with the training (level 1), how much they learned in the class (level 2), and how well they are now applying this new knowledge to their job performance (level 3). PowerLearning's level 1 evaluation is provided in Exhibit 20.1.

In the specific case study presented earlier, once the decision was made to implement the new outage management system, the author communicated with the supervisors to discuss the project and the training requirements. Attention was given to the outcomes of the training and the supervisors' responsibilities before, during, and after the training took place.

Step 4: Conduct Learner Analysis. A learner analysis is conducted to identify the characteristics of those who will be trained. The client/manager/supervisor will work with training personnel to identify the target audience for a training course or program. Together they will also identify existing learner skills, behaviors, and general ability level of any participant. This information will help define the

Exhibit 20.1. Training Strategy

In our model, the manager/client (business owners of the training) is actively involved in all aspects of the training. Note that sign-off occurs at steps 1, 2, 4, 7, 8, and 10.

PacifiCorp "Power Skills" Training Strategy

Identify Business Goals	Assess Needs	Conduct Instructional Analysis	Analyze Learners and Context	Write Performance Objectives	Develop Assessment Instrument	Develop Instruc-tional Strategy	Develop and Select Instructional Materials	Implement Instruction	Evaluate
1	2	3	4	5	6	7	8	9	10

Step 1: Identify Business Goals
    Meet with Business Owners
    Get sign-off

Step 2: Assess Needs
    Meet with Business Owners
    Get sign-off

Step 3: Conduct Instructional Analysis

Step 4: Conduct Learner Analysis
    Meet with Business Owners
    Get sign-off

Step 5: Write Performance Objectives

Step 6: Develop Assessment Instruments

Step 7: Develop Instructional Strategy
    Meet with Business Owners
    Get sign-off

Step 8: Develop and Select Instructional Materials
    Meet with Business Owners
    Get sign-off

Step 9: Implement Instruction

Step 10: Evaluate Program
    Meet with Business Owners
    Get sign-off

parameters of the planned training. Identifying the motivation of the participants, as well as interests, attitudes, and learning preferences will help determine how the training will be conducted.

In some instances, a pretest may be given to determine competency levels of the participants. Outcomes from the pretest could affect whether a person is exempt from taking the course or from some components of the course. It could also highlight possible content areas to be included in the training.

At this stage in the new outage management system training development, important decisions were made about the parameters of the training based on the skill levels of the employees who would be participating. These decisions affected the instructional strategy. It was at this time that decisions were made to include subject matter experts from the business areas affected by the new system in the actual training sessions. The skill level of the participants dictated the detail of the instructional content that was required.

Step 6: Develop Assessment Instruments. At this point in the process, the training team has worked with the client to develop the performance objectives of the training. At the same time, the level 2 and 3 evaluations will be developed. The performance objectives reflect the behavioral purpose of the training. The level 2 assessment simply determines whether the learner has mastered these objectives. The level 3 assessment simply determines whether the learner has transferred this new knowledge, skill, or attitude to the job. For most training organizations, it is assumed that level 1 assessments have previously been developed. However, if one is not available, then it would have to be developed as well. Two different types of level 2 assessments are provided (see Exhibits 20.2 and 20.3).

Because of the timing and importance of the new outage management system, a strategy was developed in which the participants would complete two types of level 2 assessments. Each participant was required to demonstrate proficiency on all tasks and corresponding objectives on the system to the instructor and also to complete a level 2 paper-and-pencil assessment specifically designed for this course. Every objective was included in the assessments, and there were no items not reflected in the objectives.

Step 7: Develop Instructional Strategy. From the input previously gathered of the learner analysis, performance objectives, and assessments, an instructional strategy can be developed. The instructional strategy

Exhibit 20.2. Level 2 Assessment—*net*CADOPS

One form of the level 2 assessment for this training of a new computer system was given as a paper-and-pencil test. The questions were carefully written to best assess if the learner knew the proper procedures, application keystrokes, and verbal information required to successfully use the application. To simulate the important tasks presented in this training, screen captures of the application were taken and the learners were asked to simulate the appropriate responses. For example, a screen capture is made of a display from the application and specific questions are asked to make a response close to the actual response. Question 6, as shown, requires the learner to circle the button on the diagram to perform a task. In actual application, the learner would actually push the button to perform the task. Both the question and actual task require the learner to accurately process the information on the page in order to make the correct decision.

*net*CADOPS 2002.0				System Outages Overview			
Find							
10	All ▾	All ▾	All ▾	All ▾	All ▾	All ▾	All ▾
	Haz.	District	Infer. Outages	Verif. Outages	Max Duration	Non Cust. Calls	Unasg. Calls
...	0	PORTLAND	0	2	3.0	1	0
...	0	ROSEBURG	0	1	1.4	0	0
...	0	YAKIMA	1	1	1.2	0	0
...	0	YREKA	1	0	0.0	0	0
...	1	COOS BAY	1	1	3.0	0	0
...	1	ALBANY	1	0	0.6	0	0
...	1	STAYTON	1	0	0.7	0	0
...	1	GRANTS PASS	1	1	0.7	0	0
...	1	MEDFORD	1	1	2.1	0	0

Answer the following questions using the System Outages Overview menu.

5) List the district(s) that show outages with hazards?
6) Circle the button on the display above to show the outages for the district with non-customer calls.

---

includes details of how the training will be delivered. Factors considered include length, location, delivery method, and materials provided.

Once the instructional strategy has been determined, then the business owner will agree to the instructional strategy and all assessments developed and will "sign off" on them. The Assessment Sign-off Form has been developed to serve as the sign-off sheet (see Exhibit 20.4).

In the new outage management system course, the training team worked together to determine the most appropriate instructional strategy. Based on the information learned from the specific goals of

Exhibit 20.3. Level 2 Assessment—EMS SCADA Basic Navigation

The level 2 assessment for this training of a new computer system was given as a competency check list. The questions carefully matched the objectives of the course. Each person taking the class was required to demonstrate competency to the instructor on each specific task listed. Various factors required this training to be conducted one on one. This task list was given out to all the learners even prior to the training, and a blank assessment was provided to all learners after completion. Distributing the checklist before the training provides the person with the important elements of the training before it starts. The learner can also use this checklist to supplement the training to help verify abilities after the training. A section of this assessment is provided here.

WS500 Navigation—Performance Assessment

The student will achieve the goal of the course by completing the presented objectives. These objectives are achieved by demonstrating competency to the instructor in the specific behaviors assigned to each objective. Students must demonstrate mastery in each objective to earn credit for this course.

| Procedure
To accomplish . . . . | Objectives
Demonstrate the
ability to . . . . | Tasks
By showing you can . . . | Demonstrated |
|---|---|---|---|
| Logging into the system | Log In | Launch WS500 from desktop | |
| | Shift Change Log In | Log in while another operator is already logged in | |
| | Log Out | Log out of the WS500 | |
| | Change Password | Change the WS500 password | |
| Working with Displays | Open Displays Using the File Method | Open the master menu (MSTR MENU) in a new window using the filter and wildcard characters | |
| | | Open a substation index display in the same window from a poke point on the Master Menu | |

Exhibit 20.3. Level 2 Assessment—EMS SCADA Basic Navigation (*continued*)

Procedure *To accomplish . . .*	Objectives *Demonstrate the ability to . . .*	Tasks *By showing you can . . .*	Demonstrated
Working with Displays (*cont.*)	Open Displays Using the File Method (*cont.*)	Open a substation one-line display in a new window from a poke point on the substation index display	
	Navigate Between Displays	Navigate to a display previously open in the active window using Display Recall buttons	
		View the display history for the window using Display Recall and select a display to open	
		Navigate to another open display using the Window drop down menu	

Exhibit 20.4. PacifiCorp Assessment Instrument Form

During step 7 of our training strategy, we meet with the business clients to review the level 2 assessments developed, approve them, and collaboratively develop the items for the level 3 assessment. We ask our clients to sign the Assessment Instrument Form on these items.

PACIFICORP

POWER
LEARNING   **Assessment Instrument Form**

Project Name: Date:
Business Owner: PowerLearning Manager:
Department: Project Assigned To:

Level 2 Evaluation (attached)

Level 3 Evaluation (attached)

Estimated Date for Level 3 Evaluation:

Signatures of Approval

Business Owners:	Date:
Power Skills:	Date:

TSF 5   Rev 8/04

the course, the learner characteristics, and the development of the objectives and corresponding assessments, it was determined that the training had to be hands-on at a company facility in close proximity to the company offices in California. It was determined that the training team would include a lead trainer and subject matter experts from company areas affected by the new system.

Management also signed off on the assessments and worked with the training team to develop together the appropriate level 3 assessment items. It was decided that the level 3 assessment would be conducted by the lead trainer in the form of an informal interview within a few weeks after the training. Furthermore, it was decided that this time would also be used to determine the next course of action if there were deficiencies found in the transfer of the learning to the workplace.

Step 10: Evaluate program. Training has been given. Level 1 (Reaction) and 2 (Learning) evaluations will be conducted immediately after the training. Feedback on the evaluations will be provided to the business owner. A time will be established to administer the level 3 (Behavior) evaluation to the business owner or designate. The purpose of the level 3 evaluation is solely to determine if there has been a transfer of training from the class to the job performance. This date should be sufficiently long enough after the end of training in order for the supervisor to determine if the skills learned in the course have been transferred to the workplace. Training staff will conduct level 3 evaluation at a later date after the end of training (see Exhibit 20.5). Training staff will meet with business owners to review level 3 results, acquire approval signatures, and determine next steps.

An interesting thing happened during the administration of the paper-and-pencil assessment during the new outage management class. Upon completion of the assessment, the class, including the supervisors, reviewed each of the questions and answers. The assessment turned into a valuable learning tool, and the participants gathered some valuable insights. The instructors, supervisors, and class participants left the class with a newfound appreciation for level 2 assessments and how they can be used as additional training tools.

Because of the unique situation that occurred after the training, the level 3 evaluation was conducted very shortly after the class. The managers were delighted beyond measure by the performance of the class participants on the job.

Exhibit 20.5. PacifiCorp Level 1 Assessment

A significant amount of effort was put into the development of our level 1 assessment provided below.

PACIFICORP
POWER
LEARNING

Course: _____   Date: _____

Instructor: _____   Location: _____

It is our sincere desire to provide you with the best possible learning experience. We take our responsibility to help you perform your job better very seriously. Please take a few moments to complete this survey about your training experience. Thanks from the entire PowerLearning training team.

About this Learning Activity...

	Strongly Disagree	Disagree	Neutral	Agree	Strongly Agree
This learning activity met my expectations.	1	2	3	4	5
This activity will help me to perform my job better.	1	2	3	4	5
The materials used in this activity helped my understanding.	1	2	3	4	5
I feel that I have learned something from this activity.	1	2	3	4	5

Was the length of the activity appropriate?   (please circle)   Too Short   Just Right   Too Long
Please provide a suggestion for improving the course (use back of sheet for additional suggestions):

About the Facilitator...

	Strongly Disagree	Disagree	Neutral	Agree	Strongly Agree
The facilitator was effective presenting the material.	1	2	3	4	5
The facilitator was knowledgeable in the subject matter.	1	2	3	4	5
The facilitator involved me in learning.	1	2	3	4	5
The facilitator managed time well.	1	2	3	4	5
The facilitator provided applicable examples/demonstrations.	1	2	3	4	5
The course objectives were clearly stated.	1	2	3	4	5
The course objectives were fully met.	1	2	3	4	5

What did the facilitator do well in the class that really helped your learning?

Exhibit 20.5. PacifiCorp Level 1 Assessment (*continued*)

What can the facilitator do to improve the learning experience:

About the Learning Experience...

	Poor	Fair	Good	Very Good	Excellent
Rate the overall ease & clarity of the enrollment process.	1	2	3	4	5
Rate the overall training facility	1	2	3	4	5

What other suggestions would you have for improving your learning experience?

About What You Learned...

Rate your productivity, BEFORE TRAINING, on a scale of 0 to 10, on the skills/knowledge you learned in this course.	0	1	2	3	4	5	6	7	8	9	10
Predict your productivity, AFTER TRAINING, on a scale of 0 to 10, on the skills/knowledge you learned in this course.	0	1	2	3	4	5	6	7	8	9	10
On a scale of 0 to 10, how much of your total working time will you be spending on tasks that require the skills/knowledge you learned in this course?	0	1	2	3	4	5	6	7	8	9	10
On a scale of 0 to 10, rate the importance of the skills/knowledge you learned in this course as it relates to your specific job?	0	1	2	3	4	5	6	7	8	9	10

revised 4/12/04

235

Benefits Experienced from Implementing
Level 2 Assessments

PowerLearning has recently begun to implement level 2 assessments in our training. In addition to being able to measure effects of our training better, we have received a number of additional benefits as a result of implementing level 2 assessments in our training programs. We found that the level 2 assessment also serves as a teaching tool. In the case study presented earlier, the answers to the assessment were reviewed with the class upon completion of the assessment. We were delighted to discover that in a couple of instances material covered during the course was clarified. We noted that students would pose additional questions that were answered by both the instructors and other classmates and led to a richer training experience.

The level 2 assessment provided a content check for the instructors. In one specific instance it was identified during the debrief time that an important point covered in the assessment was not covered in the depth that it needed to be addressed during the training. A potential problem was averted by reviewing the assessment after the class. The assessment provided a valuable and time-saving check on the training.

The use of the level 2 assessments also improves the consistency of content presented by the different trainers, because, we have found, that having the different instructors use the same level 2 assessment for a given course as a benchmark has helped us to bridge the gaps in training and learning outcomes between instructors. Differences are quickly identified and resolved before the actual training begins.

The implementation of level 2 assessments has gone smoothly and there has been complete support from the class participants for the courses we have developed. Instructors and class participants have a better idea of what is important in the class, and the level 2 evaluations enforce consistency between the instructional content and the course objectives. Development of the level 2 assessment has helped focus the training development. Extraneous material is removed from the instruction, and objectives are added and refined to better match important instructional material. This has helped streamline our courses to include only the relevant and important content.

An additional benefit is that the level 2 assessment is also being used as a teaching tool. The level 2 assessment can help validate learners' understanding and increase instructors' confidence that the class participants have mastered the material covered in the class. In situations when a student is not able to demonstrate competency, instructors are provided with a good opportunity to clarify and answer questions.

Benefits Experienced from Implementing Level 3 Assessments

It is important to note that even if students can demonstrate proficiency during training, it does not mean that they can perform the task on the job. Obviously, since job performance is more important than performance in the classroom, there is a need to check actual performance on the job after training to determine if transfer has taken place. Normally these evaluations take place long enough after the training to enable the supervisor or manager enough time to determine if the employee has transferred the skills onto the job. Kirkpatrick's Level 3 evaluation is designed to do just that.

We have integrated the development of the level 3 assessment into our training development strategy. Once we have identified the skills and tasks to be included in the training, we develop the objectives (level 2 and level 3 questions). We have the person who has requested the class, usually a manager or supervisor, review these and sign off on them. This takes place before any instructional materials are developed.

The majority of the level 3 assessments we have given have been in the format of a structured interview. During this meeting, we discuss the level 3 questions (that we had previously developed collaboratively) for each employee. We then explore next steps. We have found that we received tremendous support from management using this process and that there has been a strong sense of ownership and partnership from management. When we have followed up with the level 3 evaluation after training, we found that managers were very receptive and provided specific and useful feedback.

We have found that we have been able to develop training that better addressed the rationale for training. By jointly developing the level 2 and 3 assessments and comparing them, we were to include content that was relevant and eliminate extraneous material before extensive development had occurred. As a result, the resulting training better matches the required job performance and often has saved the company time and money.

We have also found that when these managers provided us with training development projects, they did so with an increased confidence level. These managers are proactively involved in additional training projects and are able to better articulate the outcomes they are expecting as a result of having previously gone through level 3 evaluations.

By developing and receiving approval for the level 3 questions before development of the training materials, we received better support for our training from management, developed and delivered better training, and saved the company time and money resources. These outcomes were achieved with minimal additional effort or cost.

Final Thoughts

Implementing a sound evaluation strategy into our training development has been highly effective. We agree with others that level 3 and 4 evaluations cannot be performed unless a level 2 evaluation has been previously performed. It makes sense to our training team and managers that one cannot determine if the training was effective without knowing the learning (level 2) outcomes of the training participants. We strongly believe that the success of our evaluation efforts is affected by implementing the sound methodology for developing the different assessments. We have experienced the fact that the business owners/managers' confidence and satisfaction in our training organization increased as a result of involving them strategically throughout the development of training. We found that not only were our training efforts successful, but that our training group also experienced the benefits of increased responsibility and opportunity for developing bigger training initiatives for the company.

References

Dick, Walter, Lou Carey, and James O. Carey. *The Systematic Design of Instruction.* 6th ed. Boston: Pearson, 2005.

Gagné, Robert M. *The Conditions of Learning.* 4th ed. New York: Holt, Rinehart and Winston, 1985.

Kirkpatrick, Donald L. *Evaluating Training Programs: The Four Levels.* 2nd ed. San Francisco: Berrett-Koehler, 1998.

Robinson, Dana G., and James C. Robinson. *Performance Consulting: Moving Beyond Training.* San Francisco: Berrett-Koehler, 1996.

Shrock, Sharon, and William Coscarelli. *Criterion-Referenced Test Development.* Boston: Addison Wesley, 2000.

Chapter 21

Evaluating a Coaching and Counseling Course

This practical case study comes from Spain. It describes a program of great interest to many types and sizes of organizations where "coaching" has become a critical component of training. Moving from level 2 (Learning) to level 3 (Behavior) requires the manager to encourage and help learners apply what they have learned. You will find practical subject content as well as evaluation tools and techniques that you can use and/or adapt.

Grupo Iberdrola

Gema Gongora, Training and Development Manager
Consultants
Epise, Barcelona
Juan Pablo Ventosa, Managing Director
Nuria Duran, Project Manager
Madrid, Spain

The Company

With more than 100 years of experience, Iberdrola is one of the main private electricity supply industries of the world. Its services, addressed to sixteen millions of clients—more than nine million just in Spain—are focused on the generation, transport, distribution and marketing of electricity, and natural gas. There are more than 10,000 staff members at the Iberdrola offices in Spain and Latin America.

For Iberdrola, training has strategic relevance, since it is an essential function that helps to assure the competency levels demanded of the professionals, so they can fulfill the requirements of the Strategic Plan. In the year 2000 they did 400,000 hours of training, which make for an average of about forty-one training hours per person per year. To date, training has been evaluated exclusively in regard to the participants' reaction or satisfaction level.

The corporation asked whether there was the need for an integral evaluation system to form part of its strategic guidelines. This system would allow the evaluation of training's impact on all of the company's business and units.

The Project

The Corporate Training Unit and the Training Services attached to the various companies of Iberdrola decided to attempt a common approach to the development and implementation of the guidelines for evaluation. A team of training specialists from the organization, with the collaboration of an external consultant, Epise, developed a project for the creation of a general handbook of procedures designed to evaluate training events.

Three training events were chosen to serve as a pilot, and an evaluation procedure was designed and applied to these events in accordance with Kirkpatrick's four-level model. The training events were intended for business units and dealt with widely varying subjects so that they would provide a sufficient number of cases for the creation, based on the acquired experience, of a practical handbook that met the needs of the organization. One of these training events was a face-to-face course on coaching and counseling, administered at Iberdrola Engineering and Consultancy.

The Course

The characteristics of the course are given in Table 21.1.

Table 21.1.

Course Title: COACHING and COUNSELING	Date: 28/03/01 to 30/03/01
Number of Participants: 11	Duration: 16 hours
Number of Assessed Participants: 10	Location: Madrid

Taught by: Euroresearch

Profile of the participants

- People who are going from performing the function of junior engineer to that of senior engineer. They have at least two years of experience in the company.
- They will go on to coordinate small work teams.

Course objectives

1. To make the participants aware of the importance of directing their colleagues by using a style of constant listening and personal attention.
2. To provide training in the skill of developing collaborators for the position.
3. To develop active listening skills in order to confront problems of performance or motivation.
4. To develop the skills necessary to intervene in the event of emotional or motivational conflict between colleagues.

Methodology

A completely participative method is employed. Three "coaching" and "counseling" role-playing exercises are conducted, as well as two games, in order to demonstrate some key aspects. Participants complete three questionnaires about learning style, styles of response in emotional communication, and the opening of avenues for interpersonal communication. Each theoretical explanation is followed by a practical exercise of similar duration.

Evaluation

How Are the Criteria Defined?

Having been conducted in previous years, this training event had already been designed and the educational goals necessary for the level 2 evaluation were available, but the criteria for levels 3 and 4 were not. In order to obtain this information, a workshop was conducted with participants' supervisors.

In the first part of the session, the project was presented, with an emphasis on the contribution expected from the supervisors and the benefits they would receive in exchange. In the second part, those in attendance responded collectively to the following questions:

- As regards the functions of the participants in the training event, what tasks are they responsible for that are related to the content of the course, and what criteria are used to evaluate their performance?
- What are the strategic goals of the department?
- What factors, apart from the training of the staff, have an influence on the performance of the department?

As seen in Table 21.2 the results of the workshop, were used to:

- develop tools to evaluate behavior (level 3), based on the criteria used to evaluate the tasks related to the course content.
- select criteria for the evaluation of results (level 4).

What Tools Were Used?

Level 1 Reaction.   The questionnaire usually used by the consulting firm responsible for teaching the course was employed.

Level 2 Learning.   Because the educational goals of the course included not only knowledge but skills as well, the consulting firm that gave the course was asked to conduct one test of knowledge and another of skills. For this purpose, the firm designed a questionnaire and guidelines for observation. These can be seen in Exhibits 21.1 and 21.2.

Level 3 Behavior.   A questionnaire was designed, with some generic questions and some specific ones based on the criteria for the evaluation of the tasks related to the content of the course. Exhibit 21.3 displays the most comprehensive version of this questionnaire, the one intended for the participant after the training event.

Level 4 Results.   The level 4 criteria that were selected were those that corresponded to the strategic goals of the department that were most influenced by the tasks related to the content of the course (see chart in Table 21.2). They were:

Table 21.2. Results of the Workshop with Supervisors

With regard to the functions of those attending the training event, what tasks, related to the training received, do they carry out and what are the criteria used to evaluate their performance?

Tasks	*Evaluation Criteria for the Task*
1. Motivate	– Degree of satisfaction of colleagues – Complaints by colleagues – Dedication – Contribution of new ideas
2. Assign responsibilities	– Correct the course of the project – Avoidance of "bottlenecks" – Distribution of the workload – Knowledge of colleagues

3. Know colleagues	– Be aware of information regarding:
	  – Training of colleagues
	  – Abilities of colleagues
	  – Relationship of colleagues with their surroundings
	  – Behavior of colleagues in extreme situations
	– Data regarding performance assessments
	– Rotation index (unexpected)
	– Dissatisfaction expressed to the boss

4. Resolve conflicts	– Knowledge of colleagues – Prevent conflicts from having an influence on the course of the project – As a rule, don't receive complaints from the group – Don't avoid responsibilities (hot potato) – Don't display lack of camaraderie
5. Control resources (optimize)	– If necessary: – Number of rotations – Requests for inclusion – Offering of available resources
6. Possess communication/ negotiation skills	– Identification of profiles – Attitude adjustment (positive results) – Absence of "rumor mill" due to transparency of information – Give Web-organized explanations – Brief and precise explanations

(continued)

Table 21.2. Results of the Workshop with Supervisors (*continued*)

7.	Delegate	- Don't return the delegated "item" - Excessive workload for colleagues
8.	Follow the progress of the project	- Provide feedback to colleagues - Achieve the goals set out in the planning stages - Redirect the project if necessary - Have up-to-date information
9.	Assess performance	- Results are coherent (assessor and assessed) - 360° feedback is carried out - Results can be justified
10.	Make decisions	- Result - On time - According to plan - Decisions don't need to be retaken
11.	Identify needs	- Presentation of proposals - Training needs met - Knowledge of the technical requirements for the project - No repetition in the meeting of needs - Results of the performance assessment
12.	Train colleagues	- Satisfaction of colleagues with performance assessments - Display acquired knowledge and greater independence

- Index rotation
- Meeting deadlines
- Commercial activity
- Profits
- Training given
- Internal client's satisfaction index

In order to isolate the effect of the training, it was decided that a control group would be used and that this group would be made up of individuals with characteristics similar to those of the participants in the training, and that they would be matched with each of the participants one to one. Unfortunately, it was impossible to carry out the evaluation at this level.

Table 21.2. Results of the Workshop with Supervisors (*continued*)

Chart of Goals/Tasks	
Operative	*Tasks*
• Index Rotation	Motivate Assign responsibilities Know colleagues Resolve conflicts Delegate Follow the progress of the project Assess performance
• Meeting deadlines	Motivate Assign responsibilities Resolve conflicts Delegate Follow the progress of the project Take decisions
• New breakthroughs (R+D)	Motivate

• Commercial activity
  • Enlargement strategies:
   – Number of applicants
   – Number of offers
	
	Motivate
	Possess communication/negotiation skills

• Profits	Control resources (optimize) Follow the progress of the project Take decisions
• Provide technical training	Know colleagues Assess performance Identify needs Train colleagues
Corporate	
• Internal client's satisfaction index	Motivate *Resolve conflicts* Possess communication/negotiation skills
• Meeting deadlines	Motivate Assign responsibilities Resolve conflicts Delegate Follow the progress of the project Take decisions
• Scope of training (number of hours of training per person)	Identify needs
• Degree to which plan is successfully carried out	Identify needs

Exhibit 21.1. Knowledge Test for Level 2 Evaluation

(You must remember these numbers at the end of the course)

Coaching and Counseling

Please, fill in this questionnaire related to the *Coaching and Counseling* course that has as its exclusive purpose to determine the level of learning reached once the course is over.

The content of this questionnaire is totally confidential. The answers of all the group members will be compiled in one document in order to protect the identity of the authors.

At the top of the document, please enter a combination of four numbers (that you must remember at the end of the course) for identification purposes.

To answer the questionnaire, you must indicate (in every item) to which extent the item really fits to team direction.

	For the team management this behavior is			
	Very suitable	*Quite suitable*	*Not very suitable*	*Not suitable at all*
1. Maintaining an open and personal communication with your colleagues				
2. Putting yourself in others' place and understanding their views				
3. Being polite and distant in personal relations				
4. Showing empathy to emotive expressions				
5. Considering that personal life should not be taken into account in professional life				
6. Respecting others' opinion				
7. Being inflexible with your thoughts and feelings				
8. Providing your colleagues with solutions in conflict situations				
9. Paying attention to others				

Exhibit 21.1. Knowledge Test for Level 2 Evaluation (*continued*)

	For the team management this behavior is			
	Very suitable	*Quite suitable*	*Not very suitable*	*Not suitable at all*
10. Understanding the real difficulties of the work of your colleagues				
11. Judging issues from your point of view the others' opinions without considering feelings and emotions				
12. Showing indifference to the personal conflicts of your colleagues				
13. Ignoring whenever you can the differences and brushes between team members				
14. Communicating clearly and assertively				
15. Creating a relaxed and pleasant atmosphere suitable for dialogue				
16. Appearing to be perfect without having problems				
17. Taking care of personal relations for colleagues to be fluent and positive				
18. Trying to provide solutions in conflicts between personal and corporate interests				

Exhibit 21.2. Guidelines for Level 2 Evaluation

Seminar-Workshop
Techniques for people management:
Coaching and Counseling

Impulse management or counseling
Observation notes

Name: ....

Observe the manager's behavior in regard to the verbal and the nonverbal spheres. Write down your comments for every item. At the end of the performance, grade the manager in every item and explain your scoring by writing constructive comments in the right. In the scale, 1 stands for "needs to improve substantially" and 5 stands for "excellent."

EUROSEARCH
CONSULTORES
DE
DIRECCIÓN

CHECK LIST	COMMENTS	EXAMPLES
Structure Has the skills developer followed all the stages of the skills development model?		
*In accordance with the topic	1 2 3 4 5	
*It identifies goals	1 2 3 4 5	
*It encourages discoveries	1 2 3 4 5	
*It establishes criteria	1 2 3 4 5	
*It empowers and authorizes	1 2 3 4 5	
*It recapitulates	1 2 3 4 5	
Procedure Has the chief used the required preparation for the procedure?		
*He has paid attention carefully	1 2 3 4 5	
*He has asked questions	1 2 3 4 5	
*He has made suggestions	1 2 3 4 5	
*He has given feedback	1 2 3 4 5	
*He has used "I statements"	1 2 3 4 5	
Atmosphere Has the chief created a productive atmosphere?		
*He has clarified purposes	1 2 3 4 5	

Exhibit 21.2. Guidelines for Level 2 Evaluation (*continued*)

*He has avoided value judgments	1 2 3 4 5	
*He has created a pleasant, genuine, respectful and empathetic atmosphere	1 2 3 4 5	
*Good opening and closing	1 2 3 4 5	
Summary *According to you, has this been a successful "Skills Development" session?	1 2 3 4 5	
Has the manager followed the basic counseling model?		
*Exploration	1 2 3 4 5	
*Finding new perspectives	1 2 3 4 5	
*Action	1 2 3 4 5	
How does the manager implement the basic skills of counseling?		
*Paying attention	1 2 3 4 5	
*Listening	1 2 3 4 5	
*Visual contact	1 2 3 4 5	
*Nonverbal communication	1 2 3 4 5	
*In the sort of questions used	1 2 3 4 5	
How does the manager handle the two core elements in the interview?		
*Feelings/Emotions	1 2 3 4 5	
*Empathy	1 2 3 4 5	
Summary *According to you, has this been a successful counseling model session?	1 2 3 4 5	

EUROSEARCH
CONSULTORES
DE
DIRECCIÓN

Exhibit 21.3. Questionnaire About Learning Transference

Posttest: Coaching and Counseling

Participant Questionnaire—Learning Transference

Personal Particulars
Name
Position

Supervisor or Manager Data
Name
Position

We have contacted you again to ask for your collaboration in the fulfillment of this questionnaire. The purpose is to collect the necessary data to determine the rightness of the training that you have received at the Coaching and Counseling course as an Iberdrola holding employee.

Personal particulars are essential to manage properly the answer received and the data transferred. However, we assure you that the answers received will be totally confidential: the data will be used exclusively for statistical purposes.

Once you have finished the questionnaire, please send it to:
E-mail address:

Question 1: In the last months you attended the *Coaching and Counseling* course. What have you been able to put into practice that you learned?

Nothing	A few things	A lot of things	Almost everything/everything
(1)	(2)	(3)	(4)

Question 2: If you answered "Nothing" or "A few things" in the above question, what are the main reasons that led to this?

1. The skills I learned have proved to be insufficient.
2. I didn't have the opportunity to put them into practice.
3. The supervisor didn't facilitate the implementation of these skills.
4. I didn't have the resources to put into practice what I learned.
5. Other reasons. (Please explain them).

Question 3: Do you feel your knowledge about coaching techniques is?

Insufficient	Sufficient	Good	Very good
(1)	(2)	(3)	(4)

Question 4. Next you will find a list of different behaviors related to your job. Indicate in each case the frequency in which they occur.

Activity	Almost Never	Sometimes	Often	Almost Always	No Answer
1. Provide feedback about the development of the project.					

Exhibit 21.3. Questionnaire About Learning Transference (*continued*)

Activity	Almost Never	Sometimes	Often	Almost Always	No Answer
2. Present training proposals for your colleagues to management					
3. Receive systematic (destructive) complaints from your colleagues.					
4. Unexpected changes (leaves) in the team occur.					
5. Colleagues extend their workday to complete tasks assigned.					

Question 5. Next you will find another list of different behaviors related to your job. Evaluate in each case how you perform these tasks.

Activity	Almost Never	Sometimes	Often	Almost Always	No Answer
1. Assign tasks according to the training and abilities of your colleagues.					
2. Plan explanations according to the level of the audience.					
3. Synthesize and organize ideas in explanations/ negotiations.					
4. Colleagues express their satisfaction with regard to the coordination of the team.					
5. Colleagues display greater independence in the completion of tasks.					

In case you ticked off "No answer" for any of the items, please explain.

Date / /

How Was the Evaluation Carried Out?

Level 1.   The participants completed the reaction questionnaire at the end of the last session of the course.

Level 2.   The participants took the knowledge test at the beginning and at the end of the training event. The trainer applied the observation guidelines to the role-playing activities that were conduced during the course.

Level 3.   The participants and their supervisors completed the questionnaire before the training event and again three months after the completion of the event.

What Were the Results of the Evaluation?

Level 1.   See Table 21.3.

Level 2.   See Figures 21.1 and 21.2.

Level 3.   Only three of the supervisors responded to the questionnaire that was sent to them three months after the completion of the training event, so the study is limited to the data provided by the participants. The numbering of the questions in the presentation of the results corresponds to the questionnaire displayed in Exhibit 21.3. See Figures 21.3, 21.4, and 21.5, and Tables 21.4 and 21.5.

What Are the Conclusions?

From the questionnaires, it is evident that the training event received a very positive reaction from the participants. With regard to the learning evaluation, the results are positive because:

- 100 percent of the participants assessed received a score of 17 or 18 out of a possible 18 on the test administered after the course. The results show that the participants had considerable knowledge of the subject before the course, as 60 percent of the original scores were over 15 points. As a result, the increase in the level of knowledge was not very pronounced.
- In the level 3 questionnaire, 73 percent of the participants displayed an increase in knowledge level with respect to their initial self-evaluations.

Table 21.3

1. *Organization of the Course*	Media
1.1. Following of the planned agenda	7.3
1.2. Duration of the course	8.2
1.3. Quality of the materials (manuals, overheads, etc.)	9.0
2. *Usefulness of the Course*	
2.1. Quality of the exercises	8.7
2.2. Number of exercises	8.7
2.3. Applicability at work of the knowledge obtained	7.5
3. *Content of the Course*	
3.1. The content of the course met with expectations	7.2
4. *Instructors*	
4.1. Knowledge of the subject	9.8
4.2. Quality of the explanations	9.5
4.3. Friendliness, holding of interest	9.8
5. *Services of the Center*	
5.1. Training rooms	9.2
5.2. Support equipment (overhead projector, VCR, TV, etc.)	9.7
6. *Time*	
6.1. Overall evaluation of the course	8.8
6.2. The stated objectives of the course have been achieved	9.0

However, because the information about skills learning is unavailable, we cannot consider the results to be representative of the overall efficiency of the training event.

In regard to the evaluation of behavior, the results indicated a not very high degree of applicability of the knowledge acquired during the course. Of all of the participants, only 27 percent said they had been able to apply much of what they learned. The rest said they had applied little or none of what they learned, and, of these, 75 percent said this is because the opportunity had not presented itself.

With regard to concrete behaviors observed at work, it is not possible to reach any conclusions because:

Figure 21.1. Knowledge Learning

Score range: 0–18 points

	Before	After	Difference
	18	18	0
	14	18	4
	13	18	5
	15	18	3
Participants	10	18	8
	16	17	1
	17	18	1
	17	18	1
	14	18	4
	16	18	2
Average	15	17.9	2.9

LEARNING OF SKILLS

- The lack of application distorts the results obtained. The impact the training may have had on these changes is not significant if a large proportion of the participants indicate that they have been able to apply little or none of what they learned, making it possible that other factors might have played a part in bringing about the apparent changes.
- In addition, the evaluations by the superiors, which would have served as an alternate source of information, were not available.

The results can be considered satisfactory with regard to the learning achieved by the participants. However, the desired application of this learning in the workplace has not come about. In this case, it is possible that more time and concrete opportunities might facilitate the application of the acquired knowledge.

Figure 21.2a. Results Before

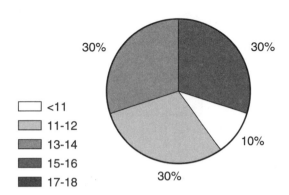

Figure 21.2b. Results After

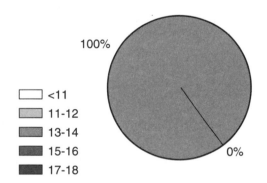

What Are the Strategic Goals of the Entity?

The objectives are described from two perspectives:

Operative

- Rotation index
- Meeting deadlines
- New breakthroughs (R+D)
- Commercial activity

Figure 21.3.

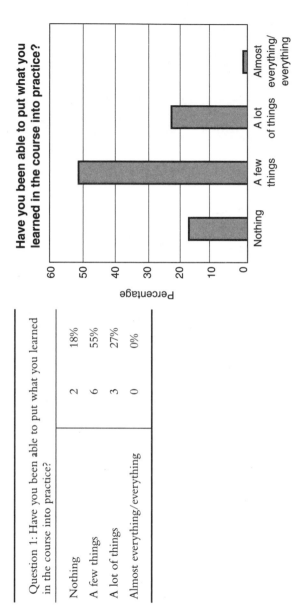

Have you been able to put what you learned in the course into practice?

Question 1: Have you been able to put what you learned in the course into practice?

Nothing	2	18%
A few things	6	55%
A lot of things	3	27%
Almost everything/everything	0	0%

Figure 21.4.

Question 2: What are the reasons for the lack of applicability of the knowledge obtained?

Reason 1:	Don't have people working under them	13%
Reason 2:	Haven't had the opportunity	75%
Reason 3:	Workload	13%

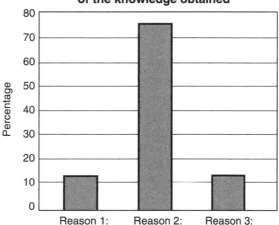

- Enlargement strategies
  - Number of applicants
  - Number of offers
- Profits
- Provision of technical training

Corporate

- Internal client's satisfaction index
- Meeting deadlines
- Scope of training (number of hours of training per person)
- Degree to which plan is successfully carried out

Figure 21.5.

Knowledge about coaching and counseling

Question 3: Do you feel your knowledge about coaching and counseling is:

	Before (n = 11)	After (n = 11)
Insufficient	64%	0%
Sufficient	27%	64%
Good	9%	9%
Very Good	0%	27%

Difference between knowledge before and after the training event:

(n = 11)	N	%
Increased	8	73%
Did not increase	3	27%

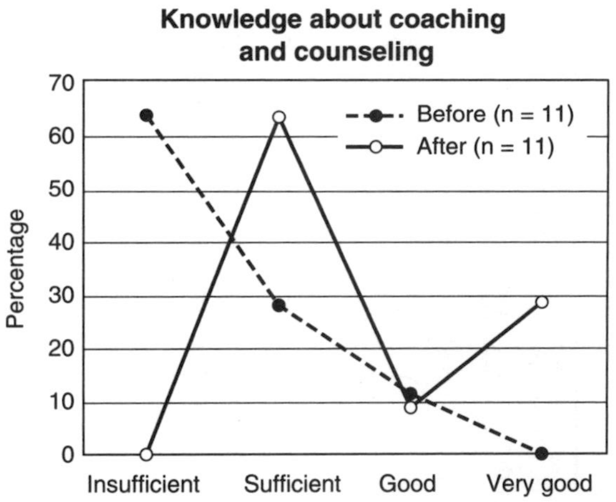

Table 21.4.

Question 4: In each case what is the frequency with which the following things occur?

4.1 Provide feedback about the development of the project

	Before (n = 11)	After (n = 11)
No answer	18%	0%
Almost never	0%	0%
Sometimes	18%	27%
Often	27%	18%
Almost always	36%	55%

4.2 Present training proposals for your colleagues to management

	Before (n = 11)	After (n = 11)
No answer	18%	9%
Almost never	18%	9%
Sometimes	36%	64%
Often	27%	9%
Almost always	0%	9%

4.3 Receive systematic complaints from your colleagues

	Before (n = 11)	After (n = 11)
No answer	0%	9%
Almost never	91%	64%
Sometimes	9%	27%
Often	0%	0%
Almost always	0%	0%

4.4 Unexpected changes in the team occur

	Before (n = 11)	After (n = 11)
No answer	9%	9%
Almost never	64%	55%
Sometimes	27%	27%
Often	0%	9%
Almost always	0%	0%

4.5 Colleagues extend their workday to complete tasks assigned

	Before (n = 11)	After (n = 11)
No answer	0%	9%
Almost never	18%	9%
Sometimes	36%	64%
Often	36%	9%
Almost always	9%	9%

Table 21.5.

Question 5: In each case, how will you perform these tasks?

5.1 Assign tasks according to the training and abilities of your colleagues.

	Before (n=11)	After (n=11)
No answer	9%	18%
Poor	0%	0%
Fair	0%	0%
Good	64%	45%
Very good	27%	36%

5.2 Plan explanations according to the audience.

	Before (n=11)	After (n=11)
No answer	9%	0%
Poor	0%	0%
Fair	18%	9%
Good	64%	64%
Very good	9%	27%

5.3 Synthesize and order ideas in explanations/negotiations.

	Before (n=11)	After (n=11)
No answer	9%	0%
Poor	0%	0%
Fair	27%	9%
Good	45%	45%
Very good	18%	45%

5.4 Colleagues express their satisfaction with regard to the coordination of the team.

	Before (n=11)	After (n=11)
No answer	9%	27%
Poor	0%	0%
Fair	36%	27%
Good	45%	36%
Very good	9%	9%

5.5 Colleagues display greater independence in the completion of tasks.

	Before (n=11)	After (n=11)
No answer	0%	18%
Poor	0%	0%
Fair	9%	0%
Good	64%	36%
Very good	27%	45%

Factors Apart from Training that Influence the Results

- Personality
- Personal surroundings
- Work environment
- Changes in geographic location
- Performance of business
- Change in the organization's strategic orientation
- Turnover of key personnel
- Assignment of resources by the organization
- Interaction with other departments or with providers or clients
- IT operating systems

Chapter 22

Evaluating a Performance Learning Model

Instead of evaluating a specific program, DAU evaluates all its programs within an enterprise learning framework they call the Performance Learning Model which includes evaluating all of its training courses, continuous learning modules, and performance support efforts totaling over 103 thousand graduates per year. Details of this evaluation include all four Kirkpatrick levels. The figures will be of particular interest.

Defense Acquisition University (DAU)

Christopher R. Hardy, Ph.D., Strategic Planner
Mark Whiteside, Director Performance and Resource Management
Ft. Belvoir, Virginia

Who We Are

The Defense Acquisition University (DAU) is a government "corporate" university for the Department of Defense, managed by the Office of the Undersecretary of Defense (Acquisition, Technology, and Logistics) (DoD USD [AT&L]). To accomplish its mission of *providing practitioner training and consulting services* to over 134,000 Department of Defense employees across fifteen career fields, DAU provides a full range of certification training (required for all 134,000 to qualify for advancement), assignment-specific training, performance support, continuous learning opportunities, and knowledge sharing.

DAU was established in 1992 and funded by Congress. DAU headquarters are located at Ft. Belvoir, Virginia, where DAU maintains a headquarters staff for centralized academic oversight, a robust curriculum development center, and an e-learning and technology development directorate. In addition, DAU has strategically located five regional campuses in areas where there is a high concentration of DoD AT&L workforce members:

- **West**—San Diego, California (serves workforce of 26,000)
- **Midwest**—Wright Patterson Air Force Base, Ohio (serves workforce of 20,000)
- **South**—Huntsville, Alabama (serves workforce of 27,000)
- **Mid-Atlantic**—Patuxent River, Maryland (serves workforce of 23,000)
- **Capital and Northeast**—Fort Belvoir, Virginia (serves workforce of 37,000). We also have the Defense Systems Management College-School of Program Managers at Ft. Belvoir for executive and international training.

What We Do

DAU's products and services include more than training. To meet all its learning and development requirements, DAU created an overarching learning strategy, the Performance Learning Model (PLM), which promotes career-long learning and achievement. The PLM includes four main thrusts:

- Certification and assignment-specific training through resident training, hybrid learning courses, and distance learning courses
- Continuous learning through DAU's continuous learning modules
- Performance support through consulting, rapid deployment training, and targeted training

- Knowledge sharing through the AT&L Knowledge Sharing System (AKSS) and Acquisition Community Connection (Communities of Practice).

By developing and adopting this new learning strategy, DAU rapidly changed the traditional training paradigm of instruction limited to the classroom, to one that provides learning solutions twenty-four hours a day, seven days a week—the concept of anytime, anywhere learning. With implementation of the PLM, the 134,000 workforce members now have more control over their career-long learning opportunities. Before adopting the PLM learning model, DAU would train on average 30,000 students per year. Now with an expanded learning platform and providing alternative delivery methods for our training, DAU graduates over 90,000 students per year from our course instruction, we support over 200,000 registered users to our continuous learning modules, and we have over 300,000 queries to our learning assets through our communities of practice. Clearly DAU has dramatically increased its reach to its customers and broadened the depth and scope of its training assets in a fairly short time frame.

Evaluation and Feedback—Our Commitment

We used to spend an inordinate amount of time and effort collecting data that left little time for actual analysis. In the last few years, we completely modernized our "back room" infrastructure and invested in business tools. This has helped to reverse the trend so that we now spend the majority of our time analyzing and acting on data. (See Figure 22.1.)

At DAU, we strive to provide our customers with an experience marked by quality products, relevant learning solutions, a responsive faculty and staff, and a continuous connection to the broader AT&L community. To ensure we meet their needs, we have established robust evaluation and feedback mechanisms for each of our products and services. Comments and results are not just put on the shelf. Each quarter the senior leaders conduct a thorough review of the results of the quarter and, where appropriate, make timely, effective enhancements to our learning solutions. To earn a "premier corporate university" evaluation is not a choice, it is an imperative.

Figure 22.1. Reversing the Trend

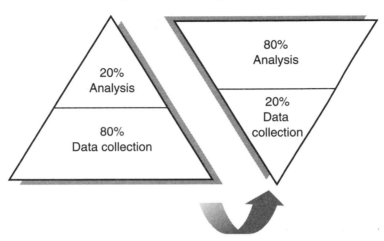

DAU evaluates all of its products and services. Evaluation plays a significant role as part of our quality reviews and as a barometer of our mission success. DAU employs several systems and the resulting data to link and assess the impact of learning on individual and organizational performance. More important, the results of its evaluation program are used to improve faculty performance, delivery, facilities, content, curricula, relevance to the job, applicability, and impact on the organization. Evaluation data, comparatives, benchmarking, and trends are also a key element in DAU's overall performance measurement program. DAU uses a holistic approach, leveraging its time accounting system, evaluation results, and cost data to afford its leadership the actionable intelligence with which it effectively manages its enterprise. By using an industry leader for its evaluation services, DAU is also able to access benchmarking data from many other learning and development organizations (over 100) throughout the world to better calibrate its performance. As Figure 22.2 shows, DAU, using a data mart, can quickly evaluate mission performance and trends, comparing measures of efficiency and effectiveness mined from various tools and legacy systems.

In theory and in actual practice, DAU adapted Dr. Don Kirkpatrick's four-level model for evaluating its learning products and services. Taking advantage of the speed and reach of technology as well as the real-time data analyses it affords, we have implemented a

Figure 22.2. DAU Data Mart

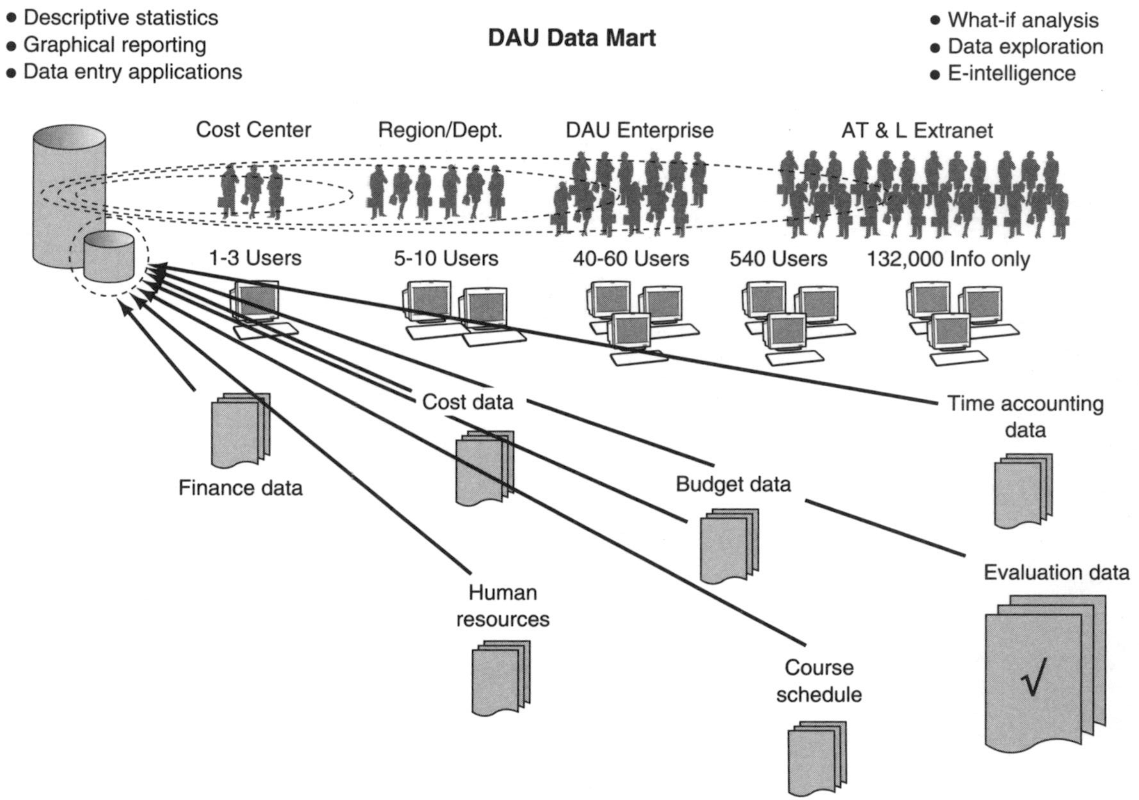

DAU Data Mart

- Descriptive statistics
- Graphical reporting
- Data entry applications

- What-if analysis
- Data exploration
- E-intelligence

Cost Center
Region/Dept.
DAU Enterprise
AT & L Extranet

1-3 Users
5-10 Users
40-60 Users
540 Users
132,000 Info only

Finance data

Human resources

Cost data

Budget data

Course schedule

Time accounting data

Evaluation data

tool that is a best-in-class web-enabled evaluation system (Metrics that Matter), developed by Knowledge Advisors. This web-based learning evaluation capability allows DAU leadership to quickly gauge how effective learning is and cost-effectively measure training impact on the individual, supervisors, and organizational performance in real time. This system provides a robust real-time analytical capability that enables leaders to make better business decisions in regard to learning products and services.

AT&L Performance Learning Model (PLM)

We evaluate and receive feedback for each of our products and services. The centerpiece of the DAU experience is the AT&L Performance Learning Model, depicted in Figure 22.3.

Figure 22.3. Performance Learning Model (PLM)

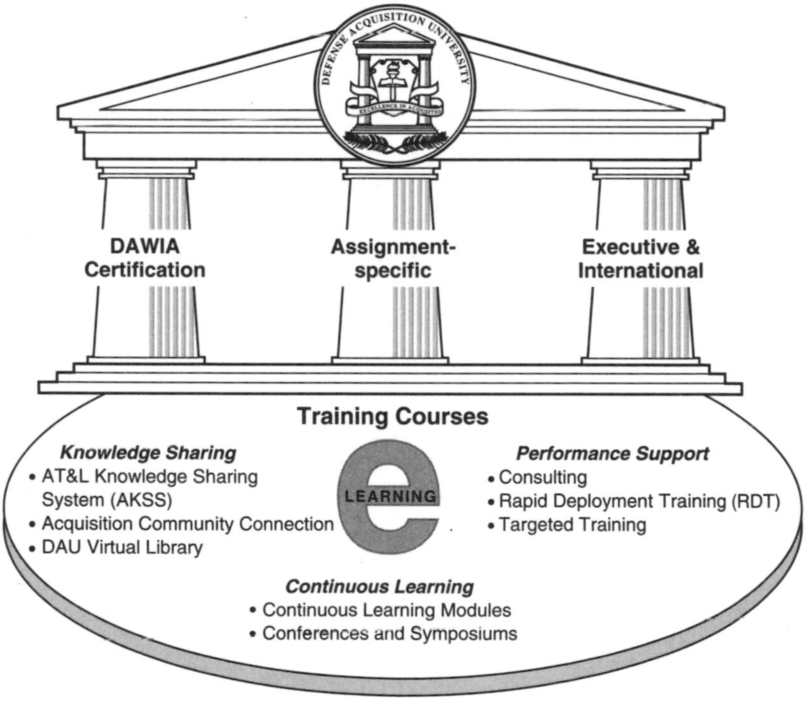

This award-winning, best-practice, and overarching learning strategy provides each member of the AT&L workforce with more control over his or her career-long learning opportunities. The PLM extends the learning experience from traditional classroom instruction to a variety of learning solutions that are available anytime, anywhere. The PLM components include: Training through web-enabled, hybrid, and classroom courses that include case-based instruction aimed at developing critical thinking skills; Continuous learning with self-paced, relevant training modules, available 24/7, to help meet continuous learning requirements and improve job performance; Performance support with rapidly delivered business solutions offered to students and their organizations and supplementing the classroom experience through on-site consulting, targeted training, and rapid deployment training; and Knowledge sharing through the AT&L Knowledge Sharing System and the Acquisition Community Connection, to connect with experts, peers, and technical resources.

Training Courses: Certification, Assignment-Specific, and Executive and International

Our more than 1,200 course offerings per year are delivered in a classroom setting at one of our five regional campuses, or ten satellite locations, or via the internet. Courses are also taught at customer sites. At the end of each course, we survey students on several aspects of the course, including course content, course work, faculty, and job applicability. For in-resident courses, students take the survey online while they are still in the classroom. In our distance learning courses (more than 300 offerings per year), students must answer the survey before they can print the course completion certificate. Faculty members and course managers have full access to the results for their courses. The faculty, academic deans, and course managers review results and work to address shortfalls. Upon completion of the course and after the students are back at work for sixty days, for selected courses we e-mail students and their managers follow-up surveys. After six months, for selected courses we attempt to determine the impact of the training on the organization.

Continuous Learning: Continuous Learning Modules

Our Continuous Learning Center (CLC) contains self-paced continuous learning modules that are available 24/7 to help meet continuous learning requirements and improve job performance. At the end of each DAU-developed Continuous Learning Module is a course feedback survey. Students must complete this survey before they receive their completion certificate. Course owners review the survey results for their course and incorporate improvements. Noncourse comments or site-specific technical questions abut the CLC are e-mailed to our help desk.

Performance Support: Consulting, Targeted Training, and Rapid Deployment Training

Our performance support services are provided to DoD and other government agencies to help them resolve individual project and agency-level acquisition problems. We also provide immediate training on new policy initiatives. At the end of each consulting effort, the customer is asked to provide feedback. Following each targeted training event, students respond to an online course survey similar to the one used for our certification and assignment-specific courses. DAU reviews the results for both consulting and targeted training efforts and incorporates improvements.

Knowledge Sharing: AT&L Knowledge Sharing System, Acquisition Community Connection, and Virtual Library

DAU hosts the AT&L Knowledge Sharing System (AKSS) and the Acquisition Community Connection (ACC). AKSS is the central gateway for all AT&L resources and information. ACC is the collaborative arm of AKSS, with a variety of knowledge communities (of practice). Users of our knowledge-sharing systems are asked to provide feedback through online comment areas. On the AKSS home page, they can just click the "We want your feedback—again" button. Users of the ACC can provide feedback through the "Contact us" link. DAU reviews comments weekly and incorporates improvements and suggestions as appropriate.

DAU Evaluation Survey Instruments

We adapted templates from Knowledge Advisors for Level 1, 3 and 4 and have their permission to share examples of our template.

Level 1—Reaction

End-of-class surveys are required from all our students in order to graduate from our courses, whether they be class, hybrid, or online. These surveys focus questions in specific subject areas, such as faculty performance in the classroom, course content/material, learning effectiveness, business results, and environment. Each focus area has multiple questions to provide for further drill down on the data, thus allowing DAU to make more informed decisions for its survey results. When DAU managers review the data from our class survey, they can do so in many different slices or dimensions. For example, DAU management can drill down into course results by region or across all regions. Survey results can be distilled down by question category or down to specific question responses. Our survey results are accessible within twenty-four hours of completion of the class by the faculty who taught the class, course managers who are responsible for that specific course, center directors for curriculum development to assess the course content results, and our deans, who are responsible for the overall delivery of all of our classes. Paper copy examples of our level 1 survey instruments are displayed in Exhibit 22.1 for both class and web-based courses.

Level 2—Learning

For all our certifications courses, we require content testing—both precourse diagnostics and end-of-course assessments. Precourse diagnostics are used to tailor delivery to meet the learning needs of the students and to help determine the extent of learning when compared to the end-of-course tests. Students must also achieve an 80 percent score on an end-of-course test to graduate. In addition, in senior-level courses that include case-based scenarios, individual student performance is evaluated by faculty with one-on-one feedback provided. Test scores are also analyzed and tracked for curricula and faculty development purposes. For low scores, we work with students to provide remediation as necessary.

Level 3—Behavior

To determine if a change in behavior has occurred attributable to the training program or learning activity, we also survey students (and

Exhibit 22.1. DAU Classroom Training—End-of-Class Survey★

Please help us improve the training program by responding to our brief survey below.

RESPONDENT INFORMATION

1. What is your primary Career Field? (Please check only one)
- O Auditing
- O Facilities Eng.
- O Life Cycle Logistics
- O Business, CE & Fin Mgmt
- O Industrial/Contract Property Mgmt
- O Production, QA & Man.
- O Contracting
- O Information Technology
- O Program Management
- O Purchasing
- O Systems Engineering
- O SPRDE & S&T
- O Test & Evaluation
- O Don't Know or NA

2. How many years of experience do you have in your career field?
- O Less than 1   O 1 to 2   O 2 to 5   O 5 to 10
- O 10 to 15   O More than 15

3. What level of DAWIA certification did you have in your primary career field prior to attending this course?
- O Don't know   O None   O Level I   O Level II   O Level III

4. Are you:
- O Military (Active)   O Civilian Government   O Industry

5. Please identify from one of the three sections below your current Military, GS or ACQ DEMO position grade level:

Active duty military personnel:
- O E 1-5   O E 6-7   O E 8-9   O O 1-3   O O 4-5   O 06   O GO

GS Personnel:
- O GS 1-5   O GS 6-8   O GS 9-11   O GS 12-13
- O GS 14-15   O SES

Acq Demo Personnel:
- O Broadband: I   O Broadband: II   O Broadband: III
- O Broadband: IV   O SES

INSTRUCTOR

Strongly Agree   Strongly Disagree
7 6 5 4 3 2 1 n/a

6. The instructor was knowledgeable about the subject.   O O O O O O O O
7. The instructor was prepared and organized for the class.   7 6 5 4 3 2 1 n/a   O O O O O O O O
8. Participants were encouraged to take part in class discussions.   7 6 5 4 3 2 1 n/a   O O O O O O O O

INSTRUCTOR (Continued)

Strongly Agree   Strongly Disagree
7 6 5 4 3 2 1 n/a

9. The instructor was responsive to participants' needs and questions.   O O O O O O O O
10. The instructor's energy and enthusiasm kept the participants actively engaged.   7 6 5 4 3 2 1 n/a   O O O O O O O O
11. On-the-job application of each objective was discussed during the course.   7 6 5 4 3 2 1 n/a   O O O O O O O O

ENVIRONMENT

Strongly Agree   Strongly Disagree
7 6 5 4 3 2 1 n/a

12. The physical environment was conducive to learning.   O O O O O O O O

COURSEWARE

Strongly Agree   Strongly Disagree
7 6 5 4 3 2 1 n/a

13. The scope of the material was appropriate to meet my needs.   O O O O O O O O
14. The material was organized logically.   7 6 5 4 3 2 1 n/a   O O O O O O O O
15. The examples presented helped me to understand the content.   7 6 5 4 3 2 1 n/a   O O O O O O O O
16. The participant materials (manual, presentation handouts, etc.) will be useful on the job.   7 6 5 4 3 2 1 n/a   O O O O O O O O
17. The case studies and exercises added value to my learning.   7 6 5 4 3 2 1 n/a   O O O O O O O O

LEARNING EFFECTIVENESS

Strongly Agree   Strongly Disagree
7 6 5 4 3 2 1 n/a

18. I learned new knowledge and skills from this training.   O O O O O O O O
19. The guest speakers (from outside DAU) were effective in contributing to my learning in this course.   7 6 5 4 3 2 1 n/a   O O O O O O O O
20. Rate your INCREASE in skill level or knowledge of this content before versus after the training. A 0% is no increase and a 100% is very significant increase.
   □ 0% □ 10% □ 20% □ 30% □ 40% □ 50% □ 60% □ 70% □ 80% □ 90% □ 100%

JOB IMPACT

Strongly Agree   Strongly Disagree
7 6 5 4 3 2 1 n/a

21. I will be able to apply the knowledge and skills learned in this class to my job.   O O O O O O O O
22. What percent of your total work time requires the knowledge and skills presented in this training? Check only one.
   □ 0% □ 10% □ 20% □ 30% □ 40% □ 50% □ 60% □ 70% □ 80% □ 90% □ 100%
23. On a scale of 0% (not at all) to 100% (extremely critical), how critical is applying the content of this training to your job success? Check only one.
   □ 0% □ 10% □ 20% □ 30% □ 40% □ 50% □ 60% □ 70% □ 80% □ 90% □ 100%

★This survey is adapted from Knowledge Advisors.

(continued)

their managers) when they are back on the job, usually three months after course completion.

Level 4—Results

Over the years, we have found that it is difficult to attribute an organization's success to just our training products and services. Other significant factors also contribute and might even be the key determinant, such as reorganization, recruiting, visionary leadership,

Exhibit 22.1. DAU Classroom Training—End-of-Class Survey* *(continued)*

JOB IMPACT (Continued)

24. What percent of new knowledge and skills learned from this training do you estimate you will directly apply to your job? Check only one.
□ 0% □ 10% □ 20% □ 30% □ 40% □ 50% □ 60% □ 70% □ 80% □ 90% □ 100%

BUSINESS RESULTS

Strongly Agree   Strongly Disagree

    7 6 5 4 3 2 1 n/a

25. This training will improve my job   o o o o o o o o
performance.

26. Given all factors, including this training, estimate how much your job performance related to the course subject matter will improve.
□ 0% □ 10% □ 20% □ 30% □ 40% □ 50% □ 60% □ 70% □ 80% □ 90% □ 100%

27. Based on your response to the prior question, estimate how much of the improvement will be a direct result of this training. (For example if you feel that half of your improvement is a direct result of the training, enter 50% here.)
□ 0% □ 10% □ 20% □ 30% □ 40% □ 50% □ 60% □ 70% □ 80% □ 90% □ 100%

28. This training will have a significant impact on: (check all that apply)

□ increasing quality   □ increasing productivity □ increasing employee satisfaction
□ decreasing costs   □ increasing sales   □ increasing customer satisfaction
□ decreasing cycle time □ decreasing risk

RETURN ON INVESTMENT

Strongly Agree   Strongly Disagree

    7 6 5 4 3 2 1 n/a

29. This training was a worthwhile   o o o o o o o o
investment in my career development.

    7 6 5 4 3 2 1 n/a

30. This training was a worthwhile   o o o o o o o o
investment for my employer.

What about this class was *most* useful to you?

_____

_____

What about this class was *least* useful to you?

_____

_____

How can we improve the training to make it more relevant to your job?

_____

_____

I would recommend that my colleagues take this course.
o Yes o No

_____

What is your overall opinion of this course?

_____

_____

Hawthorne effect, and so on. Survey questions remain fairly subjective even though quantified as value judgments. ROI data is equally suspect regardless of algorithms and clever manipulations. However, we are interested in ROI-type data, but it is not the sole determinant at DAU.

Each quarter during the Enterprise Performance Review and Analysis (EPRA), DAU reviews the quarter's performance and progress for all performance targets and selected operational metrics. Our evaluation survey data is an important part of this review. An example of the type of report we use for our reviews is shown in Figure 22.4.

Figure 22.4. DAU "Spider" Diagram Display

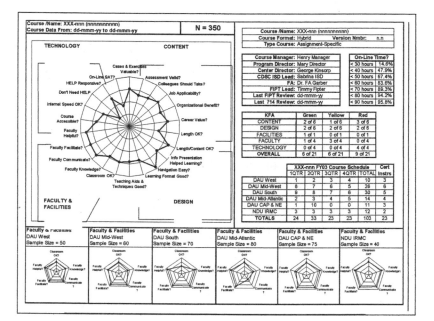

Value-Added Contributions

It is vital to show substantial evidence of "value-added contributions" to our stakeholders. We compile a compelling rationale using evidence from many sources to portray results. Though our survey data is important, summary data from many different sources is more important as we measure the total contribution across the enterprise. To link budget allocation with demonstrated results, DAU uses a formal enterprise performance review and analysis run by a resource council to review program performance based on past performance, observable results, and operational efficiencies. At the end of the year, an enterprise-wide program review is conducted during the last quarter's EPRA, and management decisions are made in regard to past performance and in regard to next year's annual performance plan and program funding and continuance. Improvements brought about by the management processes described in this chapter yield the timely and reliable financial management data necessary to achieve the remarkable results DAU has achieved. As a result, management decisions are made in the context of past trend data, and financial/personnel resources are allocated as appropriate.

An example of management's response to trend data results is in the area of course content. If survey results consistently over time show that a specific course's content is rated low in the area of currency or value of the materials on the job, a team of curriculum developers, teaching faculty, and course managers meet to reconfigure the course content in time for the next scheduled class data. Some specifics that are addressed include tracking and reporting macro models, comparative analyses and benchmarking by other organizations, and internally comparing courses, regions, faculty, delivery methods, and environments.

Building Compelling Evidence of Results for Our Stakeholders

By comparing trends in key areas such as evaluation scores, benchmarking metrics, growth in student throughput, student travel costs, and other comparatives, we look for the total enterprise's multiyear results and trends. We have been benchmarked by over eighty organizations, and through our survey application service provider (as a part of their services), we also use their survey database for comparative purposes with other learning organizations. Able to successfully meet its challenge of serving significantly increasing numbers of students with no increase in budget, DAU has improved in many areas.

Since 1998 (with a relatively flat learning and development budget investment per year) we have increased our students trained from 33,000 to 92,000 per year while at the same time reducing the faulty/staff from 643 to 540 and our student travel costs from $31,000 to $17,000 per year. Over this time, the average training cost per student has declined by 42 percent—a reduction of $1,300 per student. This translates to a projected savings in the next five years of over $50 million and a faculty savings of $10 million, allowing us to reprioritize resources into e-learning initiatives, curricula modernization, and other greater reach initiatives. Even as our cost per student has been dramatically reduced, the courses have continued to receive high marks from students and supervisors in response to survey questions. This along with our sector leadership recognition as a best-in-class corporate university provides our stakeholders with compelling evidence that DAU makes a considerable value-added contribution to the overall mission of the organization. Our sector leadership recognition can be summarized:

2002 Corporate University Best-in-Class (CUBIC) Awards

- Leader of the Year
- Best Overall Corporate University
- Best Virtual Corporate University / Best Use of Technology
- Runner-up Most Innovative Corporate University

2003—Gold Medal Winner of Brandon Hall Best Practices for e-Learning

2003 and 2004—Winner of the American Society of Training and Development BEST Award (2004 First place among eighty-three organizations worldwide)

2003 Winner of Corporate University Xchange Excellence Award for Measurement

2003—Selected in *Training* Magazine Top 100

2004—Selected by *CLO* Magazine for Two Best Practices

2004—Chief Learning Officer of the Year

Reference

Knowledge Advisors (Metrics That Matter). 222 S. Riverside, Suite 1700, Chicago, IL 60606. 312/423-8750. kbarnett@knowledgeadvisors .com.

Chapter 23

Evaluating an Information Technology Skills Training Program

This evaluation will be of special interest to readers who are looking for concepts, principles, techniques, and forms that they can adapt to similar programs. The case study measures the effectiveness of the program by evaluating at level 1 (reaction), level 2 (learning), and level 3 (behavior). The Questionmark Corporation provided software to assist in the evaluation. Be sure to read the "Summary" and "Recommendations" for ideas you may find useful.

The Regence Group

James C. Baker, e-Learning Specialist, Organizational
Development
Portland, Oregon

The Regence Group is the largest affiliation of health-care plans in the Pacific Northwest/Mountain State region. It includes Regence BlueShield of Idaho, Regence BlueCross BlueShield of Oregon, Regence BlueCross BlueShield of Utah, and Regence BlueShield (in Washington). Collectively, these four plans serve nearly three million people in four states, with more than $6.5 billion in combined revenue as of January 2004.

In 2003 Organizational Development (OD) at Regence gathered training evaluation data of an information technology skills training program for Regence Information Technology Services (RITS) using our online assessment system. RITS participated in a workforce and capacity-building training program administered by the Oregon Department of Community Colleges & Workforce Department (CCWD). The CCWD requested that both the training participants and their supervisors assess the training initially and in follow-up evaluations with an evaluation tool developed by the American Society for Training & Development (ASTD) and based on Kirkpatrick's four-level model. The responses about training, learning, and performance could be compared with other benchmark measures at Regence and at other organizations.

The Regence online training evaluation system employs the Questionmark Perception authoring and web deployment software suite to manage a broad range of classroom and online learning activities, both for individuals or teams. Using the Perception browser-based assessment forms and SQL Server database system, OD conducted online training evaluations of seventeen classes, which instructors delivered in a classroom setting. The training evaluations spanned eight months and produced a total of 490 online assessments.

Regence Online Evaluation Method

In OD at Regence, several assessment authors use the Questionmark Perception software suite to build, deliver, and report training evaluations for internal clients such as RITS. We follow this engagement process with our internal clients:

1. Collaborate on a time frame with mutual roles and responsibilities;
2. Develop and import the question wording, choices, outcomes, and scoring into the authoring tools;
3. Select a template for page layout (images, instructions, questions, submit button, and optional jump-block questions);
4. Test the evaluation in the development environment with the client;
5. Gain client approval and move the evaluation into our production environment for distribution;
6. Create an assessment schedule for participants;

7. Turn on or off the settings for log-on (anonymous or user-name and password), limit of one try, and time limit;
8. Notify the participants about the schedule with a link to their online evaluation; and,
9. At the conclusion of the session, pull the respondent data out of the database management system for analysis and reporting by participant, class, and instructor.

Online Evaluation of Levels 1, 2, and 3

Following our engagement process, OD and RITS Professional Development established a time line for the information technology skills classes with both immediate and follow-up evaluations. For the training assessments of levels 1 (reaction), 2 (learning), and 3 (behavior), we adopted the ASTD evaluation tool to benchmarking training evaluation data. Supplemental questions produced records for reporting evaluation data by participant, class, and instructor for initial and follow-up training evaluations.

Immediately after each class, participants launched our Part A online assessment of level 1 and level 2. In Exhibit 23.1 of this case study, you can see the multilevel Part A evaluation tool that we adopted from ASTD and then supplemented with other questions for reporting. Part A questions consisted of a 1–5 scale to measure reactions to statements about these categories:

- administration and logistics (prerequisites, facilities and equipment);
- content (understood the objectives, the objectives were met);
- design (method of delivery, materials, length of class time, organization);
- instruction (satisfaction with instructor);
- perceived impact (knowledge and skills increased; applicability to current job; applicability for preparing participant for other jobs in the company; training helped toward other jobs in the company); and,
- overall satisfaction with the class.

Exhibit 23.1. Part A Online Assessment Levels 1 and 2

INSTRUCTIONS: When you have completed this evaluation, click Submit.

Class name and course objectives

Your name:

Instructor name:

Questions

Choices: a. Strongly Agree b. Agree c. Neither d. Disagree e. Strongly Disagree

1. I had the knowledge and/or skills required to start this course.
2. The facilities and equipment were favorable to learning.
3. I was able to take this course when I needed it.
4. I clearly understood the course objectives.
5. The course met all of its stated objectives.
6. The way this course was delivered (such as classroom, computer, and video) was an effective way for me to learn this subject matter.
7. Participant materials (handouts, workbooks, etc.) were useful during the course.
8. I had enough time to learn the subject matter covered in the course.
9. The course content was logically organized.
10. I had an opportunity to give input to the course design or content.
11. Overall, I was satisfied with the instructor(s).
12. My knowledge and/or skills increased as a result of this course.
13. The knowledge and/or skills gained through this course are directly applicable to my job.
14. This course has helped prepare me for other job opportunities within the company or industry.
15. Overall, I was satisfied with this course.

Several weeks after each class we distributed the Part B assessment (see Exhibit 23.2). In our online Part B assessments, we asked participants to provide their names and then to answer questions about their:

- use of skills from training (opportunity to use the training, actual use of the training);
- confidence in ability to perform (extent of increase in confidence resulting from this training);

Exhibit 23.2. Part B Levels 1, 2, and 3 Online Assessment

INSTRUCTIONS: When you have completed this evaluation, click Submit.

Course name and objectives

Your name:

Questions

Choices: a. To a very great extent b. To a great extent c. To a moderate extent
d. To a small extent e. Not at all/never/rarely applicable f. Not applicable

1. To what extent did you use the knowledge and/or skills prior to attending this course?
2. To what extent have you had the opportunity to use the knowledge and/or skills presented in this course?
3. To what extent have you actually used the knowledge and/or skills presented in this course, after completing the course?
4. To what extent has your confidence in using the knowledge and/or skills increased as a result of this course?
5. To what extent did you receive the assistance necessary in preparing you for this course?
6. To what extent has the content of this course accurately reflected what happens on the job?
7. To what extent have you had access to the necessary resources (e.g., equipment and information) to apply the knowledge and/or skills on your job?
8. To what extent have you received help, through coaching and/or feedback, with applying the knowledge and/or skills on the job?
9. As a result of this course, my performance on the course objectives has changed by (%).
10. As a result of this course, my overall job performance has changed by (%).

- barriers to and enablers of transfer (training accurately reflected the job, access to necessary resources to apply the training, extent of coaching and other assistance); and,
- measures of impact (percentage changes in production and performance).

Besides the online Part B follow-up data from participants, RITS gathered follow-up training evaluations from their supervisors as part of the ASTD evaluation tool.

Table 23.1. Part A Question Choices, Descriptive Statistics, and Significance

Question Choices with Scores	Descriptive Statistics
Strongly Agree (5 points)	Highest: 4.83
Agree (4 points)	Lowest: 4.37
Neither (3 points)	Mean: 4.77
Disagree (2 points)	Mode: 4.83
Strongly Disagree (1 point)	

Training Evaluation Findings

Part A Findings

What are the results of the training evaluation in Part A? Scores indicate a consensus about the high ratings (see Table 23.1). The highest average (4.83) equals the most frequent value or mode (4.83). The mean or average (4.77) is only .05 points away from both. The results reflect very positive satisfaction on Kirkpatrick's levels 1 and 2.

The Part A training evaluation consisted of fifteen questions (see Table 23.2). One hundred thirty-nine (139) of one hundred fifty-one (151) online assessments were returned for a response rate of 92.10 percent. This return rate was above our expected two–thirds response rate because RITS Professional Development monitored participants and encouraged completion.

The consensus about the multilevel evaluation questions in Part A forms a nearly straight-line graphic (see Figure 23.1), with a relatively narrow range of 4.83 to 4.63 on a five-point scale. The lowest average (4.37) was for question 3: "I was able to take the course when I needed it" is an exception. The training schedule for these participants did not provide them as much opportunity for personal choice as they wanted.

Table 23.2. Part A Question Score and Ranking

Question Wording	Average	Ranking
1. I had the knowledge and/or skills required to start this course.	4.80	
2. The facilities and equipment were favorable to learning.	4.80	
3. I was able to take this course when I needed it.	4.37	Low
4. I clearly understood the course objectives.	4.63	
5. The course met all of its stated objectives.	4.83	
6. The way this course was delivered (such as classroom, computer, and video) was an effective way for me to learn this subject matter.	4.83	
7. Participant materials (handouts, workbooks, etc.) were useful during the course.	4.83	
8. I had enough time to learn the subject matter covered in the course.	4.77	
9. The course content was logically organized.	4.83	
10. I had an opportunity to give input to the course design or content.	4.80	
11. Overall, I was satisfied with the instructor(s).	4.83	
12. My knowledge and/or skills increased as a result of this course.	4.77	
13. The knowledge and/or skills gained through this course are directly applicable to my job.	4.83	
14. This course has helped prepare me for other job opportunities within the company or industry.	4.83	
15. Overall, I was satisfied with this course.	4.80	

Part B Findings

The question items in Part B have different wording, choices, outcomes, and scoring than question items in Part A. For example, Part A contains five-scale scoring whereas Part B scoring uses six-scale scoring. Any attempts at comparative analysis of the two parts must overcome the differences in question items in Part A immediately after the training and in Part B several weeks or months later. The Part B train-

Figure 23.1. Part A Average Scores by Line Graph

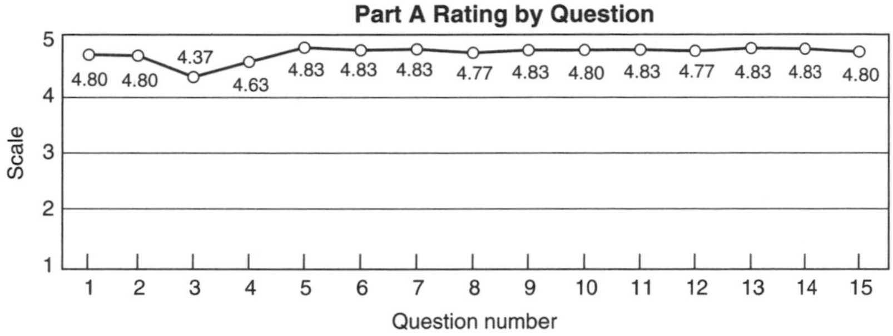

ing evaluation consisted of questions: questions 1–8 and then questions 9–10 to measure performance impact (see Exhibit 23.2).

Questions 1–8. Regarding Kirkpatrick's levels 1, 2, and 3, is there a positive consensus in the Part B 1–8 results? Maintaining a pattern from Part A, the participants show agreement and high ratings in the follow-up training evaluation (see Table 23.3).

Of the 336 online assessments, 333 were returned for a response rate of 98.10 percent for Part B questions 1–8. The rate is higher than the Part A response rate of 92.10 percent because of increased communication with participants and their supervisors by RITS Professional Development.

The mean (5.68) and mode (5.68) are high on a six-scale and are the same value (see Table 23.4), which is only .04 points from the highest average (5.72). The results in the first eight questions in Part B reflect very positive satisfaction on Kirkpatrick's levels 1, 2, and 3.

Table 23.3. Part B Questions 1–8: Question Choices, Descriptive Statistics, and Significance

Question Choices with Scores	Descriptive Statistics
To a very great extent (5 points)	Highest: 5.72
To a great extent (4 points)	Lowest: 5.63
To a moderate extent (3 points)	Mean: 5.68
To a small extent (2 points)	Mode: 5.68
Not at all/never/rarely applicable (1 point)	
Not applicable (0 points)	

Table 23.4. Part B Questions 1–8: Scores and Ranking

Question Wording	Average Score	Ranking
1. To what extent did you use the knowledge and/or skills prior to attending this course?	5.68	
2. To what extent have you had the opportunity to use the knowledge and/or skills presented in this course?	5.68	
3. To what extent have you actually used the knowledge and/or skills presented in this course, after completing the course?	5.69	
4. To what extent has your confidence in using the knowledge and/or skills increased as a result of this course?	5.72	High
5. To what extent did you receive the assistance necessary in preparing you for this course?	5.70	
6. To what extent has the content of this course accurately reflected what happens on the job?	5.63	Low
7. To what extent have you had access to the necessary resources (e.g., equipment and information) to apply the knowledge and/or skills on your job?	5.65	
8. To what extent have you received help, through coaching and/or feedback, with applying the knowledge and/or skills on the job?	5.67	

The graphical representation of this data forms a fairly straight line, one where the range is from 5.72 to 5.65 on a scale of 6. There is considerable agreement and a positive evaluation shown from the data questions 1–8 in Part B (see Figure 23.2).

Questions 9–10. Following questions 1–8 in Part B there are two questions on job performance (Table 23.5). For questions 9–10, 319 of 333 online assessments were returned for a response rate of 95.80 percent, another high response rate maintained by the good communications from RITS Professional Development with particpants and their supervisors.

What are the performance impact measures? For question 9: "As a result of this course, my performance on the course objectives has changed by 54%." For question 10: "As a result of this course, my overall job performance has changed by 24%."

Figure 23.2. Average Scores by Line Graph

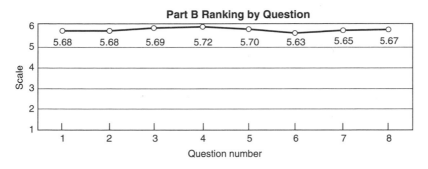

Table 23.5. Part B Questions 9–10: Scores and Ranking

9. As a result of this course, my performance on the course objectives has changed by (%).	54%
10. As a result of this course, my overall job performance has changed by (%).	24%

The findings allow us to conclude from the online training evaluations that those participants in Parts A and B and their supervisors in Part B both evaluated the training for RITS very positively. Using Kirkpatrick's model, there is significant consensus that the training was satisfying (level 1), effective (level 2), and applicable (level 3) in improving the performance of the participants.

Summary

This case study employed an ASTD training evaluation tool and online assessment methods in assessing an information technology training program. These tools and methods combined to achieve several goals:

1. Standardized question items from ASTD, based on Kirkpatrick's model, provided standardized data types for benchmark comparisons by instructors, training managers, and budget analysts;

2. Combination of Part A and Part B assessments reduced the number of training evaluations by participants, while covering levels 1, 2, and 3; and,

3. Quick and efficient online assessment processes with our client, who followed up with scheduled participants, produced timely assessments and reports and helped to produce unexpectedly high return rates.

Recommendations

In order to make training evaluation more effective for your clients, whether they are internal or external, you might give attention to these three practices.

1. When collaborating with clients to solve human performance problems, you can recognize that training is a relevant solution, and, if that is so, establish a value exchange to give (training evaluation for the client) and receive (expanded competencies on your assessment team in the Part A and B evaluation tool from ASTD, using levels 1, 2, and 3 training evaluations).

2. When you have to achieve even more desirable conditions in a training program, determine whether the two-part, multi-level assessments can be a relevant component in your action planning to close the gap.

3. When you have an action plan to implement two-part, multilevel assessments, identify how you can adopt assessment software to gather and organize the relevant training measurements to achieve an exchange of value with your clients.

Reference

Questionmark Corporation, 5 Hillandale Avenue, Stamford, CT 06902.

Chapter 24

Evaluating a Performance Improvement Program

This impressive case study evaluates programs at all four of Kirkpatrick's levels plus return on investment (ROI). Of special interest is the approach to improving communication. Not only will the case be of benefit to those involved in selling, it will also be of interest to all readers because of the forms that are included. Some of these can probably be adapted to your organization regardless of the type and size.

Toyota Motor Sales, U.S.A., Inc.

The University of Toyota
Judy E. Brooke—Supervisor, Measurement & Evaluation
Gusti Lowenberg—Manager E-Learning and M&E
Torrance, California

Organizational Profile

The University of Toyota represents an unusually forward-thinking learning organization with a fast-track history of organizational performance. At the root of the university is a rigorous effort to enhance overall sales and customer satisfaction by continually improving the performance of Toyota associates and dealers through lifelong learning. The ultimate goal of the university is to support the vision of Toyota Motor Sales (TMS), which is to be the most successful and respected automotive company in America.

The university emerged through Toyota's New Era Initiatives—an organization-wide blueprint of the future that revolves around the themes of growth, change, and development. The latter aspect of the initiative—professional development—was the seed of the university. This aspect represents the imperative to make associate and dealer development the engine of organizational excellence and industry superiority. Learning and performance improvement are recognized and rewarded through a variety of programs.

College of Dealer Education and Development (CDED)

Operating as a small service organization within the University of Toyota, the College of Dealer Education and Development is dedicated to supporting the needs of 1,400 Toyota, Lexus, and Scion dealers and over 100,000 dealership personnel. Within these dealerships, the College products and services are focused on core operations including Management, Sales, Finance and Insurance, Parts and Service, and General Administration.

The university uses a variety of education and training delivery methods, ranging from traditional, instructor-led classroom courses, conferences, seminars, and meetings to online virtual classrooms, computer-based training, and formal, documented on-the-job training. Regardless of the particular delivery mechanism, the driving innovative learning principles are expressed as "tell me, show me, let me practice, and test me." Over 2,500 class days are delivered per year along with performance consulting, e-learning, and evaluation services. The university utilizes a state-of-the-art corporate learning center and training facilities throughout the United States for delivering retail professional development courses and dealership personnel certification programs.

There are eighty full-time college associates at their corporate office located in Torrance, California. In addition, independent contractors, agency-based contingent workers for administrative support, and outsourced functions such as delivery administration are an integral part of college operations.

Evaluating a Performance Improvement Program

A large and respected automotive dealership group located on the East Coast identified the need to improve their service and financial performance. In particular, the Dealer Principal identified a need to improve the following service and financial metrics across the dealership group:

- Repair Order (RO) Count
- Labor Sales
- Average Sales/Repair Order
- Operations Count
- Average Operations Per Repair Order
- Technician Labor Hours
- Labor Sales
- Average Estimated Labor Rate (ELR)
- Vehicle Service Survey (VSS) Scores
- Lexus Service Survey (LSS) Scores

After clarifying the desired and current business results, the Measurement & Evaluation (M&E) team carefully assessed the primary service job functions, associated tasks, workflow processes, and general work environment. The key job functions responsible for service performance within the dealership group included service managers, assistant service managers (ASMs), and technician team leads. A combination of interviews and document analysis was used. The Dealer Principal agreed to allow access to financial data before and after training to enhance our analysis. The gap between the desired and current level of performance was determined to be a result of inadequate knowledge and skills, inefficient workflow processes, and an absence of effective management coaching.

As a result of the upfront analysis, a performance improvement solution was designed and presented to the Dealer Principal. In general, the intent was to send all service managers and assistant service managers from all twenty-eight dealerships in their dealer group through a comprehensive, five-week leader-led immersion training program that integrated process and job-related improvements. The specific subjects addressed are:

Power of Communication. To build a foundation for increasing overall customer satisfaction, participants learned how to use the LACE™ technique to communicate more effectively in day-to-day professional and personal activities. Objectives included:

- Value the importance of good communication in your dealings with team members, customers, and personal contacts
- Employ the components of the LACE™ process to make your daily interactions more effective
- Use "active listening" techniques and identify possible meanings behind nonverbal communication
- Use open-ended questions to get to the core reasons behind a person's concerns and use the "acid test" to resolve any open issues or concerns
- Create a Personal Action Plan and commit to using LACE™ on the job (see Exhibit 24.1 for a sample Action Plan that was used in all four classes)

ASMs in the Service Process. In this portion of the training, participants learned how their performance affects others at their dealership and how they can make a dramatic impact on retaining loyal customers. More specifically, they learned about and practiced effective communication and customer handling skills; and they practiced writing clear, concise repair orders that accurately document the process. Objectives included:

- Recognizing how your performance affects the customer, your dealership, and Toyota
- Writing clear, concise repair orders that accurately document the process while meeting legal guidelines
- Handling several customers at once, while making each one feel welcome
- Ensuring customer satisfaction through an effective delivery, in which you verify that work was completed and explain repairs and costs
- Following-up with customers to ensure their satisfaction and arrange future services
- Effectively communicating the status of repairs with your dealership team as well as with the customer

Exhibit 24.1. 30-Day Action Plan

Action to Be Taken in the Next 30 Days	People to Involve	Date to Complete	Results Expected

Managing Service Workflow. To help control workload in a high-stress environment, participants learned techniques for making sound decisions, even "when the pressure is on," through simulations and team role-plays with their peers. Objectives included:

- Organizing your schedule and managing time more efficiently at each step in the service process
- Preplanning your day using a comprehensive "to do" list that helps you prioritize tasks and track daily activities

- Using a production schedule to track appointments and vehicle status
- Managing a busy service drive while simultaneously writing effective Repair Orders
- Dispatching work based on latest start time
- Increasing customer satisfaction and retention by communicating more effectively with customers and associates

Consultative Service Selling. To increase sales and customer loyalty by developing relationships with customers through a consultative approach, participants learned how to gain the trust of customers so that the customers would rely on Toyota for advice and recommendations for service. Objectives included:

- Establishing relationships with customers that resulted in customer loyalty and retention
- Identifying appropriate sales opportunities at each stage in the service process
- Using the LACE™ technique to gather information and educate the customer
- Effectively explaining the features, functions, and benefits of maintenance and repairs to customers
- Identifying and overcoming customer objections using effective consulting skills
- Using appropriate methods to close service sales based on customer preferences
- Establishing clear customer expectations about additional service needs resulting from diagnosis and inspection
- Developing and using a tickler file to contact customers for scheduling of recommended services and future maintenance needs

Summary of Findings/Recommendations

M&E also recommended getting new hires immediately into training so that they have an opportunity to incorporate the new processes into their regular routine. This was designed to ensure that all the department employees conduct business in the same way to achieve the same outcome.

M&E also felt strongly that immersion-type training (defined as a complete department and their management attending the same training within a relatively short period of time) could produce positive departmentwide results. More specifically:

- The exit velocity gained by dealership immersion training has the potential to actually make a difference in a dealership's process and business indicators when the dealership team can get together and make decisions to implement department-wide changes.
- Making constructive changes in department processes can reduce stress, which then positively impacts attitudes of employees, even when the change does not necessarily increase their pay.
- The ASM training should have a positive impact on the ASMs and improve their performance as well as positively impacting the team leads and technicians.
- It is critical for managers to attend classes that their employees attend, especially if the classes recommend process changes that may prove to be almost impossible to implement if management does not buy into the change.

Levels of Evaluation

Overview

The Measurement and Evaluation team seized the opportunity to study the results on performance that could be realized when an entire department simultaneously experienced the same training, process improvement, and management coaching.

To prepare for the evaluation project the M&E team developed:

- An analysis of the selected classes, identifying each learning objective and correlating it to the different metrics and activities that would be associated with the project (see Exhibit 24.2 for the matrix).
- A plan to establish data collection (see Exhibit 24.3)
- A communication plan for internal and external stakeholders (see Exhibit 24.4)

Exhibit 24.2. Class Learning Objective Matrix

University of Toyota

Course	Learning Objective	ASM Observation	RO Analysis	ASM Interview	Customer Interviews	VSS/LSS Question	SM Interview	Team Ldr Interview	CRM Interview	Effective Labor Rate	Labor Sales	Lines per RO	Total Hours	Gross Profit	Avg. Sales per RO
ASMs in the Service Process	List primary and secondary internal team contact			X			X								
	Use telephone and e-mail appropriately to communicate with customers at each step of the process	X	X	X			X								
	Schedule customer appointments (gather customer information; identify and document service needs; track appt. times)	X		X	X	2	X			X	X	X	X	X	X
	Greet customers by name	X		X	X	3	X								
	Use LACE to communicate effectively	X		X	X	3	X			X	X	X	X	X	X
	Gather/verify customer information	X													
	Gather/verify VIN and mileage	X	X				X								
	Ask open-ended questions	X		X	X	3	X	X							
	Document customer requests on RO	X	X	X		3	X								
	Check service history files to ID previous repairs and recommend maintenance	X		X			X	X		X	X	X	X	X	X
	Use TDN to gather service history info (DOFU, campaigns, warranty)	X	X	X			X	X		X	X	X	X	X	X
	Verify warranty and service agreement coverage	X	X	X			X			X	X	X	X	X	X
	Agree on a time to call customers to discuss RO	X	X	X	X		X		X						
	Establish appropriate promise time	X	X	X	X		X		X						
	Assure Install "courtesy items" in vehicle before moved	X													
	Review Tech notes on RO for completeness & clarity	X	X	X			X	X	X						
	Describe diagnosis and repair to customers	X		X	X	6	X								
	Update customers on vehicle status	X		X	X		X								
	Document diagnosis and repair info on RO	X	X	X		3		X							
	Verify work on vehicle is complete (QC)	X		X			X								
	Verify completeness of RO	X	X	X			X								
	Explain completed work and costs to customers	X	X	X	X	6	X								

294

Exhibit 24.2. Class Learning Objective Matrix (*continued*)

Course	Learning Objective	ASM Observation	RO Analysis	ASM Interview	Customer Interviews	VSS/LSS Question	SM Interview	Team Ldr Interview	CRM Interview	Effective Labor Rate	Labor Sales	Lines per RO	Total Hours	Gross Profit	Avg. Sales per RO
	Apply delivery standards to active, telephone, and after-hours deliveries	X					X								
	Follow-up with customers to assure satisfaction			X		7	X								
Managing Your Workday	Explain how a service dept. makes money under a flat-rate system	X		X			X							X	
	Use a production schedule to track flat rate hour inventory			X			X	X					X		
	Explain the concept of a flat-rate hour inventory			X			X								
	Describe how the sale of flat-rate hours generates gross profit			X			X								
	Record vehicle status throughout the day on Production Schedule	X		X			X								
	Use a "to-do" list to prioritize and track daily activities (list, prioritize, review tasks during day)	X		X			X	X							
	Maintain a neat, customer-friendly work space	X				9									
	Establish a fixed time each day to pre-plan the next day's activities at the end of the previous day	X		X			X								
	Review the to-do list, review carryovers, review appts. Identify potential bottlenecks	X		X			X	X							
	Use an appointment system to schedule appointments	X		X		2	X	X							
	Calculate the svc dept daily capacity in flat rate hours	X		X			X			X	X	X	X	X	X
	Estimate time required for an operation	X		X			X	X							
	Schedule appts based on flat-rate hours (up to 80% of capacity)	X		X			X			X	X	X	X	X	X
	Stagger appointment times	X		X		3	X								
	Confirm customer appts day before	X		X			X								
	Pre-write ROs for appt customers	X		X		3	X								
	Use production schedule to track appts. and vehicle status throughout service process	X		X			X			X	X	X	X	X	X
	Use a time bucket to monitor capacity	X		X			X			X	X	X	X	X	X
	Record carryovers at the end of day	X		X			X	X							
	Record vehicle status throughout the day on Production Schedule	X		X			X								

(*continued*)

Exhibit 24.2. Class Learning Objective Matrix (*continued*)

Course	Learning Objective	ASM Observation	RO Analysis	ASM Interview	Customer Interviews	VSS/LSS Question	SM Interview	Team Ldr Interview	CRM Interview	Effective Labor Rate	Labor Sales	Lines per RO	Total Hours	Gross Profit	Avg. Sales per RO
	Dispatch work based on latest start time	X				4	X	X							
	Prioritize customer contact for authorizations and to communicate status			X			X								
	Monitor work-in-progress to ensure promise times met	X		X		4	X								
	Use a quick write-up sheet to gather complete info	X		X		3	X								
	Use an early bird system for added customer convenience	X													
Consultative Service Selling	Establish relationships with customers based on perceived value to promote customer loyalty	X													
	Identify appropriate sales opportunities at each stage in the service process	X	X			X	X			X	X	X	X	X	X
	Select an appropriate sales approach (on the drive, on the phone) based on customer and dealership preferences	X		X			X								
	Use the LACE technique to gather info and educate customer	X		X	X		X								
	Conduct vehicle walkaround while in service drive	X		X			X								
	Describe benefits of walk-around to customer	X			X										
	Select which customers and vehicles to target for walk-around	X		X			X								
	Describe what to look for during walkaround		X	X			X								
	Describe walkaround results on RO and to customer	X	X	X			X								
	Document walkaround inspection results on RO	X		X			X								
	Communicate walkaround results to customer	X		X		3	X								
	Check service history files to identify maintenance needs (ASM1)	X		X		3	X	X		X	X	X	X	X	X
	Use a service menu to present maintenance needs	X		X		3	X			X	X	X	X	X	X
	Explain features, functions & benefits of maintenance	X		X		3	X			X	X	X	X	X	X
	Quote consistent prices to customers	X		X		3	X								
	Overcome customer concerns regarding price, product and convenience/time	X		X		3/6	X								

Exhibit 24.2. Class Learning Objective Matrix (*continued*)

Learning Objective	ASM Observation	RO Analysis	ASM Interview	Customer Interviews	VSS/LSS Question	SM Interview	Team Ldr Interview	CRM Interview	Effective Labor Rate	Labor Sales	Lines per RO	Total Hours	Gross Profit	Avg. Sales per RO
Obtain customer authorizations for diagnosis & inspection	X		X			X	X							
Use appropriate techniques to close service sales (Acid Test)	X	X	X											
Explain/educate customer about purpose and benefits of diagnosis or inspection	X	X	X											
Establish customer expectations that diagnosis or inspection may result in add'l repair needs/costs	X	X	X											
Offer customer opportunity to pre-authorize repairs	X		X			X	X		X	X	X	X	X	X
Validate technician recommendations thru discussion w/Tech			X				X							
Use telephone or e-mail to present add'l service needs and obtain authorization	X	X	X	X		X			X	X	X	X	X	X
Use telephone or e-mail to present future maintenance needs	X		X	X		X			X	X	X	X	X	X
Describe work completed	X		X	X		X								
Educate customer about importance of future maintenance	X		X	X		X			X	X	X	X	X	X
Determine best time and method for follow-up with customer	X	X	X	X		X								
Offer to contact customer to schedule future maintenance or deferred repairs	X	X	X	X		X			X	X	X	X	X	X

Exhibit 24.3. Evaluating a Performance-Improvement Program: Data Collection Plan

University
of Toyota

		Job Category Affected	Pre-Study	30-Day Follow-Up	120-Day Follow-Up	End of Study
				When Data is Collected:		
1	Service Manager Interviews	Service Managers	X	X		X
2	ASM Interviews	ASMs	X		X	X
3	Team Leader Interviews	Team Leaders	X			X
4	CR Manager Interviews	CR Manager (CRM)	X			X
5	Management Telephone Interviews	Fixed Ops Directors, Svc Mgrs, CRM	X			X
6	Customer Interviews	Selected customers in dealership waiting rooms	X			X
7	RO Analysis	ASMs	X			X
8	ASM Observation Check Lists	ASMs	X			X
9	Action Plan Observations	Service Managers		X		
10	Action Plan Follow-Up	ASMs			X	
11	Customer Complaints from CRM	CR Manager (CRM)	X			X
12	Effective Labor Rate	Service Managers	X			X
13	Labor Dollars	Service Managers	X			X
14	Lines per RO	Service Managers	X			X
15	Technician Hours	Service Managers	X			X
16	Gross Profit	Service Managers	X			X
17	Average Sales per RO	Service Managers	X			X
18	President's Award Winner	Internal	X			X
19	VSS Lights	Internal	X			X
20	Employee Certification Status	Internal	X			X

- A project time line identifying major milestones (see Exhibit 24.5)

To assess behavior and results, the M&E team conducted:

- Pre-training telephone interviews with the service managers (see Exhibit 24.6).
- Pretraining in-dealership observations of ASMs (see Exhibit 24.7 for Observation Checklist).
- Pretraining in-dealership interviews with ASMs/team leaders (see Exhibit 24.8 for ASM interview worksheet and Exhibit 24.9 for team leader interview worksheet).
- Telephone follow-up with managers thirty days after training to determine if ASMs' action items on their individual action plans were being transferred to the job (see Exhibit 24.10 for service manager and ASM follow-up worksheet).
- Telephone interviews with each ASM 120 days after training

Exhibit 24.4. Evaluating a Performance-Improvement Communication Plan

University of Toyota

Communication Plan

Stakeholder Groups	Stakeholder	Type of Communication	09/09/02	09/16/02	09/23/02	09/30/02	10/7-11/4	12/09/02	02/09/02	05/09/02	06/09/02
C	Sales & Marketing	Project Status	Meeting	E-mail	E-mail	E-mail	E-mail	E-mail	E-mail	E-mail	E-mail
		Timeline	Meeting								
		Study Results									Meeting
D	Associate Dean	Project Status	Meeting	E-mail	E-mail	E-mail	E-mail	E-mail	E-mail	E-mail	
		Timeline	Meeting								
		Study Results									Meeting
E	UOT Vice President	Project Status	Phone								
		Study Results									Meeting
D	Facilitators (4)	Project Status		Phone							
		Interviews/Data Gathering		Phone							
		Study Results					Mail				E-mail
	CDED Team	Project Status	E-mail								
		Study Results									Meeting
DEALERSHIP CONTACTS	Dealership Executive Management Staff	Project Status		Phone	Phone	Visit		E-mail	E-mail	E-mail	
		Timeline		Phone							
		Interviews/Data Gathering									
		Study Results									
	Service Managers/ Directors	Project Status			Phone	Mail		E-mail	Phone		Phone
		Interviews/Data Gathering			Phone	Visit					
		Timeline									
	Customer Relations Managers	Project Status			Phone	Visit		E-mail	Phone	Visit	
		Interviews/Data Gathering			Phone						
		Timeline									
	Assistant Service Managers (ASMs)	Project Status			Phone	Visit		E-mail	Phone		
		Interviews/Data Gathering			Phone						
		Timeline									
	Technicians/ Team Leaders	Project Status			Phone	Visit		E-mail	Phone	Visit	
		Interviews/Data Gathering			Phone						
		Timeline									

Project Status includes initial project introduction as well as ongoing status of the overall education evaluation. Everyone will receive a project status with the initial contact; however, not everyone will receive an ongoing project status/update.

Interviews/Data Gathering includes requesting hard data from a number of sources including DMS reports from Service Managers, financial statement data from Business Management, etc.

Study results can be provided on an as-needed/requested basis outside the contacts listed above.

Exhibit 24.5. Evaluating a Performance-Improvement Program: Project Time Line

University of Toyota

Project Timeline

Task	8/26	9/2	9/9	9/16	9/23	9/30	10/7	10/14	10/21	10/28	11/4	11/11	11/18	11/25	12/2
Develop project and communication plans	→→														
Start gathering data	→	→													
Survey fools for first level stakeholder interviews		→→													
Interview facilitators for coaching class			→→												
Conduct phone interview with stakeholders			→→												
Review learning objectives and do gap analysis			→→												
Service Managers attend Coaching class				●											
Develop baseline survey tools				→→											
Develop management coaching tools				→→											
Refine baseline survey tools and conduct additional phone interviews prior to dealer visits					→→										
Conduct gap analysis on ASM courses					→→										
Conduct dealer visits						→									
Conduct Power of Communication							●								
Conduct ASMs in the Service Process									●						
Conduct Managing Your Workday										●					
Conduct Consultative Service Selling											●				
Capture metrics and analyze					←—————————————————————→										
Conduct follow-up dealer visits (180 days-- June, 2003)															6/03
Publish study findings (July, 2003)															7/03
Publish case study (August, 2003)															8/03

to obtain their perspective on learning transfer based on their action plans (see Exhibit 24.11 for ASM follow-up worksheet example).

- In-dealership ASM observation follow-up six months after training (see Exhibit 24.7).
- In-dealership interviews with ASMs, team leads, and cashiers (see Exhibits 24.12, 24.13, and 24.14).

In addition, level 1 feedback was collected and reported to reveal trends and areas to be addressed. Level 2 results were tracked and reported (Item Analysis Report) to help monitor effectiveness, as well as to ensure the achievement of learning objectives and continuous improvement of the program. The ROI calculation focused on improvement in labor sales pre- and poststudy compared to the direct costs of the program.

Exhibit 24.6. Evaluating a Performance-Improvement Program: Service Manager
Pretraining Interview Worksheet

Name of Service Manager:

What factors in your dealership environment seem to make it easy or difficult to put
into practice what you learn at a class?

_____
_____
_____
_____
_____

Do you think management supports your personal training?

_____
_____
_____

Do you have a process in place in the service department for the ASMs activities
during the course of a day? If so, what is the process and how was it communicated
to them?

_____
_____
_____
_____
_____

Do your ASMs make their own service appointments?

_____
_____
_____

What percent of your business do you think is appointments? _____

Are appointments staggered throughout the day? _____

Do the ASMs conduct a vehicle walkaround when writing up service? _____

Do the ASMs use service menus? _____
_____
_____

Are the ASMs instructed to contact customers during the day to provide a status of
the vehicle? _____
_____
_____

Do the ASMs call the customer to explain the repairs or wait until they pick up
their car? _____
_____
_____
_____

Exhibit 24.7. Evaluating a Performance-Improvement Program: Service Drive
Observation Checklist

Service Advisor:	Customers in Service Drive				
Team Color:	1	2	3	4	5
DURING SERVICE WRITE-UP					
Prewritten ROs for appointments					
Quick write-up sheet to gather info					
Prompt/courteous greeting (active)					
Introduction/customer's name					
Friendliness					
Check customer's vehicle history					
Listen actively to customer (eye contact)					
Ask open-ended questions					
Confirm customer's concern					
Educate/explain next steps					
Take notes while talking to customer					
Vehicle mileage captured					
Obtain/verify customer's phone number					
Estimate given/signature obtained					
Conduct vehicle walkaround					
Communicate walkaround to customer					
Use service menu					
Establish appropriate promise time					
Overcome any customer concerns about price, product, and convenience					
Install courtesy items on customer's vehicle					
CUSTOMER CALL DURING SERVICE					
All information gathered before making call					
If left voice mail message – concise & accurate					
Update/call customer to give vehicle status					
Reconfirm pickup/promise time					
Review repairs and costs with customer					

Exhibit 24.7. Evaluating a Performance-Improvement Program: Service Drive
Observation Checklist (*continued*)

Service Advisor:	Customers in Service Drive				
Team Color:	1	2	3	4	5
ACTIVE DELIVERY					
Actively greet customer on return					
Review RO with customer					
Walk customer to cashier					
Contact customers via phone to ensure satisfaction					

Evaluation Objectives

The overall objectives of the evaluation were:

- To establish a baseline on service department performance metrics as they relate to course performance objectives, dealership learning environment, and customer satisfaction
- To measure and evaluate the application of the performance-improvement solution on job performance in the service department
- To discover the most effective techniques for measuring performance improvement in the dealership environment
- To communicate all findings to university management and the Dealership Group
- To evaluate dealership management's role in the transfer of learning for performance improvement.

Upfront Analysis

Each dealership service department was surveyed for a three-month period prior to training to create a baseline measurement for analysis. Table 24.1 illustrates the overall results of this analysis—essentially, the current state of performance against the identified business metrics.

In addition, the M&E team conducted a series of observations and

Exhibit 24.8. Evaluating a Performance-Improvement Program: ASM Pretraining
Interview Worksheet

Name of ASM:

Number of years at the dealership: _____

Number of years with the dealer organization: _____

Number of years in automotive industry: _____

Number of years as an ASM: _____

Why do you attend training classes?

_____

_____

Is what you learn at a training class easy to apply on the job? Why/why not?

_____

_____

What factors in your dealership environment seem to make it easy and/or difficult
to apply what you learn at a training class?

_____

_____

Can you tell me at least one thing you learned at a training class that you are still
using on the job?

_____

Do you think management supports your personal training efforts? _____

_____

_____

Is there a process in place in your service department so that all the ASMs know
what they need to do during the course of a typical day? If so, what is that process,
and how was it communicated to you?

_____

_____

Do you make your own service appointments? _____

What percent of your service business do you think is appointments? _____

_____

Do you try to stagger appointments throughout the day? _____

_____

Do you conduct a walkaround when writing up a vehicle for service? _____

_____

Do you use a service menu? _____

_____

Do you use a production schedule to track a customer's vehicle status throughout
the day?

_____

_____

Exhibit 24.8. Evaluating a Performance-Improvement Program: ASM Pretraining
Interview Worksheet (*continued*)

Do you contact customers during the day to provide a status of the vehicle's repair?

_____

_____

Do you personally call customers to explain repairs or do you wait until the customers picks up their vehicle after servicing?

_____

_____

What do you think you need to learn to be more successful?

_____

_____

What indicators (such as lines per RO) would you like us to gather to help evaluate
your performance improvement after attending the new ASM classes?

_____

_____

What is the best way to communicate with you throughout the course of our
study?
E-mail _____
Telephone _____
Fax _____

interviews to investigate the learning environment, existing management practices, and workflow processes, including pretraining telephone interviews with the dealer group customer relations manager
and service managers; pretraining in-dealership observations of the
ASMs; and pretraining in-dealership interviews with ASMs and team
leaders.

To capture the individual ASM pretraining three-month averages
at the dealership, M&E used the months of August, September, and
October 2002 and compared them to the posttraining three-month
averages of May, June, and July 2003. This was necessary because many
of the ASMs employed at the dealership at the time of the training
intervention were not at the dealership during the three-month
period we used with all other dealerships (May, June, July 2002). All
dealerships used the same three-month period for posttraining calculations (May, June, July 2003). For individual ASM and additional
dealership improvement numbers, more comprehensive analysis
reports were generated.

Exhibit 24.9. Evaluating a Performance-Improvement Program: Team Leader
Pretraining Interview Worksheet

| Name of Group/Team Leader: |
| Name of Dealership: |

What would you consider the top concerns you have with the way you receive an
RO from an ASM?

_____
_____
_____
_____
_____
_____
_____

Is work generally dispatched as it comes into the shop so that you get the oldest
work in first (except when there's a rush)?

_____
_____
_____
_____
_____
_____

Do either you or the ASM check the customer's service history file to identify if
any routine maintenance is needed on a customer's vehicle?

_____
_____
_____

Do you use Additional Service Request forms (or something similar) when you
identify additional needed repairs or maintenance on a vehicle? If you do, does the
ASM generally get it approved by the customer?

_____
_____
_____
_____
_____

Exhibit 24.10. Evaluating a Performance-Improvement Program: 30-Day Action Plan Follow-Up

Dealership	Class	ASM Manager	Action Plan Items	Results
	ASMs in the Service Process	Service Manager	Implement the NVH interview sheet for better diagnosis	Using haphazardly, not as much as probably should.
			Involve the Parts Dept. in all aspects to increase customer satisfaction	With special order parts (SOP), when something goes haywire, they meet with parts to try to figure out what happened and what they can do.
			Track comebacks	This is an ASM issue. They are not advising svc mgr when a comeback happens (it's like a 4-letter-word!). Svc mgr usually finds out when the customer calls to complain. This is still being worked on.
	Managing Your Workday		Keep pens in my nite drop box	Easy one . . . definitely done!
			Have add'l person to help with phone calls during peak hours	Same person who does SOP follow-up also helps out with phones.
			Track efficiency and productivity	Tracking monthly. Used to track only dollars, but now tracks all. Posts the numbers daily and this has generated considerable interest.
	Consultative Service Selling		Walkaround by all ASMs	Stopped when the weather was 28 below. Now that the weather is nice they need to start doing this again.
			Deemphasize checkout fees and give ASM more flexibility about	Svc mgr met with ASMs to implement a procedure that instead of always throwing money at a

(continued)

Exhibit 24.10. Evaluating a Performance-Improvement Program: 30-Day Action Plan Follow-Up (*continued*)

Dealership	Class	ASM Manager	Action Plan Items	Results
			initial estimates	customer, approach with a soft-sell stance first. If no opposition continue; If opposition, stop asking for money.
			Expand active delivery—we still do not make the customer feel the value—apply acid test	Have been doing active delivery and feel this may be one of the reasons they achieved the highest recognition possible this year.

Exhibit 24.11. Evaluating a Performance-Improvement Program: 120-Day Action Plan Follow-Up

Dealership	Class	ASM Manager	Action Plan Items	Results
	ASMs in the Service Process	ASM	Write-up—write clear ROs that both the tech and I can understand clearly.	4/28-Improved, but still more to go. Specific improvement in the areas of customer and product knowledge.
			Appointments—schedule appointments better—give more specific times as well as reminder call the day before.	4/28-A lot better . . . maybe 80% improvement. Cashier is now calling the day before as reminder, and Domingo is scheduling lighter so the shop is not as stressed out.
			QCI—do a QCI on all vehicles with a specific complaint to make sure all concerns are addressed by the customer in a satisfactory way.	He has incorporated this with repeat customers—he also does test drives with them. His goal is to do with all.
	Managing Your Workday		Prewrite up to speed-up morning rush.	They tried this, but it was not successful. When a customer is a no-show, the numbering sequence is off, and the voided-out tickets go against the RO count.
			Have a "to-do" list so I don't forget tasks.	Been doing this. Keeps a notepad on his desk.
			Manage techs' time better for more productivity.	Now gets techs' schooling schedules, and techs let him know when they are out on vacation or sick so he can schedule better.
	Consultative Service Selling		Build relationships with customers to gain trust.	He is more people-friendly now that he is more comfortable and has a higher confidence level.
			Identify customers' concerns better so that I can tend to their needs better.	He attributes a lot of his progress in this area and the next to the role model that his service

(continued)

Exhibit 24.11. Evaluating a Performance–Improvement Program: 120-Day Action Plan Follow-Up (*continued*)

Dealership	Class	ASM Manager	Action Plan Items	Results
			Sell benefits to customers so they are able to understand and weigh the differences.	manager provides. This is the first car company experience he has and he's been through three SMs. His current SM is really helping him a lot. Also, facilitators provided really good options on stuff rather than just one way. This has opened up doors for him to see other ways to do things.

Exhibit 24.12. Evaluating a Performance-Improvement Program: ASM Posttraining Interview Worksheet

| Name of Dealership: |
| Name of ASM: |
| Team Color: |

Is what you learned at the recent ASM classes easy to apply on the job? Why/Why Not?

_____

_____

What factors in your dealership environment seem to make it easy or difficult to apply what you learn at a training class?

_____

_____

Can you tell me at least one thing you learned at the ASM classes that you are still using on the job?

_____

_____

Do you think management supports your training efforts?

_____

_____

What percent of your service business do you think is appointments? _____

Do you try to stagger appointments throughout the day? _____

What do you think you need to learn to be more successful as an ASM?

_____

_____

_____

_____

What have you learned based on the follow-up telephone calls that related to your Action Plans:

_____

_____

_____

_____

_____

_____

_____

Level 1 Reaction

A Level 1 survey consisting of closed and open-ended questions was administered by the instructor at the end of each course. All participants were asked to provide feedback about their confidence, learning experience (i.e., level of detail, difficulty of the content, relevance, exercises, facilitator knowledge, facilitation skills, and usability of

Exhibit 24.13. Evaluating a Performance-Improvement Program: Team Lead Post-training Interview Worksheet

| Name of Dealership: |
| Name of ASM: |
| Team Color: |

What would you consider the top concerns you have with the way you receive an RO from an ASM? _____

_____

_____

Last November you identified the following items as top concerns:

_____

_____

_____

Now that the ASMs have attended the three ASM training classes and six months have passed, what are your top concerns?

_____

_____

_____

Is work generally dispatched as it comes into the shop so that you get the oldest work in first (except when there's a rush)? _____

_____

Do either you or the ASM check the customer's service history file to identify any routine maintenance needed on the customer's vehicle? _____

_____

Does the ASM generally get the additional service requests you identify on an RO approved by the customer? Is he/she doing better than six months ago?

_____

_____

Is there any other area specifically in which you feel the ASM for your team has improved?

_____

_____

_____

_____

_____

Exhibit 24.14. Evaluating a Performance-Improvement Program: Cashier Post-training Interview Worksheet

Name of Dealership:	
Name of ASM:	
Team Color:	

Are you getting a lot of questions from customers regarding completed work as compared to six months ago? (Be as specific as possible.)

_____

_____

_____

Are you experiencing fewer confrontations with customer over inaccurate invoicing/billing than six months ago? (Be as specific as possible.)

_____

_____

How often is there a difference between what customers are quoted and actually pay?

_____

_____

_____

Have you found that since the ASM training last November (the last six months), customer's attitudes at the cashier's window have improved?

_____

_____

_____

Has this positive/negative change impacted your job so that you could say your job is now easier? If so, how? (Can you be specific?) _____

_____

_____

_____

_____

Are there any other differences you have noticed with the customers since the ASMs took the four days of training last year?

_____

_____

_____

_____

_____

Table 24.1

2002 3-mo. Avg.	RO Count	Labor Sales	Avg. Sales/RO	Op Count	Avg. Ops/RO	Tech Hrs	Labor Sales	Avg. ELR
Total	33,125	$3,540,876	$110.25	64,061	2.11	66,311.84	$3,540,876	$76.84

materials), and satisfaction with the location, food, and beverages. A standard form was used to enable the surveys to be scanned and tabulated quickly. Students were asked to rate items using a forced-choice, six-point Likert scale. Open-ended comments were compiled into a general report and analyzed for opportunities for program improvement.

Level 2 Learning

To help measure each student's ability to achieve the learning objectives, a level 2 knowledge assessment was administered at the end of each course by the instructor. These assessments were not set up for "pass" or "fail." Rather, they were used as an integral part of the learning process. The instructors would review each question to reinforce key learning points and address any remaining questions or concerns. A standard form was used to enable the surveys to be scanned and tabulated quickly. An Item Analysis Report was generated for each course to help monitor program effectiveness and facilitate continuous improvement of the design and delivery of the program. Participants also completed individual Action Plans at the end of each course.

Level 3 Behavior and Level 4 Results

Posttraining interviews and observations were conducted to assess transfer and impact, including:

- Telephone follow-up with managers thirty days after training to determine if ASMs' action items on their individual Action Plans were being transferred to the job.
- Telephone interviews with each ASM 90 to 120 days after training to obtain their perspective on learning transfer based on the action items outlined in their Action Plans.
- In-dealership ASM observation follow-up six months after training as well as in-dealership interviews with ASMs, service managers, team leads, and cashiers.
- Pre- and postanalysis of business financial/numeric indicators of success.

All students from all of the four individual dealerships were included in the level 3 and 4 assessments. Trained M&E staff conducted the interviews using an interview guide, and they noted observations using a checklist.

Return on Investment (ROI)

The ROI calculations completed by the M&E team focused on improvement in labor sales pre- and poststudy compared to the direct costs of the program.

Evaluation Results

Results from the M&E evaluations conducted are highlighted in Table 24.2.

Reaction

Overall, participant reaction within the individual courses was positive as illustrated in the sample of total scores in Table 24.2.

Learning

Although the focus of evaluating learning was dynamically managed by the instructors and facilitated through the action-planning process, a knowledge-based assessment was used. Overall, participants performed well.

For instance, 47 percent of the participants answered all questions correctly in the ASMs in the Service Process and Managing Your Workday courses and 30 percent in Consultative Service Selling. Most other participants only missed one or two questions.

Table 24.2

Course	Participant Reaction Samples
ASMs in the Service Process	Total satisfaction score = 4.75/5.0
Consultative Service Selling	95% strongly agreed or agreed that they would recommend the class to others.
Managing Service Workflow	96% strongly agreed or agreed that they would recommend the class to others.

Behavior/Results

All ASMs studied experienced improvement in each of the business impact areas targeted except average operations per repair order (RO), which showed a very slight overall decrease of .03. These individual improvements rolled up into an overall improvement in all the dealerships' indices combined. The four dealerships in the study showed a 19 percent increase in labor sales, a 4 percent increase in average sales per repair order, a 10 percent increase in technician hours, and an 11 percent increase in their effective labor rate; 97% of one of the dealership's VSS scored questions showed a statistically significant increase of over .05 points—an excellent improvement for this dealership.

For pretraining three-month averages, see Table 24.1; for posttraining three-month averages, see Table 24.3; and for combined overall-improvement three-month averages, see Table 24.4. Not only did the business-impact indicators show an improvement in the service department operations, but also the ASMs and team leads felt that the job-specific training they received as a group improved their performance. The ASMs reported that their new abilities to communicate more effectively with customers and to better plan and manage their workday schedules resulted in improvements of dollar volume across the board for the dealerships studied.

Additional results have been documented through the thirty-day and ninety-day follow-up action-planning activities. For example,

Table 24.3. Posttraining Three-Month Averages

2003 3-mo. Avg.	RO Count	Labor Sales	Avg. Sales/RO	Op Count	Avg. Ops/RO	Tech Hrs	Labor Sales	Avg. ELR
	35,650	$4,189,042	$119.29	69,850	2.11	71,890.05	$4,189,044	$83.62

Table 24.4. Combined Overall Improvement—Three-Month Averages

	RO Count	Labor Sales	Avg. Sales/RO	Op Count	Avg. Ops/RO	Tech Hrs	Labor Sales	Avg. ELR
Totals	2,525	$648,167	$35.14	5,789	0.00	5,578.21	$648,167	$6.77

two significant process changes, Change in Appointment Interval and Use of Route Sheets, elicited high praise from the ASMs. Not only were the ASMs positive about the process changes, but the technician team leads were impressed with the improvement that the ASMs made in their dealerships. The icing on the cake for these employees is that the increase in the business indicators did, in fact, result in an increase in their pay—something that did not go unnoticed by most of them.

Of the three Toyota dealerships in this study, only the one dealership with the lowest VSS scores had enough of a response rate to allow a statistically significant comparison between pre- and post-training. The response rate for the other two Toyota dealerships did not have enough of a response rate to allow for any statistically significant judgments about their pre- versus posttraining scores.

ROI

As illustrated in Table 24.5, the ROI for the program was calculated to be 551.15 percent overall. Even after a 50 percent adjustment to allow for any other external factors that might have influenced the dealerships' improvement, the ROI for the program was 275.57 percent.

Intangible Benefits

An influencing factor that cannot be ignored is signature. Of special significance is the fact that the dealership that experienced the highest turnover rate during the study was not negatively impacted on its VSS or its financial indicators. To the contrary, it realized strong improvement in all areas tracked. Measurement & Evaluation feels that there is a strong correlation between dealership improvements—even with high turnover—and established processes that a dealership has in place. Established processes are the vehicles by which a dealership can initiate and implement successful changes in a department.

In addition, M&E feels that this dealership's improvement—even with high turnover—shows the importance of getting new hires immediately into training so that they have an opportunity to incorporate the new processes into their regular routine, to ensure that all the department employees are conducting business in the same way to achieve the same outcome.

Table 24.5

Dealership	# Mgrs	# Classes	Total Mgr Classes	# ASM	# Classes	Total ASM Classes	TOTAL CLASSES	Cost/ Class	Daily Lost Work Cost	Meal Cost per Person	Total Cost
4 Total	7	5	35	20	4	80	115	$175.00	$1,000	$25.00	$138,000

Improvement in Labor Sales Pre- and Poststudy		Return on Investment		Recalculated Return on Investment
$689,630		551.15%		275.57%

Evaluation Reporting

The results of the study were communicated through a variety of media, including face-to-face meetings, phone conferences, and e-mail. Aggregated level 1 results were reported to university management, curriculum designers, facilitators, and stakeholders to reveal trends and opportunities for improvement. Level 2 knowledge assessment results were presented immediately to students as part of the learning process and then tracked and reported within the college for continuous improvement of the design and delivery of the program. Level 3, 4, and 5 results were presented to the Dealer Principal, communicated to the Toyota educational community through the News-Scope newsletter and e-mails, shared with dealerships nationwide through the *En-gage* dealership magazine, and reported to Toyota's Customer Services Division and Signature Group. At its discretion, the Dealer Principal communicated the results of the evaluation internally.

As a result of this successful evaluation effort, the M&E team has become a strategic partner in determining solutions and reporting results leading to increased participation in University of Toyota interventions. The evaluation effort also revealed significant learning opportunities for the college, including the value of sending everyone in a department to the same training within a short time period. Setting up the department for process improvement and change and creating a consistent, established process within a department can result in measurable improvement, even if the department experiences significant turnover—which was the case in one of the dealerships in the study.

In addition, the findings from this evaluation strongly support the value of addressing knowledge, managerial coaching, and process improvement as an integrated performance-improvement solution. Professional practitioners such as performance technologists, program designers, and evaluators can apply structural elements of this solution and the associated evaluation methodologies within their own organizations, regardless of the type of job function involved. The findings from this case study also can be used as an example to foster managerial support, resources, and funding for an integrated approach that incorporates evaluation at all levels. A number of other lessons have been learned:

1. Careful needs assessment minimized overall costs of development by streamlining deliverables to desired outcomes and business objectives.
2. A comprehensive evaluation strategy provided important feedback to program administrators, participants, and local management, which in turn enabled continuous process improvements.
3. A holistic approach to performance improvement (addressing not only the knowledge of the worker but the workflow service process and workplace) yielded greater business results.
4. The action planning helped to ensure transfer and long-term institutionalization of desired processes and behaviors.
5. Clearly identified business metrics appropriately led the design, implementation, and evaluation of a program to the desired goals.
6. Participation in the overall process by local management and staff facilitated greater transfer and implementation of desired behaviors by the individual participant.

Chapter 25

Evaluating a Career Development Initiative

While the name of the organization is disguised upon request, this is an actual case study describing the evaluation effort for a career development initiative. This initiative was implemented as a solution strategy for increased efficiency in a dynamic manufacturing environment for a global company employing more than 9,600 employees worldwide. Evaluation was done at all of Kirkpatrick's four levels plus return on investment (ROI). Solutions included an intensive training program with business-oriented performance objectives; self and manager assessments of critical skills; and a Development Discussion action plan to help participants apply critical skills toward operational and individual performance priorities. Evaluation results showed a positive link between participants' applied behaviors learned from training and desired business results.

Innovative Computer, Inc.

Holly Burkett, M.A., SPHR, CPT
Principal, Evaluation Works
Davis, California

Background and Business Need

The Career Development Initiative began as a strategy to build organizational capacity and bench strength due to the ongoing challenge of retaining top management and technical talent.

Given a shrinking labor pool of experienced managers, rising costs of recruiting outside talent, and an alarming lack of organizational depth in developing leaders from within, this was deemed a business-critical issue. The intent of the initiative, then, was to place greater emphasis on partnering with employees as a means of creating business and leadership solutions that would enhance the viability of the organization as a world-class operation. The evaluation purpose was to measure the business impact and cost benefit of the solution.

Evaluation Framework

Implementing a results-based evaluation effort begins with a proven evaluation framework. Donald Kirkpatrick (1974) created a four-level method of categorizing evaluation data that has been used as a frame of reference for decades. In the 1980s, Jack Phillips expanded upon this framework to incorporate a fifth level of evaluation for capturing the financial impact of training programs or return on investment (ROI). This framework (shown below) includes techniques for isolating the impact of a training solution and also provides for a sixth data measure: intangible benefits, which are those benefits that have not been converted to monetary value, such as increased morale, improved teamwork, or increased job satisfaction.

Kirkpatrick's Four Levels	Phillips' Five Level Framework
Level 1: Reaction	Level 1: Reaction and Satisfaction
Level 2: Learning	Level 2: Learning
Level 3: Behavior	Level 3: Application and Implementation
Level 4: Results	Level 4: Business Impact
	Level 5: Return on Investment

Since the evaluation objective of this initiative was to measure the cost benefit of the solution, the measurement strategy integrated Kirkpatrick's and Phillips's evaluation framework, with an emphasis on Phillips's methodology for isolating training's impact and calculating ROI.

Evaluation Planning: The Linking Process

By planning early, clear direction about the schedule, scope, and resource requirements of a results-based evaluation effort can be provided. In this case, preliminary planning included defining business needs and linking those to specific objectives and measures through a documented data collection plan. This plan served to communicate the type of data to be collected, how it would be collected, when it would be collected, and who was responsible for collecting it.

As shown in Table 25.1, defined business needs drove level 4 results or impact objectives (increased operational capacity) and impact measures (increased labor efficiencies, increased productivity). The needs analysis uncovered gaps between current and desired job-task behaviors, which then determined specific level 3 behavioral or application objectives (employees will conduct development discussion with managers within sixty days of program completion).

The skill/knowledge gaps determined specific learning needs, which were reflected in level 2 learning objectives for the program. Specifically, as shown in the data collection plan, participants will identify skills, talents, and development opportunities through completion of self and manager prework assessments. Finally, learning preferences appeared as level 1 reaction objectives (achieve 4.0 out of 5 on Overall Satisfaction). With this approach, the training process had built-in evaluation components and the Career Development program was developed with job performance and business results in mind.

Another planning step involved examining the organizational targets set for the types of programs to be evaluated at each level. It is not necessary to evaluate all programs at all levels. Most best practice organizations define specific criteria for programs requiring a comprehensive, detailed analysis and will target approximately 20 percent of programs annually for evaluation at level 4.

This particular initiative had components that fit the typical criteria for higher levels of evaluation, which included:

- Long-term viability
- Importance to overall strategic objectives
- High visibility
- Senior management interest

Table 25.1. Data Collection Plan

HRD Initiative/Performance Improvement Program: BETA Career Development Initiative

Evaluation Level	Objective(s)	Data Collection Method	Data Sources	Timing	Responsibilities
1	Reaction/Satisfaction • To measure participant satisfaction with career development training • Achieve 4.0 on Overall Satisfaction and Relevance rating(s) • 80% identify planned actions	• Reaction Questionnaire • Impact Questionnaire	• Participants, managers, supervisors • Steering committee	• After each session • During session • 30, 60 days	• HRD consultant • Participants • Managers • Steering committee
2	Learning • Identify individual skills, talents, and development opportunities per self & manager assessment inventories • Demonstrate proficiency with Development Discussion guidelines	• Skill Practice exercises, simulations • Skill assessment prework (self, manager)	• Participants • Managers • HRD facilitator	• During session • Before/during • One week after	• Participants • Managers • HRD consultant
3	Application Behavior • Complete Development Discussion with manager within 60 days of program completion • Apply critical skills/knowledge to designated performance priorities within 60 days of program completion	• Individual action and development plans • Team project • Follow-up session(s)	• Participants • Steering committee • Managers	• During action plan implementation • 2 months after program	• HRD consultant • Project Sponsor • Steering Committee • Participants • Managers

Table 25.1. Data Collection Plan (*continued*)

	Broad Program Objective(s)	Measures/Data	Data Collection Method/Instruments	Data Sources	Timing	Responsibilities
4	Impact/Results					
	• To measure extent to which applied critical skills/knowledge impacted strategic goal of increasing labor efficiency • Increased operational capacity, increased labor efficiency		• Performance monitoring • Impact Questionnaire	• Steering committee • Department recorder data • Participants	• 2 months after action plan implementation	• HRD consultant • Subject matter experts • Participants • Managers
5	ROI					
	• To measure return on investment with performance improvement strategy • Achieve 120% ROI or greater		• Cost benefit analysis • Impact Questionnaire • Estimates • Historical data	• Estimates • Productivity, labor efficiency (cycle time, rework)	• 2 months after action plan completion • 3 months after program	• HRD consultant • Subject matter experts • Participants • Managers • Steering committee

Data Collection Plan adapted from J. J. Phillips, *Return on Investment in Training and Performance Improvement Programs*. 2nd ed. Boston: Butterworth–Heinemann, 2003. Used with permission.

In fact, given the business-critical nature of this initiative and the expenditure of time, resources, and expertise allotted to the training solution, level 5 (ROI) objectives were also established in the planning stage, as shown in Table 25.1.

The Training Solution

Based upon needs assessment data, a Career Development program, with corresponding assessment instruments, was used as a performance improvement strategy. The primary output of the program was an employee-driven Development Discussion Plan focusing on the following skill categories:

- *Talents*: Manager and I agree about my strengths
- *Job Gaps*: Manager and I don't agree about skill's importance
- *Skill Gaps*: Manager and I don't agree about my skill level
- *Development Needs*: Manager and I agree that my skill level is lower than job requires

The intent was two-fold. First, the process was meant to help employees develop leadership skills by providing clarity about:

- organizational and job performance priorities
- skill strengths and improvement areas
- growth opportunities

Second, the Development Discussion process was meant to help managers clarify performance priorities through a structured feedback tool. Given the important role of managers in reinforcing this initiative, a transfer strategy was developed as part of the evaluation plan. Table 25.2 shows the transfer strategy matrix used in this effort.

This document was rolled out in initial briefings about the project and had strong senior managment support. This executive support was instrumental in holding managers accountable for supporting employees' performance objectives throughout all phases of solution implementation. In communicating the vision for a results-based effort, the transfer matrix helped dispel the notion of evaluation as an

Table 25.2. Transfer Strategy Matrix for Career Development Initiative

Role	PLANNING *Before*	IMPLEMENTATION *During*	EVALUATION *After*
Steering committee	• Help define performance, business objectives. • Participate in assessing skill gaps. • Co-facilitate "kick-off" sessions or briefings. • Require attendance at scheduled briefings.	• Attend, co-facilitate select implementation sessions. • Communicate importance of learning, performance, & business objectives. • Assist in collecting, analyzing, converting data	• Participate in reviewing evaluation plan. • Reinforce follow-up and application of Action Plans. • Recognize individuals for successful completions. • Assist in removing barriers to application. • Provide incentives. • Serve as mentor, resource.
Managers, Supervisors	• Support HRD in defining performance objectives. • Attend briefing sessions prior to implementation. • Reinforce trainee participation. • Complete prework assessments.	• Remove barriers to trainees' attendance. • Provide coverage for individuals in training. • Attend sessions as available. • Directly discuss Development Discussion action plan.	• Reinforce follow-up and application of Development Discussion Action Plans. • Assist in removing barriers to application. • Ensure resources are available. • Monitor performance progress with employee Development Plan.

(continued)

Table 25.2. Transfer Strategy Matrix for Career Development Initiative *(continued)*

Role	PLANNING	IMPLEMENTATION	EVALUATION
	Before	*During*	*After*
		• Implement employee Development Plan. • Ask trainees about training progress.	• Continue implementing evaluation plan.
Human Resource Development (HRD)	• Link objectives to identified needs.	• Communicate importance of learning, performance, & business objectives.	• Conduct Action Planning sessions.
	• Customize curriculum to meet desired objectives.	• Assess trainees for reaction, learning, and skill/knowledge transfer.	• Facilitate 60-day follow-up sessions.
	• Incorporate benchmarked transfer strategies into course design.	• Facilitate prework.	• Report results to key stakeholders.
	• Design data collection instruments, evaluation plan(s).	• Teach the Action Planning process.	• Use results for continuous improvement.
		• Implement evaluation plan/tools; collect, analyze, report results data.	
Trainees	• Assist HRD in job/task analysis.	• Attend full program.	• Apply critical skills on the job.
	• Attend briefing sessions.	• Complete self-assessment inventories.	• Seek support from supervisor in implementing Development Plan.
	• Complete pre-assessment survey and prework.	• Demonstrate active participation in skill practices.	• Implement Development Plan.
		• Complete Development Discussion action plan.	• Identify barriers to application.
			• Complete 60-day Impact Questionnaire.

Adapted from Broad, Mary L. and J. Newstrom, *Transfer of Training*. Addison–Wesley Publishing, New York, N.Y. 1992.

"add-on" activity occurring at the end of a training program. It also established a foundation of shared ownership for training results.

Defining specific responsibilities of all stakeholders was critical to the success of this results-based evaluation effort. For example, management and stakeholder input was needed to ensure that the needs assessment included specific business-impact measures. Subject matter experts, participants, and line managers were needed to provide technical expertise in defining business measures and converting those measures to monetary value. These individuals were also a key resource in defining barriers to on-the-job application of learned skills and knowledge.

Shared responsibilities were necessary then to:

- Align solutions with business needs
- Show how the intervention affected organizational as well as individual performance
- Identify environmental issues that enabled or deterred the performance-improvement solution
- Determine the relevancy of the instructional design to participants' daily job
- Determine if and how the performance gap was closed

This approach not only served to validate HRD work but also secured support and cooperation for implementing value-added training solutions going forward.

Training Objectives

The following objectives were communicated to pilot participants in briefing sessions led by HRD and the senior executive team. Specifically, the business purpose was conveyed as follows: "This . . . (effort) . . . ensures our viability as a world-class factory. . . . The end result will be a supportive work environment, with a flexible workforce, capable of supporting our strategic vision and mission."

Impact/Results Objectives

- Increase operational capacity in meeting factory strategic goals.

- Increase labor efficiency.
- Increase organizational agility and flexibility.

Application/Behavior Objectives

- Complete Development Discussion with manager within sixty days of program completion.
- Apply critical skills and talents toward execution of prioritized job tasks.
- Communicate with manager about barriers or problems in achieving goals.

Learning Objectives

- Define critical skills required for job effectiveness.
- Define skill gaps.
- Identify talents.
- Identify developmental needs.
- Demonstrate proficiency with Development Discussion guidelines.

Reaction Objectives

- Mean rating of 4.0 out of 5.0 achieved on recommending program to others.
- Mean rating of 4.0 out of 5.0 achieved on relevance of program to daily job.
- 80 perccent report planned intention to conduct Development Discussion with their manager within sixty days of the workshop.

Data Collection

Reaction.   Level 1 data was collected at the end of the program and again during the Impact Questionnaire. Project sponsor and management reaction was also collected through an impact questionnaire at the end of the project.

Learning.   Level 2 data was measured during the training through skill practices, role plays, and training simulations. Learning exercises focused on participants' demonstrated ability to identify the critical skills needed to execute defined performance priorities as well as participants' demonstrated ability to conduct a Development Discussion with their manager, in accordance with the Development Discussion guidelines provided.

Application/Behavior. Level 3 data—on-the-job behavior change—was measured through an Action Plan, in which training participants outlined detailed steps to accomplish specific goals connected to program objectives. Specifically, as shown in Exhibit 25.1, participants (a) identified planned actions based upon learned skills and (b) estimated the business impact of those actions. The action planning process answers such questions as:

- What steps or action items will be taken as a result of learning?
- What on-the-job improvements or accomplishments will be realized with applied skills/knowledge?
- How much improvement can be linked to the program?

A sixty-day Impact Questionnaire was also used to assess participants' application of the Development Discussion. Participants were also asked to identify: (1) the extent to which they applied the performance objectives (as previously noted) from the program back on the job, after training and (2) the extent to which their applied behavior influenced their job effectiveness on a scale of 1 to 5, with 5 being "Completely Enhanced" and 1 being "No Change."

Impact/Results. Level 4 data was also collected with both the Development Discussion Action Plan and the sixty-day Impact Questionnaires, where participants estimated the business impact of their applied behaviors and began the process of moving from level 4 to level 5 by converting those impact measures to monetary value. To be conservative and adjust for potential error rates, this data conversion process included participant confidence levels with their estimates.

The following shows a series of sample questions from the Impact Questionnaire (Phillips 1997) that are intended to capture this data:

- As a result of this program, what specific actions will you apply based upon what you have learned?
- How often will you apply this behavior and under what conditions?

Exhibit 25.1. Action Plan for Career Development Initiative

Name: _____ Instructor Signature: _____ Follow-up Date: _____

Objective To apply skills and knowledge gained from Career Development Program Evaluation Period _____ to _____

Improvement Measures: Productivity; Labor Efficiency; Rework; Communication; Customer Response; Other

Action Steps	Analysis
As a result of this program, what specific actions will you apply based upon what you have learned:	What specific unit of measure will change as a result of your actions?
1. Initiate Development Discussion with immediate supervisor, within 60 days of program completion.	1. Increased productivity
2. Participate in monthly developmental meetings to monitor progress toward goals.	2. Increased labor efficiency
3. Provide status reports on performance priorities on a weekly basis, or as determined.	3. As a result of the anticipated changes in productivity and efficiency, please estimate the monetary benefits to your department over a one-month period. $24,000
4. _____ _____	4. What percent of this improvement can be directly attributed to skills/knowledge gained from this initiative? 60%
	5. What is the basis of your estimate? *Improved project management and time savings; estimated reduction in meeting time with manager from 8 hrs to 6 hrs. a month x base salary hourly wage.*
Comments: This program shows that the company cares about my career growth because it's given me the tools I need to manage my own path and get the resources I need to feel satisfied and productive on the job. It helps having my supervisor and me on the "same page" with project and performance priorities. The Development Discussion	6. What level of confidence, expressed as a percentage, do you place on the above estimate? (100%=Certainty and 0%=No Confidence) 70%

332

Exhibit 25.1. Action Plan for Career Development Initiative (*continued*)

planner gives a great structure for supervisory meetings.	7. What other factors, besides training, may contribute to benefits associated with these changes? <u>New project management software</u>
Intangible Benefits:	
Improved relationship with my immediate supervisor, better ability to view performance priorities in relation to the "big picture."	8. What barriers, if any, may prevent you from using skills or knowledge gained from this program? <u>New product launches, conflicting priorities.</u>

Action Plan adapted from J.J. Phillips, *Return on Investment in Training and Performance Improvement Program*, 2nd ed. Boston: Butterworth–Heinemann 2003. Used with permission.

- What specific unit of measure will change as a result of your actions?
- As a result of these anticipated changes, please estimate the monetary benefits to your department over a one-month period.
- What is the basis for your estimate?
- What level of confidence, expressed as a percentage, do you place on the above estimate? (100 percent = Certainty and 0 percent = No Confidence)
- What other factors, besides training, may contribute to benefits associated with process improvements changes?

To ensure strong response, the questionnaire was administered during a ninety-minute follow-up session, scheduled two months after training. Employees were expected by management to attend and were on paid company time.

Data Analysis and Results

Isolation and Data Conversion

Since many factors influence performance improvement, a credible evaluation strategy will include techniques for isolating the direct impact of a training solution. While Jack Phillips (1997) cites several methods for isolating impact, one of the most commonly used approach is the use of participant and/or manager estimates. The effectiveness of this approach rests on the assumption that participants are capable of estimating how much of a performance improvement is related to training. Because their actions have produced the improvement, participants typically have very accurate input on the issue. In this case, estimates were obtained by asking a series of questions in the Impact Questionnaire items, including:

- What percent of this improvement can be directly attributed to the application of skills/techniques/knowledge gained in the training program?
- What is the basis for this estimation?
- What confidence do you have in this estimate, expressed as a percent?

Table 25.3. Example of Participant Estimates with Career Development Initiative

Participant	Annual Improvement Value (A)	Basis of Estimate	Confidence Level (B)	Isolation Factor (C)	Adjusted Value (D)
1	$36,000	Improvement in project efficiency. Estimated time saved problem solving. ($3,000 month x 12)	85%	50%	$15,300
2	$30,000	Improvement in engineering project life-cycle, "cradle to grave" completion. Estimated time savings ($2,500 a month × 12)	75%	80%	$18,000

- What other factors contributed to this improvement in performance?

In accordance with Phillips's ROI methodology, once the isolation factors were determined, the Level 4 data was converted to monetary value, as shown in Table 25.3.

For instance, Participant 1 estimated that his applied actions would lead to improved project efficiencies. The monetary value of project efficiency was based upon units of time savings. Monthly time savings were annualized to the amount of $36,000. This value was then adjusted for error by Participant 1's confidence factor of 85 percent (A × B) and the isolation factor of 50 percent (A × B × C = D), which attributed 50 percent of monetary benefits *directly* to the training initiative. The adjusted values in column (D) were totaled for all participants and then used as cost benefit data and compared to program costs in the final ROI calculation.

Results

Table 25.4 shows a streamlined Impact Study report, where results were summarized and communicated to senior management. These results include the following:

Table 25.4. Streamlined Impact Study for Career Development Initiative

ROI Impact Study

Program Title: Career Development

Target Audience (Pilot): First- and second-line Managers/Supervisors; Professional Staff

Duration: 1 day

Technique to Isolate Effects: Participant estimation, trend analysis

Technique to Convert Data to Monetary Value: Historical costs, internal experts, estimates

Fully Loaded Program Costs: $83,300

Reaction, Satisfaction, Planned Action	Learning	Application/ Behavior	Impact/ Results	Return on Investment	Intangible Benefits
Overall satisfaction rating: 4.8	Participants completed self-assessment of	94% conducted a Development Discussion with their manager within 60 days of workshop.	Monetary benefits of increased productivity: $187,000	ROI (%) = Net Program Benefits Costs $195,700 $83,300 = 235% ROI	Improved relationship with immediate manager
I would recommend this program to others: 4.8	• skills		Monetary benefits from increased efficiencies: $92,000		Increased perception that employer cares about employee's career growth
Program was relevant to my daily job: 4.5	• gaps	76% apply critical skills from Development Discussion Plan.			Increased confidence in job role
	• talents				
	• development				
	• needs				

Table 25.4. Streamlined Impact Study for Career Development Initiative (*continued*)

92% reported intention to conduct a Development Discussion with their manager within 60 days of the workshop.	I have a better understanding of my Performance Priorities for the next 6–12 months: 4.48 I have a better understanding of my development needs as they relate to my current position: 4.37 I have a better understanding of my talents as they relate to my current position: 4.26	
	52% are enhancing development through development plans approved by their manager.	Improved ability to view performance priorities in relation to "big picture" Anticipated plan to stay with employer for next 12 months.

Streamlined report adapted from Patricia P. Phillips and Holly Burkett, "Managing Evaluation Shortcuts," InfoLine Issue OIII, Alexandria, VA: American Society for Training and Development, 2001.

Reaction (Level 1).

- Overall satisfaction rating: 4.8
- I would recommend this program to others: 4.8
- Program was relevant to my daily job: 4.5
- 92 percent reported intention to conduct a Development Discussion with their manager within thirty days of the workshop

Learning (Level 2).   Through skill practice exercises, observation, and peer feedback, participants successfully demonstrated key communication and feedback skills associated with conducting Development Discussions. In addition, participants completed self-assessment of skills, gaps, talents, and development needs.

Additional Learning Outcomes.

- I have a better understanding of my performance priorities for the next six to twelve months: 4.48
- I have a better understanding of my development needs as they relate to my current position: 4.37

Application/Behavior (Level 3).

- 94 percent conducted a Development Discussion with their manager within sixty days of workshop.
- 76 percent apply critical skills from Development Discussion Plan.
- 52 percent are enhancing development through development plans approved by their manager.

Impact/Results (Level 4).   Business result measures, analyzed sixty days after the program, substantiate that employees who applied structured Development Discussion practices significantly impacted targeted measures of labor efficiency and productivity. For example, responses to the questions: "Indicate the extent to which you think this training has influenced the business measures in your own work or your work unit," and "What is the basis of your estimate?" included such responses as:

- Increased productivity—based upon improved time management

- Increased labor efficiency—based upon reduced meeting time with manager around project priorities

ROI (Level 5), Based on Phillips (1997).   In moving from level 4 data to level 5 ROI results, two core steps were followed. In step one, participants were asked to convert their reported business improvements to monetary value. For instance, as shown in the Action Plan depicted in Exhibit 25.1, participants estimated the value of improved productivity based upon units of time savings over a monthly period, which was then annualized as a cost benefit. As shown in Table 25.3, estimates were adjusted to account for other influences upon improvement (the isolation factor) as well as for participant confidence levels. To be conservative, extreme or questionable data was omitted from the ROI calculation. The total reported monetary benefits associated with partipants' applied actions and corresponding business improvements were:

Monetary Benefits of Business Results (directly attributable to training)

- Monetary benefits of increased productivity: $187,000
- Monetary benefits from increased efficiencies: $92,000

In step two, the costs of the program were tabulated and fully loaded to include all cost categories, such as analysis costs, development costs, delivery costs, and evaluation costs. The adjusted values from step one were then used as level 5 cost benefit data and compared to the program costs tabulated in step two, for the final ROI analysis and calculation.

The ROI calculation for this study is:

$$\text{ROI (\%)} = \frac{\text{net program benefits}}{\text{program costs}} \times 100$$

Net cost benefits:

$$\frac{\text{Increased productivity (\$187,000)} + \text{increased efficiencies (\$92,000)}}{\text{Fully loaded program costs (\$83,300)}} = (279,000)$$

ROI:

$$\frac{\$279,000 \text{ (attributable to training)} - \$83,300 \text{ (program costs)}}{\$83,300 \text{ (program costs)}} = 2.35 \times 100 = 235\% \text{ ROI}$$

Intangible benefits linked to the program but not converted to monetary values included:

- Improved relationship with immediate manager
- Increased perception that employer cares about employee's career growth
- Increased confidence in job role
- Improved ability to adapt to change
- Improved ability to view performance priorities in relation to "big picture"
- Anticipated plan to stay with employer for next twelve months

Conclusions

Overall, project success was defined by tangible business results that showed improved measures of productivity and labor efficiency (including time savings). Evaluation results showed a link between improved business measures of productivity and labor efficiency and the Career Development focus of aligning employees' critical skills and developmental opportunities with prioritized performance goals, as defined in the participatory Developmental Discussion. The intangible benefits associated with this effort were also considered significant by senior management. Recommendations from the pilot offering included:

- Ensure that participants and managers are briefed about the time and resource requirements of program involvement in advance.
- Increase accountability of management staff to complete preassessment work in a timely manner.
- Increase accountability of management staff to hold Development Discussion within thirty days of program completion.

- Conduct quarterly progress check meetings with participants (managers/subordinates).
- Promote program benefits in intra-net communication vehicles.
- Ensure that employee talents, development needs, and critical skill gaps noted in individual Development Plans are closely aligned with the annual and midpoint performance appraisal process.

Implications and Recommendations for HRD Professionals

Integrating results-based evaluation into the organizational mainstream is simply a matter of helping stakeholders define which initiatives are adding value. By evaluating training programs with business results in mind, HRD functions can be better aligned with organizational strategy and be perceived in a more credible light.

A results-based HRD culture, however, typically involves changing old habits and practices of designing and delivering HRD solutions and does not occur overnight. HRD staff can enhance organizational capability and evaluation readiness by managing the implementaion as a change effort. They can brief mid- and senior-level managers on the importance of results-based evaluation to the business; conduct employee workshops and address resistance; invite people to participate as reviewers and evaluators; establish a cross-functional evaluation advisory group; and position results-based evaluation as a process improvement strategy and not a performance management tool for training staff.

Ultimately, this is not the sole responsibility of the HRD function. Cooperation and dedication of individuals and groups across all organizational levels are needed. As with any change effort. Preparation and planning are only half the journey. A big challenge for implementing a results-based evaluation effort is maintaining the integrity of the process over time so that it is more than a "flavor of the month."

These transition planning actions will help with the challenges:

- Move from simple to complex.
- Build credibility by developing internal evaluation skills.

- Leverage information, best practices, and tools from the growing network of evaluation experts in the HRD field.

Summary

Integrating a results-oriented evaluation strategy into the overall
training assessment, design, development, and delivery life-cycle adds
credibility to the HRD function by increasing training alignment
with business needs. While achieving a results-based approach can be
time-consuming, labor intensive, and sometimes perceived as threatening, with proper transitional planning around a proven framework,
realistic evaluation targets, and shared ownership of results, the process
can be implemented in a practical, systemic manner.

References

Burkett, Holly. "Evaluation: Was Your HPI Project Worth the Effort?"
performance evaluation chapter. In *HPI Essentials*. Alexandria, VA:
American Society for Training and Development, 2002.
————. *Program Process Improvement Team*. Vol. 3, *Action: Return on Investment*. Edited by Patricia P. Phillips. Alexandria, VA: American Society
for Training and Development, 2001.
Kirkpatrick, Donald L. *Evaluating Training Programs: The Four Levels*. 2nd
ed. San Francisco: Berrett-Koehler, 1998.
Phillips, Jack J. *Handbook of Training Evaluation and Measurement Methods*.
3rd ed. Houston: Gulf Publishing, 1997.
————. *Return on Investment in Training and Performance Improvement Programs*. 2nd ed. Boston: Butterworth-Heinemann, 2003.
Phillips, Patricia P., ed. *Return on Investment*. Vol. 3. Alexandria, VA: American Society for Training and Development, 2001.
Phillips, Patricia P., and Holly Burkett. "Managing Evaluation Shortcuts."
Info Line Issue 0111. Alexandria, VA: American Society for Training
and Development, 2001.

Chapter 26

Evaluating the Four Levels by Using a New Assessment Process

This case study describes a new process for upgrading data collection methods for level 1 (reaction) and level 3 (behavior). It uses a team approach with a more structured and uniform approach to the assessment process. The approach will be used to evaluate all classroom courses; the exhibits will be of particular interest.

Army and Air Force Exchange Service (AAFES)

Steven Jablonski, Educational Support Manager
Dallas, Texas

The Army and Air Force Exchange Service (AAFES) brings a tradition of value, service, and support to its 11.5 million authorized customers at military installations in the United States, Europe, and in the Pacific. For 109 years, AAFES has provided support to troops serving around the world. In recent years, it has provided support to the military fighting horrific forest fires in the continental United States, to our troops working the Olympic Games in Utah, and to U.S. and allied troops participating in Operation Enduring Freedom, Operation Joint Guardian, Operation Joint Forge, and Operations Northern and Southern Watch. AAFES was in the shadow of the impact site at the Pentagon and at Ground Zero in New York City supporting rescue efforts in the wake of the September 11 attacks. In 2003 through the present, AAFES has provided unfaltering support to our service members and allies in Operation Iraqi Freedom despite the adverse and threatening conditions. The service operates thousands of facilities worldwide, with more than 12,000 facilities in more than thirty-five countries and in all fifty states. These include 3,150 retail facilities, of which 205 are main stores on Army, Air Force, and Marine installations around the world. For members of the Army and Air Force family, AAFES is also a major source of employment. Approximately 31 percent of the 47,323 AAFES associates are military family members.

AAFES Corporate University has developed a plan to integrate Kirkpatrick's four levels of evaluation with current technology available within the company. This plan focuses on upgrading data collection methods for level 1 and level 3 evaluations in 2005.

Under the leadership and guidance of LaSharnda Beckwith, Vice President of Learning, more emphasis is being placed on the assessment process. In the past, individual instructors were responsible for gathering and analyzing the feedback provided by the associates who attended training. Ms. Beckwith has adopted a more structured and uniform approach to the assessment process by establishing a team that is dedicated to the development and analysis of all of Corporate University's assessment efforts.

The Educational Support Team, directed by Steve Jablonski, was formed in late 2004. After analyzing the current assessment process and exploring several different options for administering assessments, Steve's team selected an online option to facilitate the administration of assessments within AAFES. The Microsoft Office SharePoint Portal Server 2003 was launched companywide in 2004. This tool provides a survey feature that Corporate University can use to administer assessments and obtain feedback from the associates who attend courses. The Web portal also provides the ability to run reports through Excel spreadsheets and convert the data to an Access database for more detailed analysis. All of these efforts would be more labor-intensive without the aid of this online tool.

The plan for the newly established assessment process is that it will evaluate all classroom courses taught by the Corporate University staff during the 2005 training season. These will include courses such as Basic Project Management, The Manager's Mind-Set, Goal Setting in AAFES, Operational Management, Advanced Softlines Merchandising, Food Financial Management, General Managers' Command and Communication, and Fundamentals of Supervision.

Level 1 evaluations will be conducted in a two-step process for 100 percent of the classes taught by Corporate University. The first step involves a pencil-and-paper assessment that will be passed out to associates during the training session (see Exhibit 26.1). This evaluation provides an instructor with immediate feedback on the course material

Exhibit 26.1

Course Title	Date	Instructor
Location	Your Job Title	Your Grade

Directions: Please take a few minutes and give us your evaluation of the training program you completed. We want to know how useful this program will be to you on your job and if changes should be made to the content. This information is for statistical purposes only and we ask that you be honest when answering. After completion, return all evaluations to HQ AAFES HR-U.

Enter the number of the rating which best describes each statement listed below using the following scale.

4-Strongly Agree	3-Agree	2-Disagree	1-Strongly Disagree
	0-Not Applicable		

CONTENT	RATING
1. The content of the course matched the stated objectives.	
2. The difficulty level was about right for me (neither too difficult, nor too easy).	
3. The exercises and examples were realistic and true-to-life.	
4. The instructional methods (lecture, discussion, role-play, etc.) were effective.	
5. What was the weakest part of the course and how could it be improved?	

RELEVANCE TO MY JOB	RATING
1. The skills/knowledge taught in this course were applicable to my job.	
2. This course will help me do my job better.	

LEARNING MATERIALS	RATING
1. The printed material was easy to read and understand.	
2. The workbooks/handouts were well organized.	
3. I can use the printed material given to me in class as a reference on the job.	

THE INSTRUCTOR	RATING
1. Presented the materials clearly.	
2. Explained how each activity related to the overall objective.	
3. Encouraged class participation.	

OVERALL	RATING
1. The discussion topic accomplished the stated objectives.	
2. This program was worth the time spent away from my job.	

presented and the associates' facilitation skills. The second step uses the Web portal and has been designed to collect associates's reactions to the class after having had up to a week to reflect on the training. This evaluation is similar to the one given in the classroom. The instructor is asked to direct the associate to a URL that will allow access to the online assessment both during the class and in a postclass e-mail. We anticipated a drop in the response rate but have seen the quality of responses improve significantly in the classes that have been taught early in the training calendar. This improvement can be attributed to the associate having time to analyze and reflect back on the information provided in the class and not having to rush to complete the level 1 "smile sheet." The educational support team will review the feedback and provide an analysis to the instructors and their supervisors for review.

Level 2 evaluations will be conducted for 80 percent of the courses taught. These assessments will be delivered by the instructor in the form of a pre- and postclass test (Exhibit 26.2). In order for associates to receive course credit in their personnel records, they must pass the posttest with a score of 80 percent or higher. Instructors will compare the results from the pre- and post-class tests to evaluate the questions and see if any patterns exist that require the adjustment of future training or modification of test questions. The tests have been developed by the course designers and will test to ensure that the course objectives have been met during the training session.

Level 3 evaluations will be conducted for 60 percent of the courses taught. These assessments will be conducted in a two-step process. The evaluations have been developed by the assessment team in coordination with the subject matter experts, designers, and trainers of the courses. The assessments seek to determine if the associates have experienced any behavior change as a result of attending the training. Depending on the course requirements, the first step will have the instructor send associates an e-mail directing them to the portal survey sixty to ninety days following successful completion of the course (see Exhibit 26.3). The second step attempts to validate the associates' behavior change by sending a similar, online survey to the associates' supervisor two weeks later. Using the portal allows for faster and more economic analysis of the data collected. The educational support team will review the feedback and provide an analysis to the instructors and their supervisors for review.

Level 4 evaluations will be conducted for 3 percent of the courses taught. The evaluations have been developed by the assessment team in

Exhibit 26.2.

---

1. **Associates showing expensive items to a customer should show no more than this many at one time:**

   a. 1   b. 2   c. 3   d. 4

2. **Greeters should do their best to completely secure the shopping bags of customers entering the store:**

   a. True   b. False

3. **Cameras should be considered for small stores who have concerns about physical security.**

   a. True   b. False

4. **While associates are checking for concealed merchandise at register, they should detain any customer concealing items.**

   a. True   b. False

5. **In-store quarterly refresher loss prevention training should include:**

   a. Intranet tutorials   c. Topic in store meetings
   b. Safety & Security personnel assisted training   d. All of these choices

6. **Define a "detention":**

   _____
   _____
   _____

7. **A store's unobserved losses are typically only _____ % of the actual losses.**

8. **When it comes to physical security, which of the following is the most important physical condition:**

   a. Trimmed shrubs and bushes   c. Having a good peep hole
   b. Locating trash cans near the exit door   d. Good lighting

9. **What is the percentage of robberies that occur just before or after closing?**

   a. 33%   b. 25%   c. 50%   d. 75%

10. **This person must approve any one person closing operation:**

    a. Store Manager   b. General Manager   c. Region Vice President

11. **Do your best to estimate the amount of loss after a robbery and inform the authorities.**

    a. True   b. False

12. **ARFIS automatically tracks customers who:**
    a. don't have ID cards   b. don't have receipts   c. make frequent purchases.

13. **Monthly, what % of refund customers should be called (with or without receipt)?**

    a. 5%   c. 15%   e. None of these choices

    b. 10%   d. 20%   *(continued)*

Exhibit 26.2. (*continued*)

14. **There is not presently a tutorial available for shoplifting prevention, but one is coming soon.**

    a. True   b. False

15. **One should avoid conducting training only with the associate that has not appropriately followed an internal control as it occurs. This would make sure more of your staff was trained together at a future point in time.**

    a. True   b. False

16. **This is the #1 organizational characteristic that contributes to employee dishonesty:**

    _____

17. **List two acceptable reasons for a price override:**

    _____

    _____

18. **You should assign an associate to prepare a price change voucher for the total listed on the price difference report each week.**

    a. True   b. False

19. **When providing a customer an adjustment for a price discrepancy or a sales promotion 30-day guarantee, the adjustment key under refunds on the cash register will take care of your accountability.**

    a. True   b. False

20. **Name three ways the store capture rate may be improved:**

    _____

    _____

    _____

21. **When an item doesn't capture, adding it to ASAP will fix this problem.**

    a. True   b. False

22. **A customer laptop awaiting repair is not considered critical while in your store.**

    a. True   b. False

23. **This report is used to determine what did not capture daily:**

    a. Daily Sales Error Report   d. SD RPOS Sub department Rings Report
    b. Price Difference Report
    c. Tlog Report

24. **An item that shows E and F in ASAP under item inquiry does not capture.**

    a. True   b. False

Exhibit 26.2. (*continued*)

---

25. **When creating local promotions in the ISP, use the file that starts with this number to ensure markdowns are being booked to the SPS:**

    a. 1   b. 2   c. 3   d. 4

26. **You should control the following people in your store:** (*circle all that apply*)

    a. Vendors   b. Military inspectors   c. General Manager

27. **Transaction voids may be made occasionally a few transactions after the voided transaction, when the void has nothing to do with customer service.**

    a. True   b. False

28. **Under what circumstance is refund approval required for an AAFES employee?**

    _____

29. **Security tape should be available at each cash register in your store.**

    a. True   b. False

30. **List one good reason for a department ring, other than equipment failure:**

    _____

31. **List three significant potentially negative outcomes of using departmental rings:**

    a. _____
    b. _____
    c. _____

32. **What categories of merchandise are required to be treated as Critical?**

    a. _____
    b. _____
    c. _____

---

coordination with the subject matter experts, designers, and trainers of the courses. Depending on the course requirements, the instructor will send an e-mail to the associates 90 to 180 days following successful completion of the course. The e-mail will link the associate to an assessment located on the Web portal. This type of assessment will be valuable in the analysis of several of Corporate University's core business classes such as Advanced Softlines and Financial Management. The educational support team will be able to measure the results of the training by looking at such factors as sales growth in the softlines department, markdowns,

Exhibit 26.3. Sample E-mail Message

To:
From: jablonski@aafes.com
Subject: Manager Mind-Set Survey

Based on your attendance in the course Manager's Mind-Set at Ft. Jackson, I would like to thank you for taking the time out of your busy schedule to improve your skills with self-development. As mentioned during the course, the final portion to receive credit is incumbent upon you providing us with feedback. I would appreciate you taking a few minutes to give Corporate University your personal evaluation and observations of this training program. I want to know how useful this program has been to you and if the skills learned are being applied on the job. The survey that you're about to take will list the principles and skills of the Manager's Mind-Set. A second survey will be provided to your supervisor, who will then validate your application of lessons learned.

Click here to access the survey and respond to each question. Please complete the survey before *7 January 2005.*

In advance, thank you for your participation.

Steve Jablonski
Manager, Educational Support
Corporate University

---

inventory control, and so on, and compare the current results with the results prior to the associate attending the course. Again, using the portal will make the data analysis more efficient and economical. The information derived from the analysis will be used to brief management on the course results and impact.

Summary

Corporate University is very enthusiastic about the integration of Kirkpatrick's four levels of evaluation and the Microsoft Office Share-Point Portal Server in 2005. The use of the Web portal brings greater efficiency to the assessment process because AAFES associates are allowed the flexibility to answer an assessment outside of the training session, the use of the web portal speeds up the data collection phase of the assessment process, and the system has the built-in ability to generate reports in Excel and Access. This integrated model provides Corporate University an excellent structure with which to evaluate training and associate learning in a meaningful way.

Chapter 27

Evaluating a Training Program at All Four Levels

This case study from Cisco Systems illustrates how an organization can evaluate a program at all four levels. The study was done jointly by an internal training professional and an outside consultant. The first step was to identify the desired business results. From this basis, the training program was planned and implemented.

Cisco Systems, Inc.

Peg Maddocks, Manager of Training
for WorldWide Manufacturing
Cisco Systems, Inc., San Jose, California
Ingrid Gudenas, President
Effective Training Solutions, Fremont, California

Background

Silicon Valley–based Cisco Systems, a worldwide leader in the highly competitive networking industry, is a rapidly growing company with a critical goal to keep costs down and profits high. Cisco manufactures computer networking equipment and had revenue of $6.8 billion in fiscal year 1997, with a 189 percent increase in new jobs from 1996–1998, bringing the total number of employees to about 11,000. Cisco is recognized for its profitability and low operating expenses. A key strategy in staying profitable is its emphasis on frugality in every activity while enhancing productivity through the use of information systems business tools.

Manufacturing can be a source of high operating costs, while inventories are kept up to ensure delivery to the customer and where hiring costs sometimes outpace revenues. Cisco Manufacturing balances the need to hire and the cost of hiring more people by implementing tools to increase the productivity of existing employees. Often, reengineering a process and eliminating "paper trails" can have a tremendous effect on the bottom line. The challenge has always been how to train hundreds of people simultaneously to correctly use a new work process when it changes virtually overnight.

The Challenge

One example of this challenge was the new return-to-vendor (RTV) process, which was costing Cisco a significant percentage of its operating expenses in write-offs and loss of productivity. The write-offs were financial losses we incurred every quarter that cut into our profitability. Cisco manufactures routers and switches, which consist of a chassis and a set of printed circuit boards. Often the boards in the plant need to be returned to the vendor for a variety of reasons, including simply updating the components on them. This process was completely manual, with every returned circuit board being tracked using a paper process and being physically handed off to five separate work groups. Production workers would reject a board and forward it with a paper rejection request to the plant materials group. Then an engineer and buyer would determine whether to return it to the supplier. Cost Accounting would get involved as an "inspector" to ensure paperwork was properly filled out. Finally, the board would be shipped back to the vendor from the dock. Often, when it came time to receive the credit from the supplier, there were scattered records of the board being sent or received or the paperwork would be so inaccurate that Cisco could not be reimbursed.

Traceability is always a challenge in a manual process. For each board returned—and there are thousands over the course of a year—at least five departments were involved, some RTV cases were open for 30 to 120 days while people retraced the return process, and the average time to return the boards lasted five to seven days. Worst was the expense of the write-offs Cisco experienced every quarter due to untraceable returns.

Implementing the Training Project

Cost Accounting drove this project with a goal to reduce write-offs, eliminate at least one head count, and increase the speed of returning boards and receiving the credit. The Information Systems Department worked with a representative from each of the groups involved to reengineer and automate the process. Once redesigned, the paper process would be completely computer-based and all of the sign-offs could be done on line. Tracking would be accurate and timely, and the write-offs would be eliminated. On completion of the programming, the Cost Accounting Department gave the plant three weeks to train over 130 people in the new process. All process participants needed to start using the approach simultaneously for it to work, and the paper process would be "turned off."

Up to that point our Training Department had not been involved. When Cost Accounting asked us for help, we agreed, on the condition we use a training approach we knew would guarantee a successful implementation. In the past, new process training had been done by a series of department meeting demos and a question-and-answer process. Once the process was implemented, experts would spend many hours a day answering questions and fixing problems until everyone was proficient. This could take months, depending on the complexity of the procedure.

The first step in the training project was to identify the business results that would prove that the training had been successful and that the business problem had been solved. This was fairly easy, because the Cost Accounting Department had identified overall performance measures for the business and had preexisting data. In addition, our Information Systems Department had implemented a reporting process a few months back that tracked performance by buyer and by product line, which helped us measure more specific results. We identified five distinct level 4 measures and targets and two level 3 measures and targets, which we will explain later in this case study.

100% Proficiency™ Training Method

We decided to use the 100% Proficiency™ training method, which was developed by Effective Training Solutions (ETS), a California-based training and consulting firm. Through years of training work with high-tech manufacturers, other companies, and government agencies, ETS found that traditional classroom teaching methods were not workable when applied to the demand for rapidly developed proficiency that exists in today's high-tech industry.

The 100% Proficiency™ training method is not classroom training. It is self-paced, yet its structure, its guided supervision by a trained facilitator, and its unique study and training facilitation tools distinguish it from other self-paced learning. This training system is taught to client organizations, which then apply it to their particular training needs. The method of learning results in employees who are fully proficient and who:

- Have all the necessary knowledge to do their jobs well
- Are fully able to rapidly and correctly execute the actions called for in their jobs
- Are able to use good judgment when necessary

The 100% Proficiency™ training system is based on research conducted by L. Ron Hubbard in the 1960s and published as a lecture series. This research showed that training could be improved by shifting responsibility for and control of learning to the student. By setting the standard at 100 percent and giving the student relevant learning skills, the trainer's role shifted from a teacher or trainer to one of coaching and verifying proficiency. This system has demonstrated level 4 results for manufacturing as well as software training.

The core of this system is the "checksheet," which provides a road map for the trainee to follow, with an exact sequence of steps, including study of work procedures and other documents as well as practical exercises that orient an employee to equipment or to the software application. The checksheet also ensures that students practice or "drill" with hands-on exercises sufficiently to become fully proficient *during* training. This is different from traditional training in which students are expected to become fully proficient *after* training. In Cisco's situation, this difference was critical.

Inherent in the 100% Proficiency™ system is that students are given reference material in the form of documents, work procedures, or specifications and are provided with instruction on how to learn so that they can succeed in self-paced learning. (Without this instruction, students can have a difficult time with the self-paced nature of this approach.) The training materials for the RTV process consist of the checksheets, written by the Training Department, and the procedures and work instructions, written by three subject matter experts (SMEs), who designed the new process (a cost accountant, a buyer, and a materials coordinator from the plant). To implement the training, the SMEs provided a train-the-trainer to a trainer/coach from every department. A demo of the new process was provided; then the trainers worked through the checksheet and practiced the new process in a lab or at their desks over a week's time. The department trainers used the same approach to train their department over the next two weeks. All trainers attended a training course on coaching skills for the 100% Proficiency™ training approach.

During the training itself, these trainers were available to answer questions and to help students as needed. An important responsibility for the trainers was to provide students with "trainer checkouts." The checksheet indicated to a student when a "trainer checkout" was required, but the student would ensure that he or she was ready for the checkout prior to requesting it. During the trainer checkout the trainer verified that the student was fully proficient by watching the student perform the exact task. This was the level 2 measure throughout the program. There was no pretest because students were being taught skills they previously did not have; thus, a pretest would have been irrelevant. During the checkout, a trainer signed off only after the student demonstrated full proficiency, thereby verifying the acquisition of the skill being taught.

These trainer checkouts were interspersed throughout the checksheet; there was one final trainer checkout at the end of each checksheet in which students had to put everything together and demonstrate that they were able to do the whole task rapidly and accurately. In other words, full proficiency was required in order for a student to complete a checksheet and be signed off by the trainer. This level 2 measure on the actual task to be performed on the job removed any mystery about level 3. Students had been so thoroughly measured regarding proficiency *during* their training that we expected they would have few training-related difficulties in using these new skills on the job *after* training.

Once the training was complete, the paper process was "turned off." In other words, Cost Accounting would no longer accept manually written shipping authorizations, and the product could not return to the vendor without the online process being complete.

Training Measures

We were able to implement all four levels of evaluation for this project. For level 1, we conducted a survey three weeks after the training program via e-mail (see Exhibit 27.1). Students were asked how they liked the training, what they learned, and how to improve it next time. We also conducted a focus group in which we asked users to evaluate the effectiveness of the new work process, the training and support materials, the training effectiveness, and the logistics of the training (that is, the demo, labs, and "at-my-desk" practice). Trainers also received informal solicited and unsolicited feedback about training effectiveness.

Level 2 was imbedded in the training process, as discussed above, because students were "tested" by their trainer as they performed the activities on the system.

Level 3 was measured in the following two ways:

1. Trainers observed students over a weeklong period after they had signed off their checksheets but before the new process went "live" to see how quickly they were performing the RTV process and how many errors they were making. They also tracked the volume and cycle time of RTVs being processed by each buyer and then coached those who were having trouble.

2. Trainers and the Cost Accounting Department noted a stunning and immediate reduction in the number of questions asked about how to do RTVs and were rarely asked to solve process problems anymore. The buyers were clearly implementing the new process.

Level 4 was measured in the following five ways, as predetermined before we began the training project:

1. Reduction in the dollar amount of write-off for untraceable RTVs. (The goal was elimination of this type of write-off.)

Exhibit 27.1. Survey for Level 1

To: Mfg-buyers
From :   Peg Maddocks <pmaddock@cisco.com>
Subject: Sock it to us—we need your opinion
Cc:
Bcc:
X-Attachments:

Hello,

Recently you were trained in the new Auto SA/RTV process. The method we used was called High Performance Training, in which a coach assigned to your department was first trained and then in turn trained you. Ideally, you were given a demo in the training room and then given a "checksheet" that directed you through self-paced exercises.

Your coach was to "check you out" to ensure that your questions were answered, your exercises were complete, and that you thoroughly understood how to use the new tool. Please help us evaluate this training so we can improve it the next time we roll out a new process or tool.

Please reply to this e-mail by 11/20 . . . it's quick and easy!

Thanks,

Peg

Your job title:

1. How much do you use the Auto SA/RTV process?

   _____ Often (several times a day)

   _____ Some (several times a week)

   _____ A little (once in a while)

   _____ Never

2. How were you trained in the new process? (check all that apply)

   _____ Demo by coach

   _____ Used the checksheet, procedure, work instructions, and Maserati to practice

   _____ Used the procedure and work instruction without checksheet

   _____ Coach answered my questions/showed me how to find my own answers

   _____ Coach checked me out to see if I was proficient

   _____ Learned completely on my own

   _____ Didn't get trained/not using the tool

3. If you were trained using a checksheet, how much did it help you learn?

   _____ It helped me a great deal

   _____ It helped me a bit

   _____ It interfered with my learning

   _____ Didn't use checksheet

(continued)

Exhibit 27.1. Survey for Level 1 (*continued*)

---

4. If you used a checksheet, what *did* you like about it?

5. If you used a checksheet, what *didn't* you like about it?

6. If you had a coach, what did the coach *do well*? Optional: What was your coach's name?

7. If you had a coach, what could the coach *do better* next time?

8. Overall, how would you rate this form of training?

    _____ Liked it a lot

    _____ Liked it somewhat

    _____ Didn't like it much

9. Overall, how can we improve training in manufacturing on oracle and business tools?

---

2. Decrease in queue and reduced aging of RTVs in the system. (In the old process, buyers who were not proficient in the manual process or who had many RTVs would build up a backlog of RTVs to be completed, some as many as ninety days old. When this happened, Cisco was not collecting the credit from the vendor and the boards were aging, potentially becoming outdated.)

3. Reduction in the dollar value of RTV inventory in the plant at any given time waiting for the process to complete.

4. Immediate increase in productivity in the Cost Accounting Department by eliminating the inspection, verification, and resolution of problems related to RTVs. (As a result, Cost Accounting did not have to hire an additional person, which would have been done otherwise.)

5. Immediate increase in productivity in the buyer and material handling groups because of the new process and because

subject matter experts would no longer be required to answer questions and solve process problems.

The major result that the company wanted to see was the elimination of the write-offs due to nontraceable RTVs. Within one quarter these write-offs were reduced by 100 percent. Another measure was the on-hand inventory due to RTVs. At first the number of returns in the system went up by about 10 percent as people used the new process and increased their queues. But within four weeks, the cycle time for the return of boards was reduced from seven to ten days to three days, and RTV inventory moved quickly out of the stockroom and back to the vendor. As far as productivity, one person in Cost Accounting was able to focus on other projects because she was no longer receiving RTV paper authorizations and buyers were no longer asking for help. Productivity among buyers went up by a minimum of 10 percent (ability to process more returns quicker). All of this was measurable by reports developed to track the returns in the system. The trainers in each department increased their productivity by 10 to 30 percent depending on how many RTVs a department had who no longer needed to resolve issues and answer questions about the process.

Conclusion

All in all, this program was very successful. In conjunction with the implementation of an improved business process, the training facilitated a quicker financial return to the business because of the method used. The following are factors that contributed to our success:

- The training was focused on solving a real business problem; because of this the business partners were fully committed to making it work.
- The training measures were identified by the business partners and agreed to before the training began. The results were to be collected by the business, and this made measurement of the training fairly straightforward.
- The Training Department did not own the training process. Process designers wrote the reference materials, and experts in each group were able to customize the process details for their

students' situations. In this way we were able to train 130 people over a two- to three-week period.

- The 100% Proficiency™ training method ensured consistency across groups and proof of proficiency via the checkouts. The materials continue to be used successfully by the coaches to train new hires and transfers.
- Training continued on the job because the students received reinforcement and feedback from their trainers and managers as a normal course of the business measurement process.

This training project was perceived by the business managers and the participants as the most successful information systems training program they had ever experienced. Cost Accounting was impressed with the success of its implementation and the results. The trainers were relieved when few people asked them for help after the system went live, and our Training Department was perceived as a real business partner. As a result, there is now a requirement in Manufacturing that all new processes be introduced using the 100% Proficiency™ training method and that the business owners, information systems developers, and Training Department measure and communicate the results at all four levels of evaluation.

Index

DONALD L. KIRKPATRICK is Professor Emeritus of the University of Wisconsin and a widely respected teacher, author, and consultant. He has over thirty years' experience as Professor of Management at the University of Wisconsin and has held professional training and human resource positions with International Minerals and Chemical Corporation and Bendix Corporation.

He is the author of eight "Management Inventories" and six books, including: *Managing Change Effectively; Improving Employee Performance Through Appraisal and Coaching,* 2nd edition; *Developing Supervisors and Team Leaders; How to Plan and Conduct Productive Business Meetings;* and *No-Nonsense Communication.* The first two titles received the "best book of the year" award from the Society For Human Resource Management (SHRM).

Don is a past president of the American Society for Training and Development (ASTD), and in 2004 he received its highest award, Lifetime Achievement in Workplace Learning and Performance. In 1997, he was inducted into the exclusive *Training* magazine's Hall of Fame.

He received his B.B.A., M.B.A., and Ph.D. degrees from the University of Wisconsin; the title of his Ph.D. dissertation was "Evaluating a Human Relations Training Program for Supervisors." Don is best known for developing the four-level model for evaluating training programs, which is used all over the world; the book has been translated into Spanish, Polish, and Turkish. He lives in Pewaukee, Wisconsin, and is a senior elder at Elmbrook Church, Board Chairman of South Asian Ministries, and an active member of Gideons International.

JAMES D. KIRKPATRICK has worked in the field of organizational development for over 15 years. He works for Corporate University Enterprise, Inc., as its Senior Consultant for Evaluation Services, where his main responsibility is the delivery of the Kirkpatrick Evaluation Certification Program to organizations and individuals. Prior to his new position, from 1997 to 2004, Jim was the Director of the Corporate University for First Indiana Bank in Indianapolis, where he was responsible for the bank's Balanced Scorecard Management System, Leadership Development, Training, and the Career Development Program.

Jim has worked as a management consultant in the fields of health care, education, finance, manufacturing, not-for-profits, and government, and he has also had relevant experience as a career consultant and clinical psychologist. He has given workshops and consulted in a number of U.S. cities as well as in Canada, England, the Netherlands, Colombia, Australia, India, and Malaysia. Jim and his father, Don Kirkpatrick, have a new book out, *Transferring Learning to Behavior: Using the Four Levels to Improve Performance* (Berrett-Koehler, 2005). Cofounder of the downtown Indianapolis Organizational Development Network and on the board of the American Red Cross, Jim has a Ph.D. in Counseling Psychology from Indiana State University and a master's degree in Education from the University of Wisconsin.

Berrett–Koehler
Publishers

Berrett-Koehler is an independent publisher dedicated to an ambitious mission: *Creating a World That Works for All*.

We believe that to truly create a better world, action is needed at all levels—individual, organizational, and societal. At the individual level, our publications help people align their lives with their values and with their aspirations for a better world. At the organizational level, our publications promote progressive leadership and management practices, socially responsible approaches to business, and humane and effective organizations. At the societal level, our publications advance social and economic justice, shared prosperity, sustainability, and new solutions to national and global issues.

A major theme of our publications is "Opening Up New Space." Berrett-Koehler titles challenge conventional thinking, introduce new ideas, and foster positive change. Their common quest is changing the underlying beliefs, mindsets, institutions, and structures that keep generating the same cycles of problems, no matter who our leaders are or what improvement programs we adopt.

We strive to practice what we preach—to operate our publishing company in line with the ideas in our books. At the core of our approach is stewardship, which we define as a deep sense of responsibility to administer the company for the benefit of all of our "stakeholder" groups: authors, customers, employees, investors, service providers, and the communities and environment around us.

We are grateful to the thousands of readers, authors, and other friends of the company who consider themselves to be part of the "BK Community." We hope that you, too, will join us in our mission.

A BK Business Book

This book is part of our BK Business series. BK Business titles pioneer new and progressive leadership and management practices in all types of public, private, and nonprofit organizations. They promote socially responsible approaches to business, innovative organizational change methods, and more humane and effective organizations.

Berrett–Koehler
Publishers

A community dedicated to creating
a world that works for all

Visit Our Website: www.bkconnection.com

Read book excerpts, see author videos and Internet movies, read our authors'
blogs, join discussion groups, download book apps, find out about the BK
Affiliate Network, browse subject-area libraries of books, get special discounts, and more!

Subscribe to Our Free E-Newsletter, the *BK Communiqué*

Be the first to hear about new publications, special discount offers, exclusive articles, news about bestsellers, and more! Get on the list for our free
e-newsletter by going to **www.bkconnection.com**.

Get Quantity Discounts

Berrett-Koehler books are available at quantity discounts for orders of ten or
more copies. Please call us toll-free at (800) 929-2929 or email us at **bkp
.orders@aidcvt.com**.

Join the BK Community

BKcommunity.com is a virtual meeting place where people from around the
world can engage with kindred spirits to create a world that works for all.
BKcommunity.com members may create their own profiles, blog, start and
participate in forums and discussion groups, post photos and videos, answer
surveys, announce and register for upcoming events, and chat with others
online in real time. Please join the conversation!

MIX
Paper from
responsible sources
FSC® C012752

FSC
www.fsc.org